HEXED

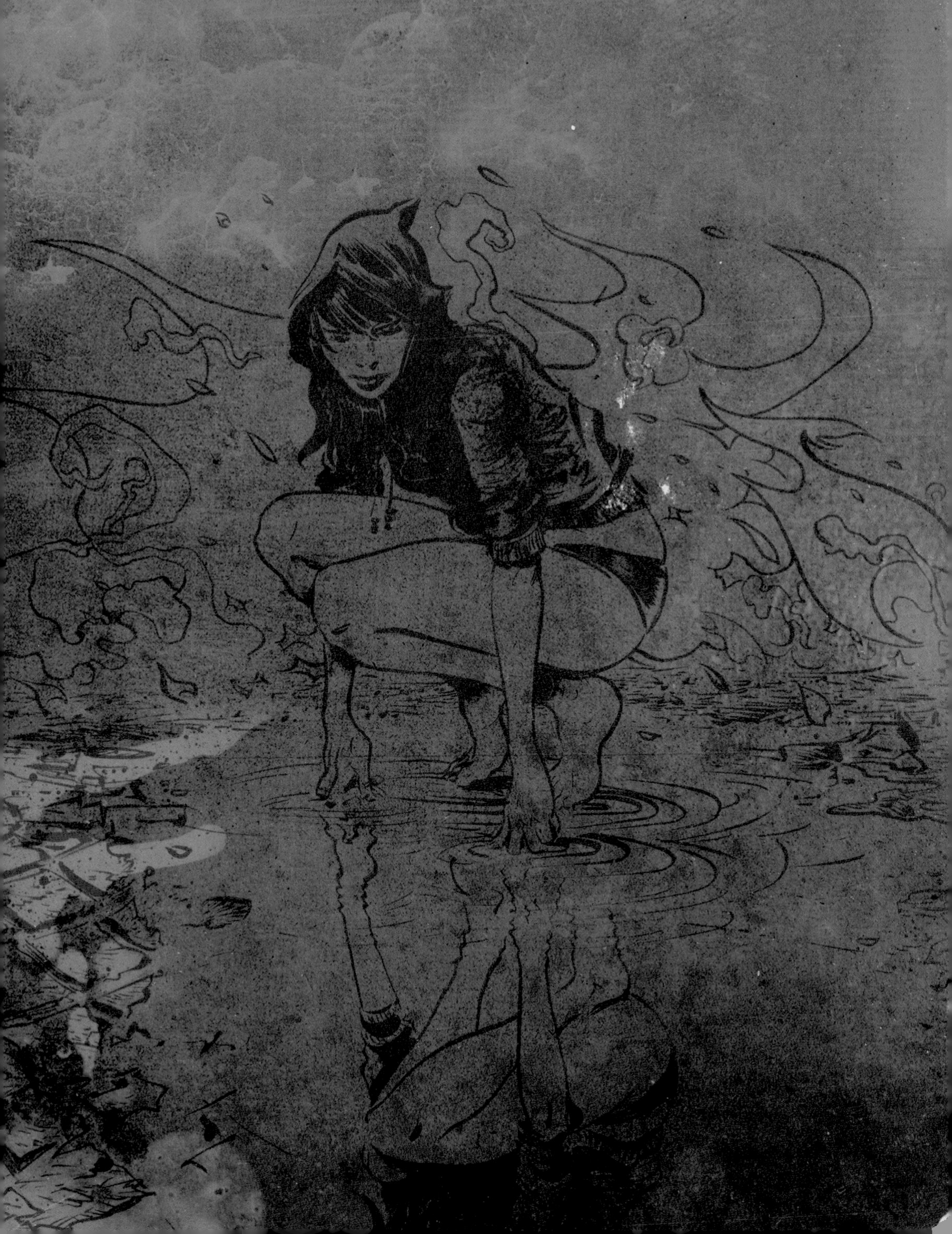

Ross Richie - Chief Executive Officer
Mark Waid - Chief Creative Officer
Matt Gagnon - Editor-in-Chief
Adam Fortier - VP-New Business
Wes Harris - VP-Publishing
Lance Kreiter - VP-Licensing & Merchandising
Chip Mosher - Marketing Director
Bryce Carlson - Managing Editor

Ian Brill - Editor
Dafna Pleban - Editor
Christopher Burns - Editor
Christopher Meyer - Editor
Shannon Watters - Assistant Editor
Eric Harburn - Assistant Editor
Adam Staffaroni - Assistant Editor

Neil Loughrie - Publishing Coordinator
Brian Latimer - Lead Graphic Designer
Erika Terriquez - Graphic Designer
Travis Beaty - Traffic Coordinator
Ivan Salazar - Marketing Assistant
Kate Hayden - Executive Assistant

For information regarding the CPSIA on this printed material, call: (203) 595-3636 and provide reference #EAST — 70410. A catalog record of this book is available from OCLC and from the BOOM! Studios website, www.boom-studios.com, on the Librarians Page.

BOOM! Studios, 6310 San Vicente Boulevard, Suite 107, Los Angeles, CA 90048-5457. Printed in USA. First Printing, Trade Paperback.
ISBN: 978-1-60886-045-6

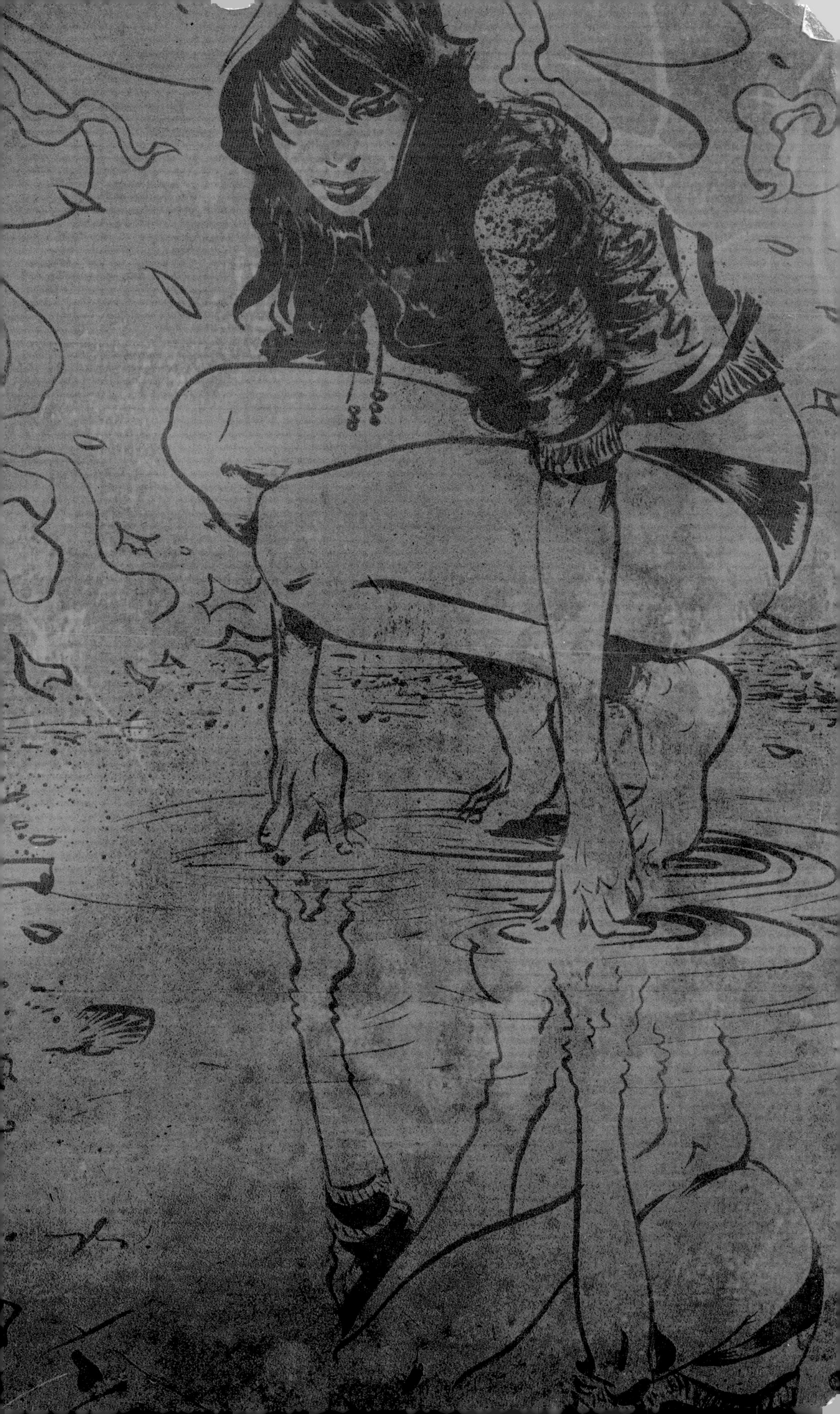

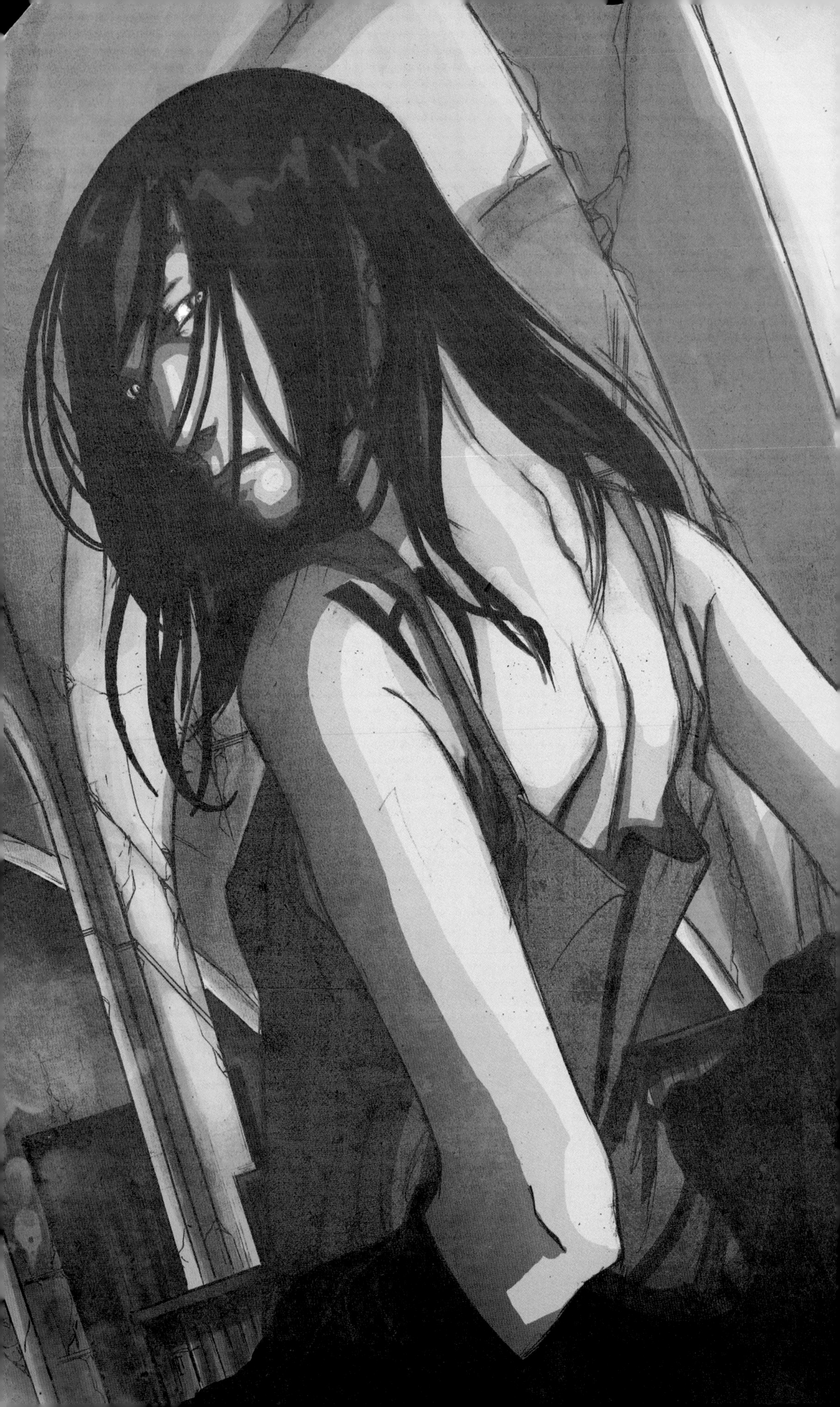

HEXED

CREATED AND WRITTEN BY
MICHAEL ALAN NELSON

ART BY
EMMA RIOS

COLORS BY
CRIS PETER

LETTERS BY
MARSHALL DILLON

COVER ART
PAUL POPE

EDITOR
MATT GAGNON

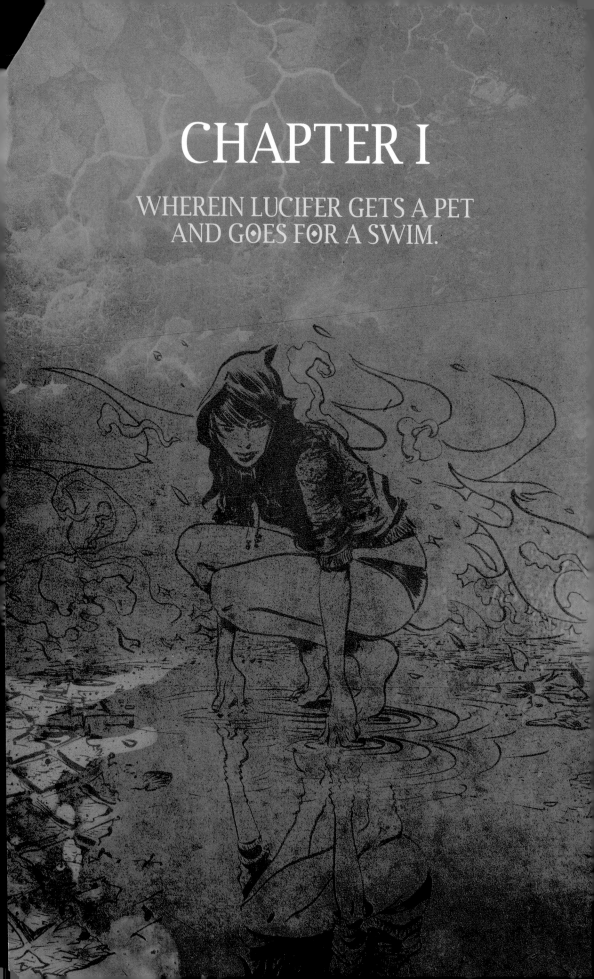

CHAPTER I

WHEREIN LUCIFER GETS A PET AND GOES FOR A SWIM.

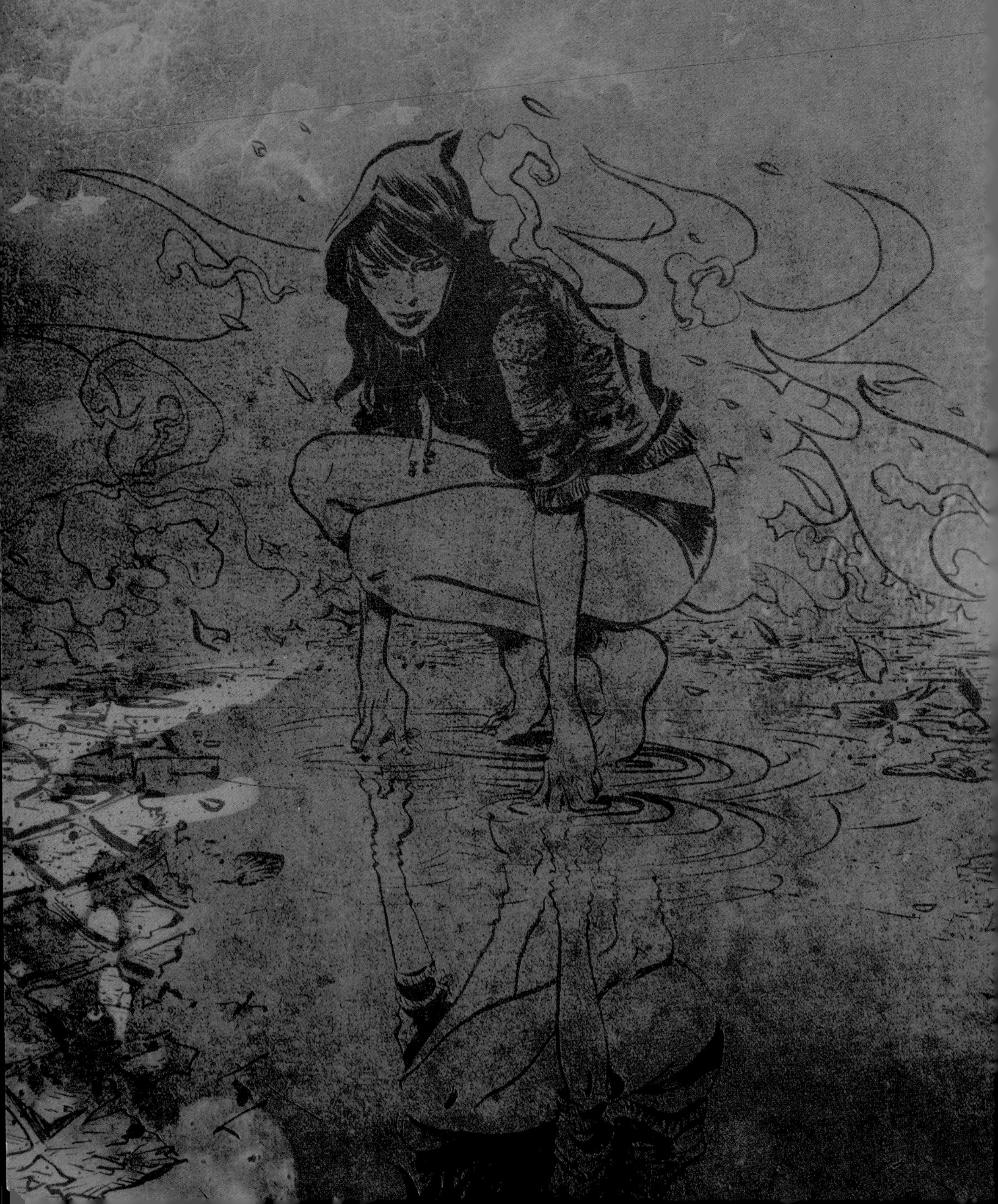

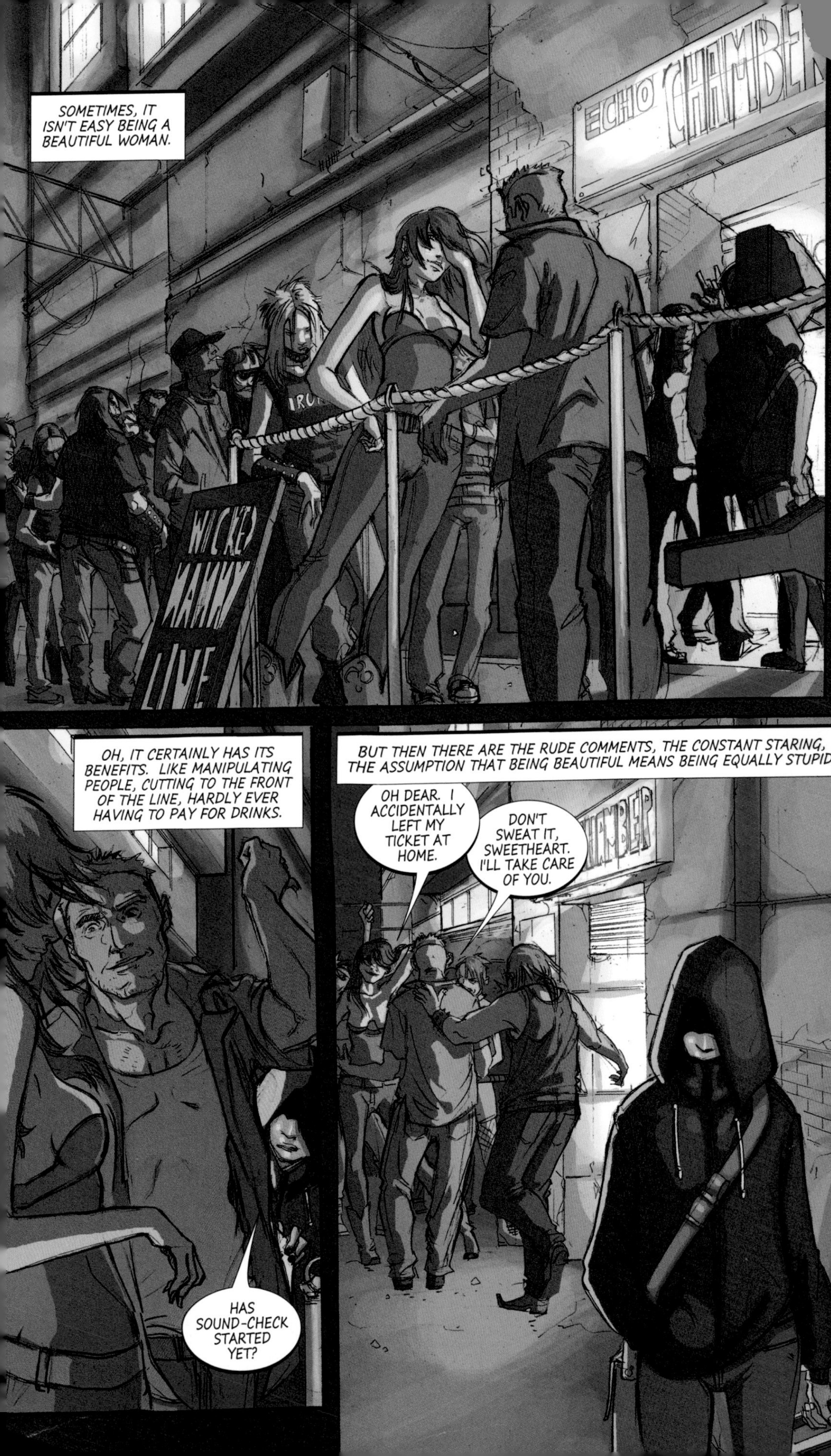
SOMETIMES, IT ISN'T EASY BEING A BEAUTIFUL WOMAN.
OH, IT CERTAINLY HAS ITS BENEFITS. LIKE MANIPULATING PEOPLE, CUTTING TO THE FRONT OF THE LINE, HARDLY EVER HAVING TO PAY FOR DRINKS.
HAS SOUND-CHECK STARTED YET?
BUT THEN THERE ARE THE RUDE COMMENTS, THE CONSTANT STARING, THE ASSUMPTION THAT BEING BEAUTIFUL MEANS BEING EQUALLY STUPID.
OH DEAR. I ACCIDENTALLY LEFT MY TICKET AT HOME.
DON'T SWEAT IT, SWEETHEART. I'LL TAKE CARE OF YOU.

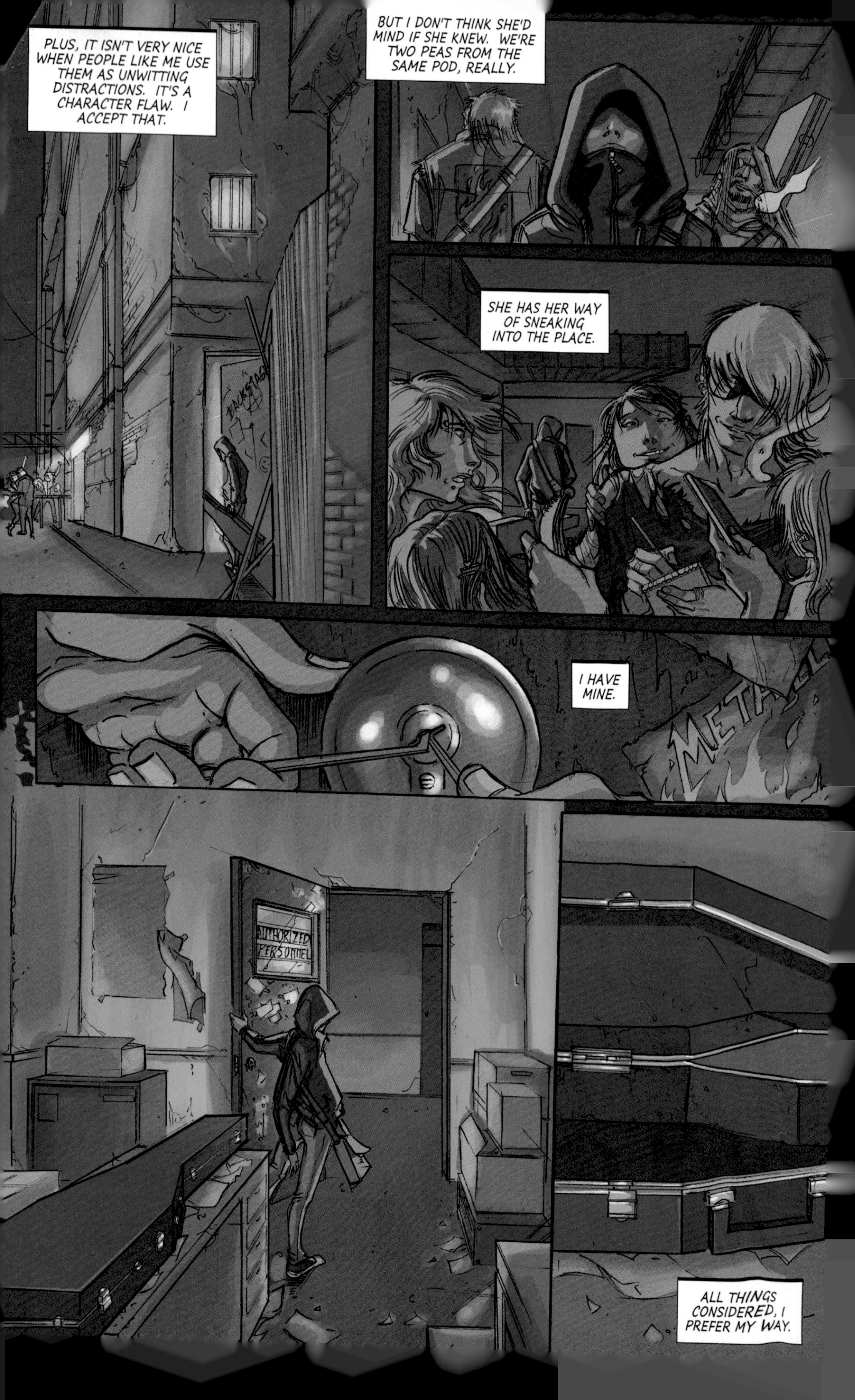
PLUS, IT ISN'T VERY NICE WHEN PEOPLE LIKE ME USE THEM AS UNWITTING DISTRACTIONS. IT'S A CHARACTER FLAW. I ACCEPT THAT.
BUT I DON'T THINK SHE'D MIND IF SHE KNEW. WE'RE TWO PEAS FROM THE SAME POD, REALLY.
SHE HAS HER WAY OF SNEAKING INTO THE PLACE.
I HAVE MINE.
AUTHORIZED PERSONNEL
ALL THINGS CONSIDERED, I PREFER MY WAY.

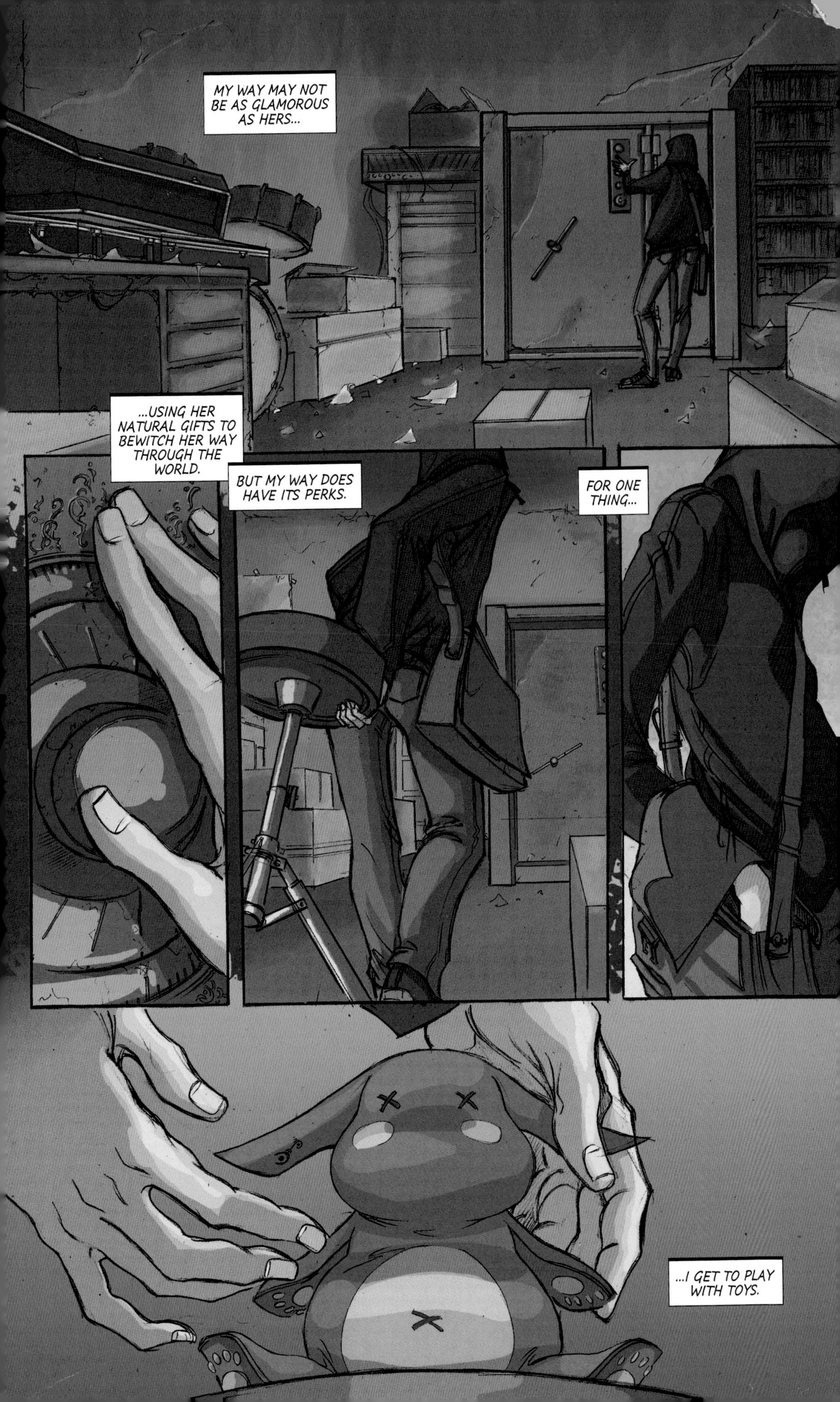
MY WAY MAY NOT BE AS GLAMOROUS AS HERS...
...USING HER NATURAL GIFTS TO BEWITCH HER WAY THROUGH THE WORLD.
BUT MY WAY DOES HAVE ITS PERKS.
FOR ONE THING...
...I GET TO PLAY WITH TOYS.

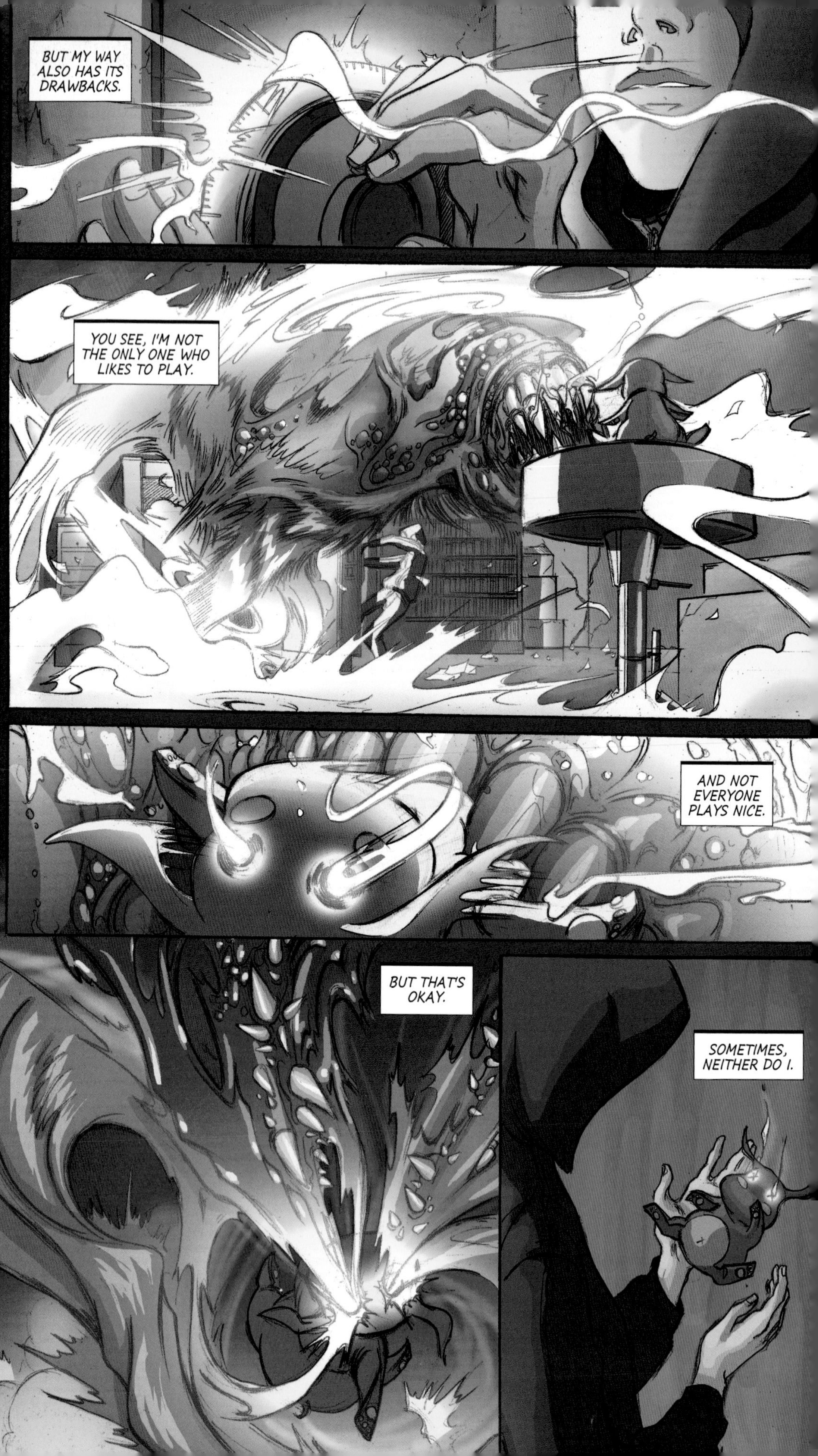
BUT MY WAY ALSO HAS ITS DRAWBACKS.
YOU SEE, I'M NOT THE ONLY ONE WHO LIKES TO PLAY.
AND NOT EVERYONE PLAYS NICE.
BUT THAT'S OKAY.
SOMETIMES, NEITHER DO I.

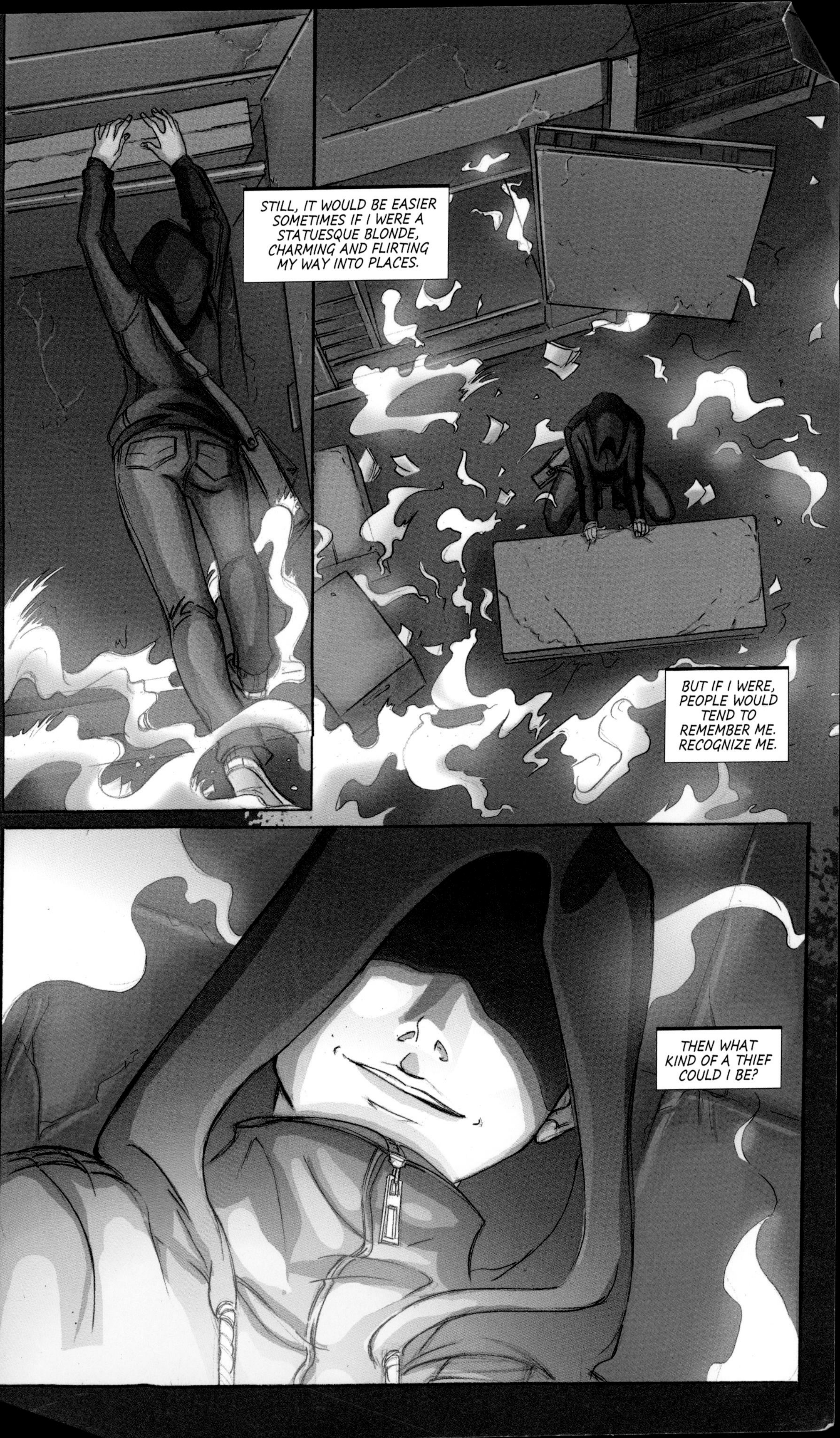
STILL, IT WOULD BE EASIER SOMETIMES IF I WERE A STATUESQUE BLONDE, CHARMING AND FLIRTING MY WAY INTO PLACES.
BUT IF I WERE, PEOPLE WOULD TEND TO REMEMBER ME. RECOGNIZE ME.
THEN WHAT KIND OF A THIEF COULD I BE?

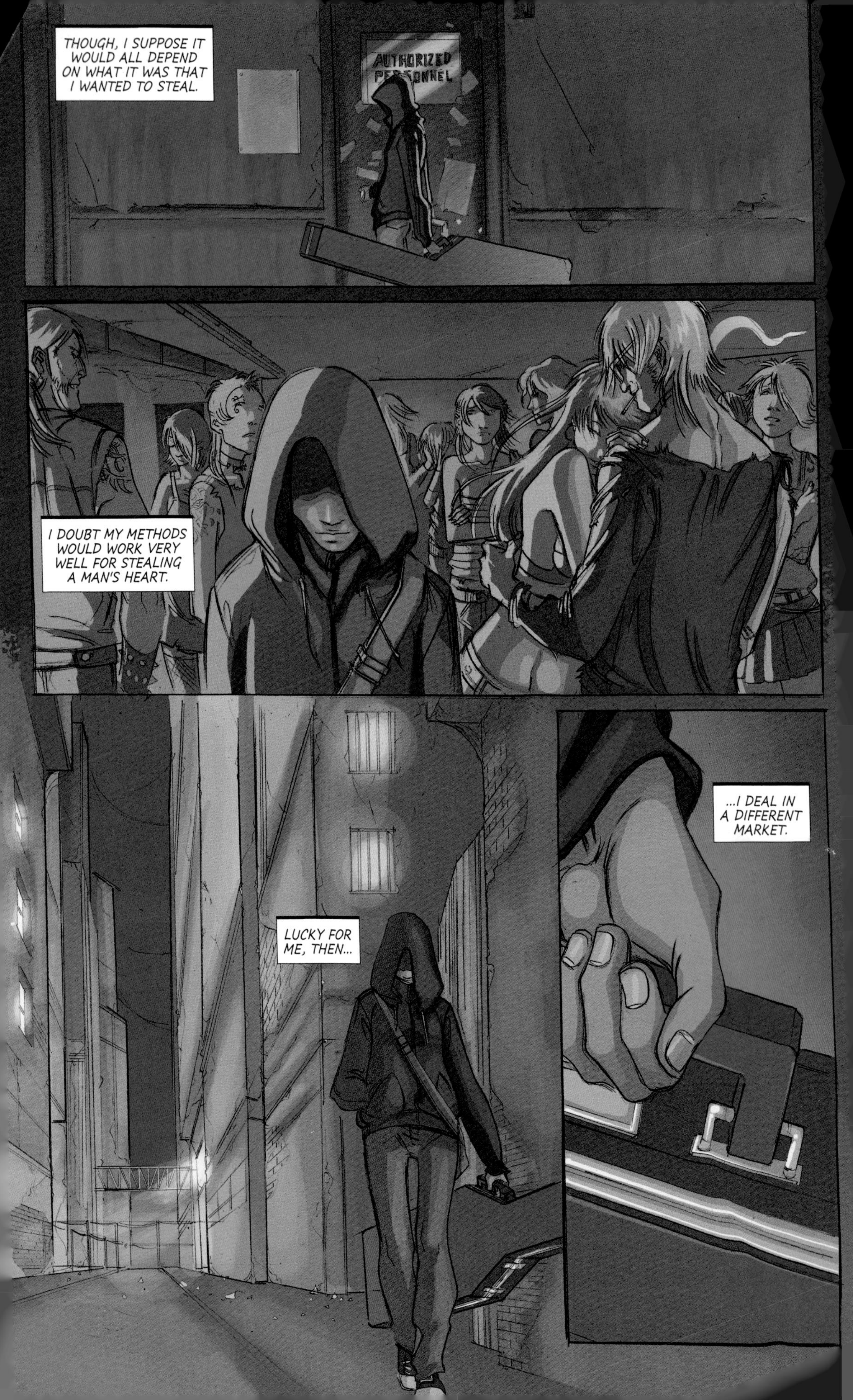
THOUGH, I SUPPOSE IT WOULD ALL DEPEND ON WHAT IT WAS THAT I WANTED TO STEAL.
AUTHORIZED PERSONNEL
I DOUBT MY METHODS WOULD WORK VERY WELL FOR STEALING A MAN'S HEART.
LUCKY FOR ME, THEN...
...I DEAL IN A DIFFERENT MARKET.

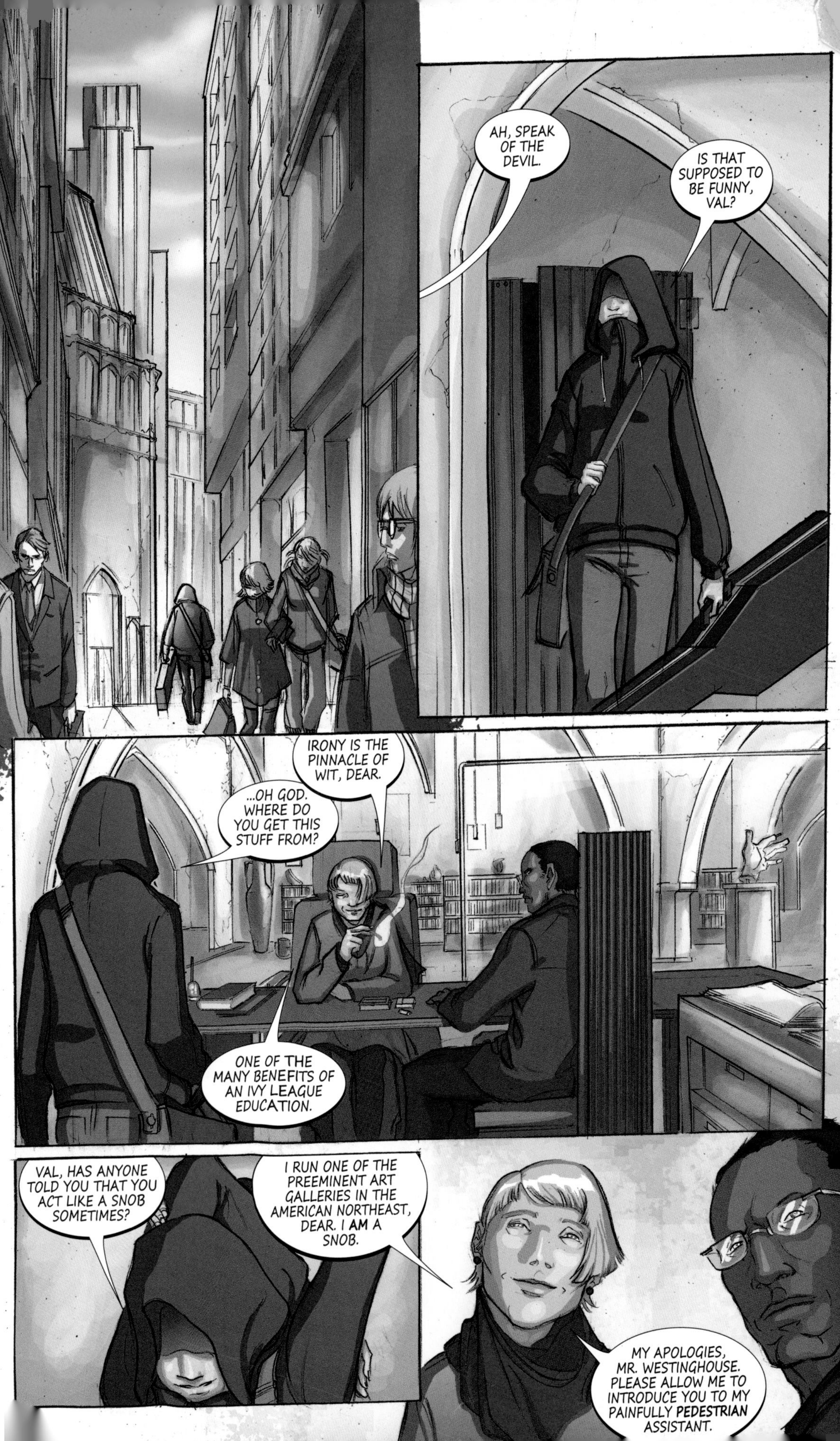
AH, SPEAK OF THE DEVIL.
IS THAT SUPPOSED TO BE FUNNY, VAL?
...OH GOD. WHERE DO YOU GET THIS STUFF FROM?
IRONY IS THE PINNACLE OF WIT, DEAR.
ONE OF THE MANY BENEFITS OF AN IVY LEAGUE EDUCATION.
VAL, HAS ANYONE TOLD YOU THAT YOU ACT LIKE A SNOB SOMETIMES?
I RUN ONE OF THE PREEMINENT ART GALLERIES IN THE AMERICAN NORTHEAST, DEAR. I AM A SNOB.
MY APOLOGIES, MR. WESTINGHOUSE. PLEASE ALLOW ME TO INTRODUCE YOU TO MY PAINFULLY PEDESTRIAN ASSISTANT.

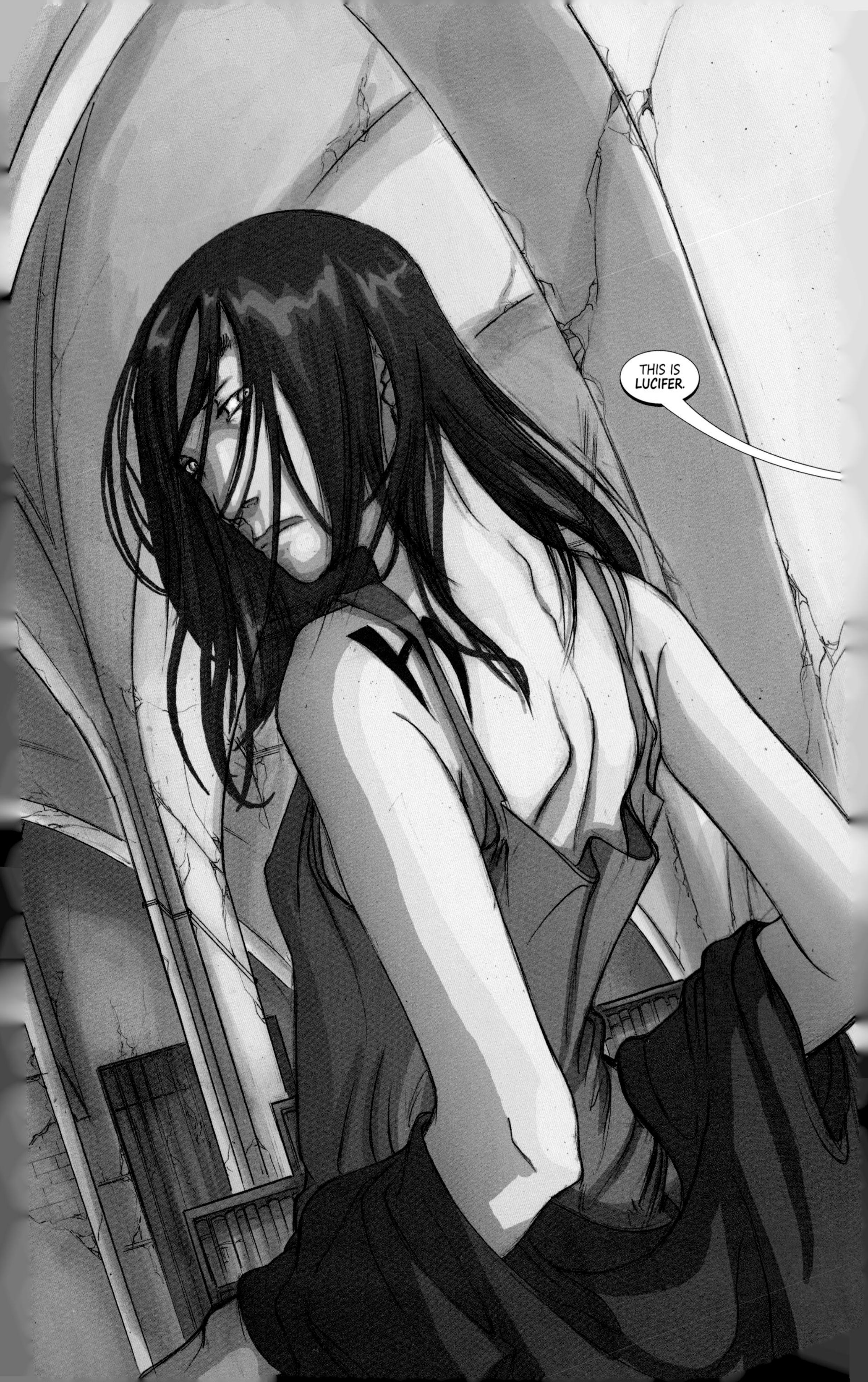
THIS IS LUCIFER.

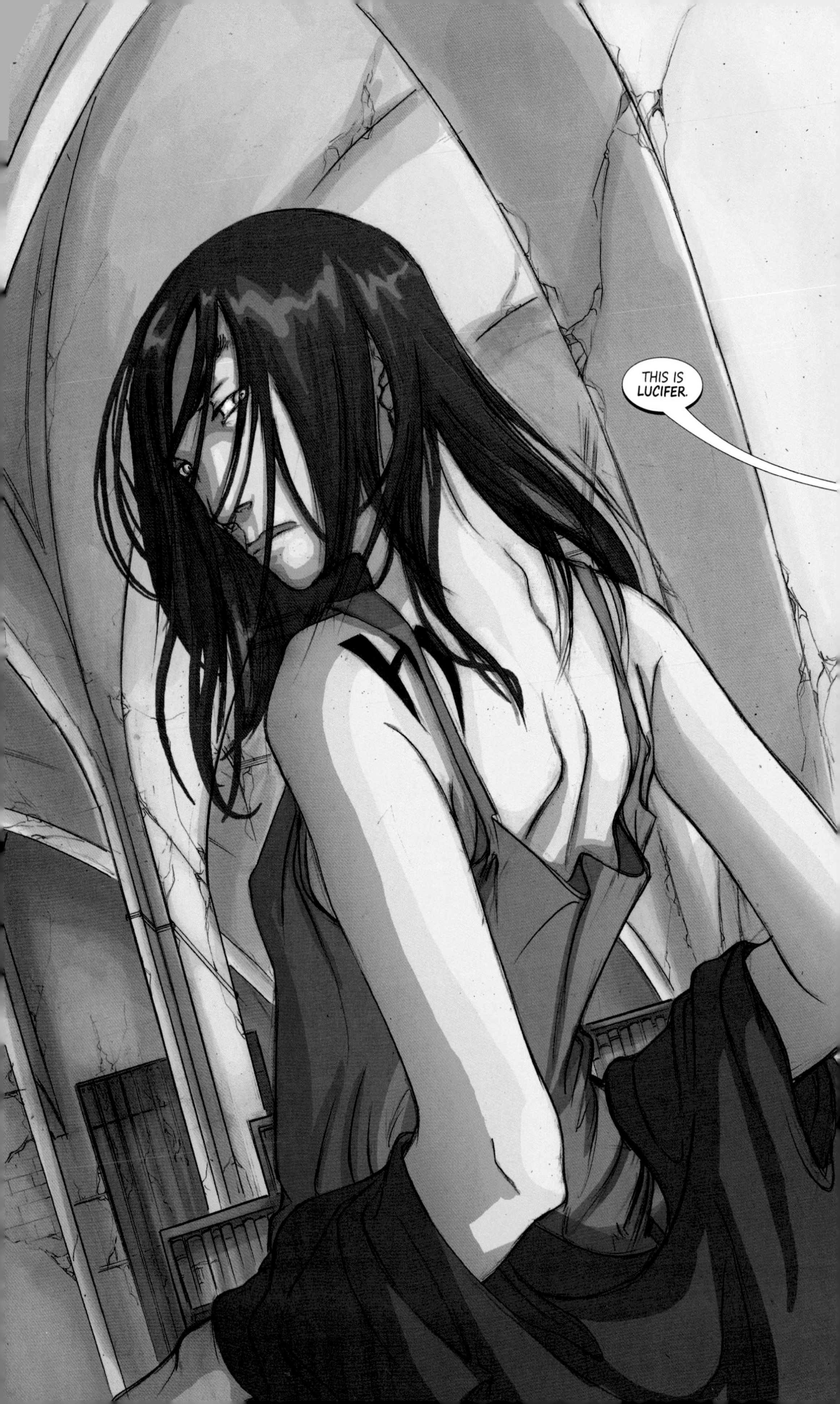
THIS IS LUCIFER.

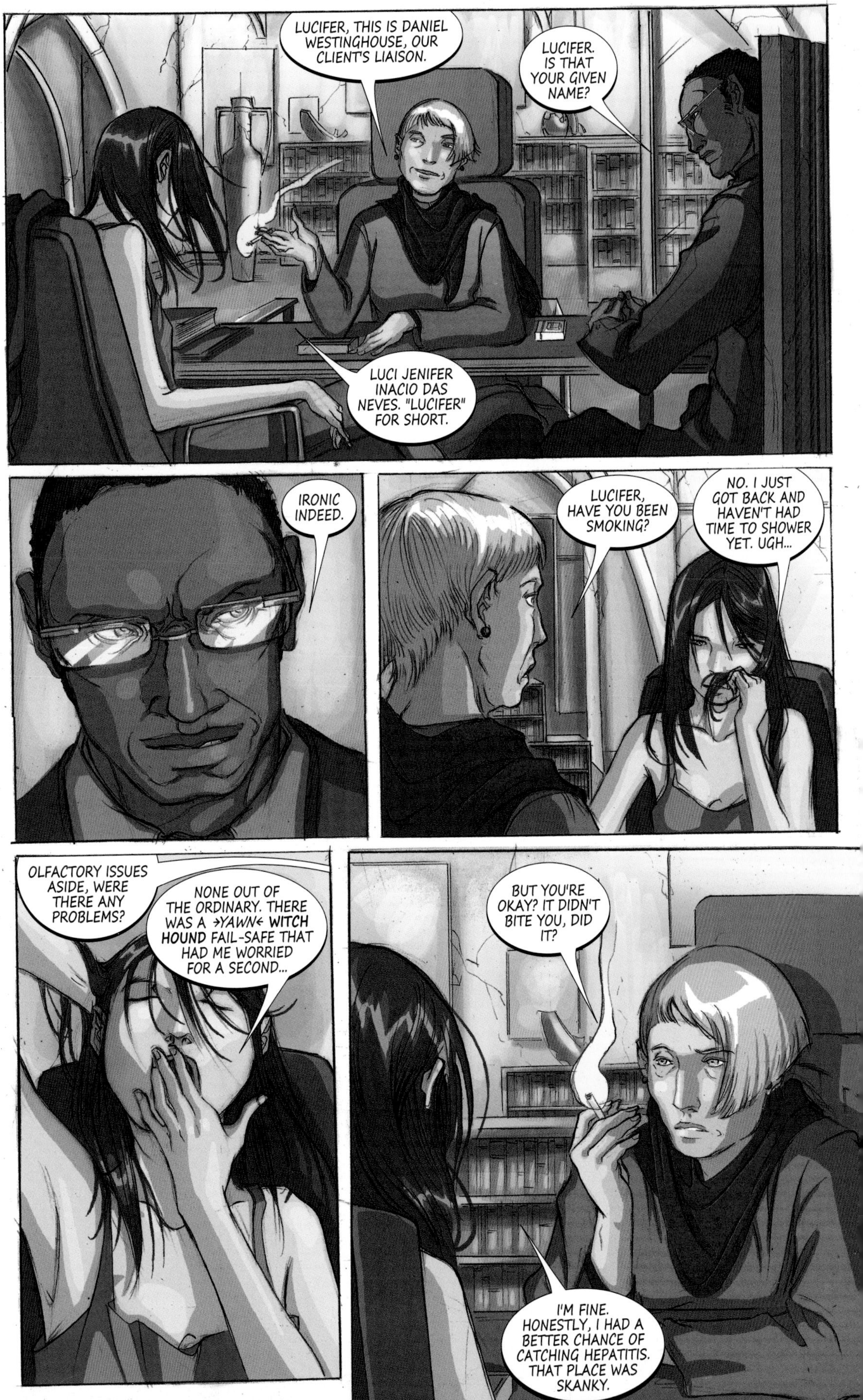
LUCIFER, THIS IS DANIEL WESTINGHOUSE, OUR CLIENT'S LIAISON.
LUCIFER. IS THAT YOUR GIVEN NAME?
LUCI JENIFER INACIO DAS NEVES. "LUCIFER" FOR SHORT.
IRONIC INDEED.
LUCIFER, HAVE YOU BEEN SMOKING?
NO. I JUST GOT BACK AND HAVEN'T HAD TIME TO SHOWER YET. UGH...
OLFACTORY ISSUES ASIDE, WERE THERE ANY PROBLEMS?
NONE OUT OF THE ORDINARY. THERE WAS A →YAWN← **WITCH HOUND** FAIL-SAFE THAT HAD ME WORRIED FOR A SECOND...
BUT YOU'RE OKAY? IT DIDN'T BITE YOU, DID IT?
I'M FINE. HONESTLY, I HAD A BETTER CHANCE OF CATCHING HEPATITIS. THAT PLACE WAS SKANKY.

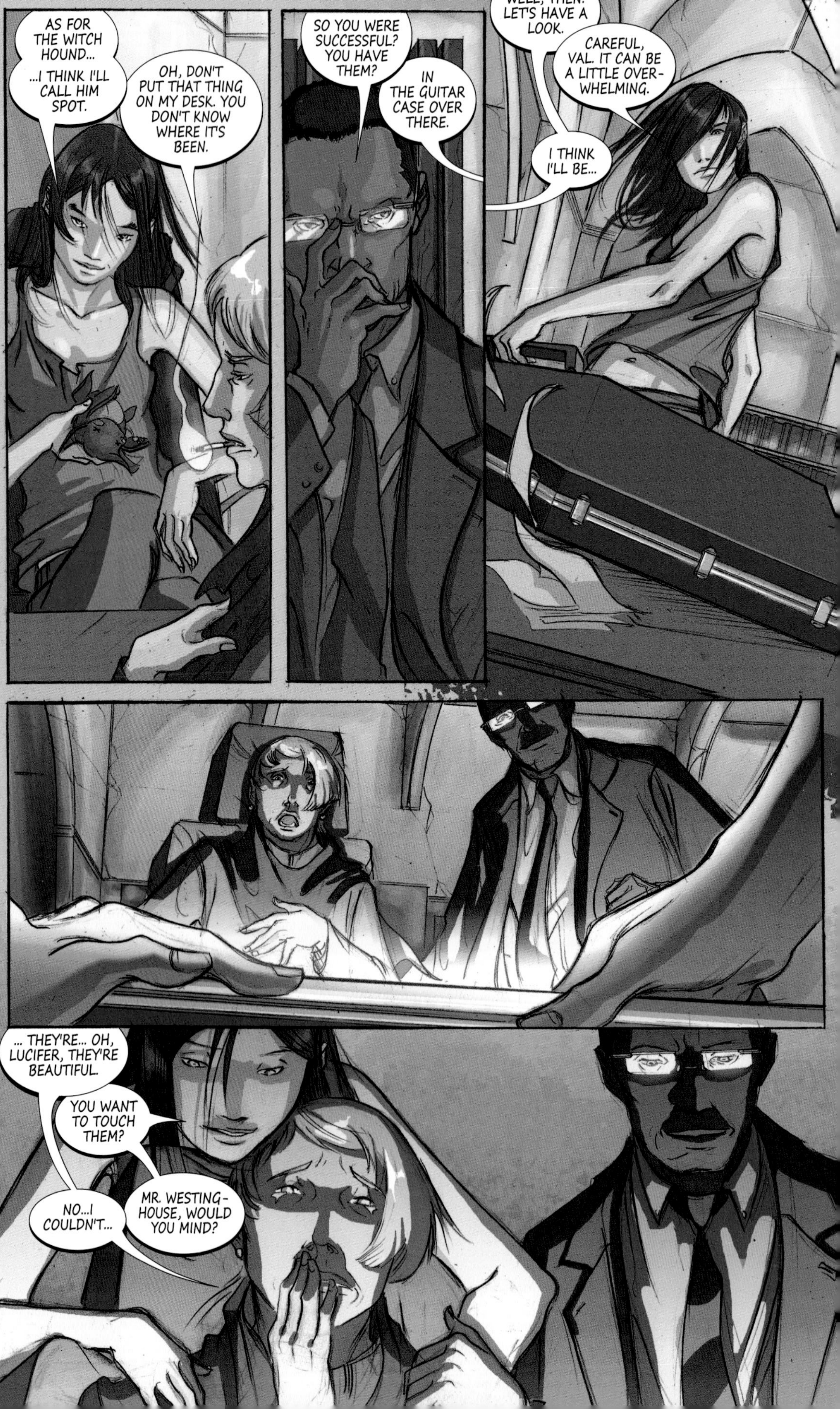
AS FOR THE WITCH HOUND...
...I THINK I'LL CALL HIM SPOT.
OH, DON'T PUT THAT THING ON MY DESK. YOU DON'T KNOW WHERE IT'S BEEN.
SO YOU WERE SUCCESSFUL? YOU HAVE THEM?
IN THE GUITAR CASE OVER THERE.
WELL, THEN. LET'S HAVE A LOOK.
CAREFUL, VAL. IT CAN BE A LITTLE OVER-WHELMING.
I THINK I'LL BE...
... THEY'RE... OH, LUCIFER, THEY'RE BEAUTIFUL.
YOU WANT TO TOUCH THEM?
NO...I COULDN'T...
MR. WESTING-HOUSE, WOULD YOU MIND?

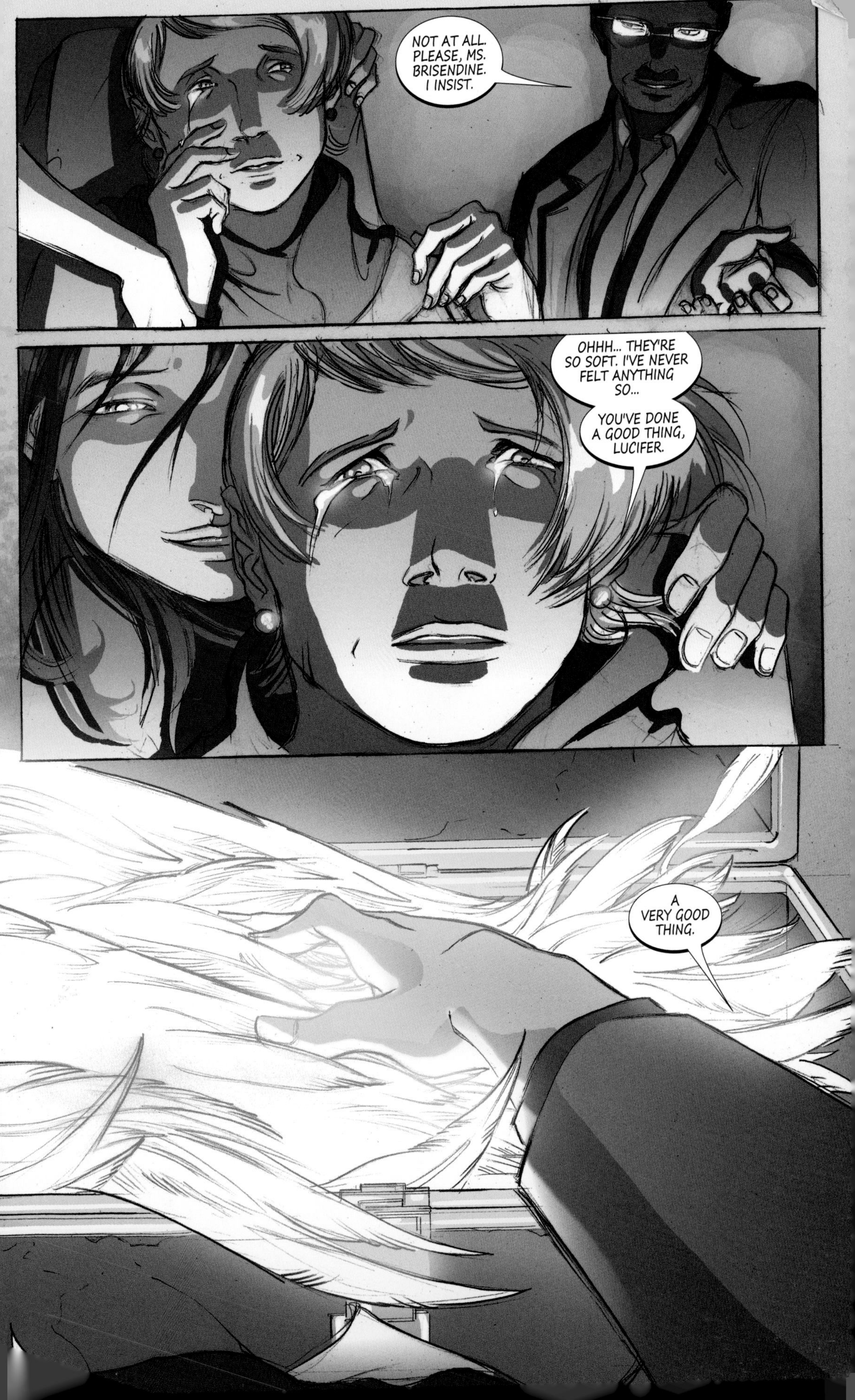
NOT AT ALL. PLEASE, MS. BRISENDINE. I INSIST.
OHHH... THEY'RE SO SOFT. I'VE NEVER FELT ANYTHING SO...
YOU'VE DONE A GOOD THING, LUCIFER.
A VERY GOOD THING.

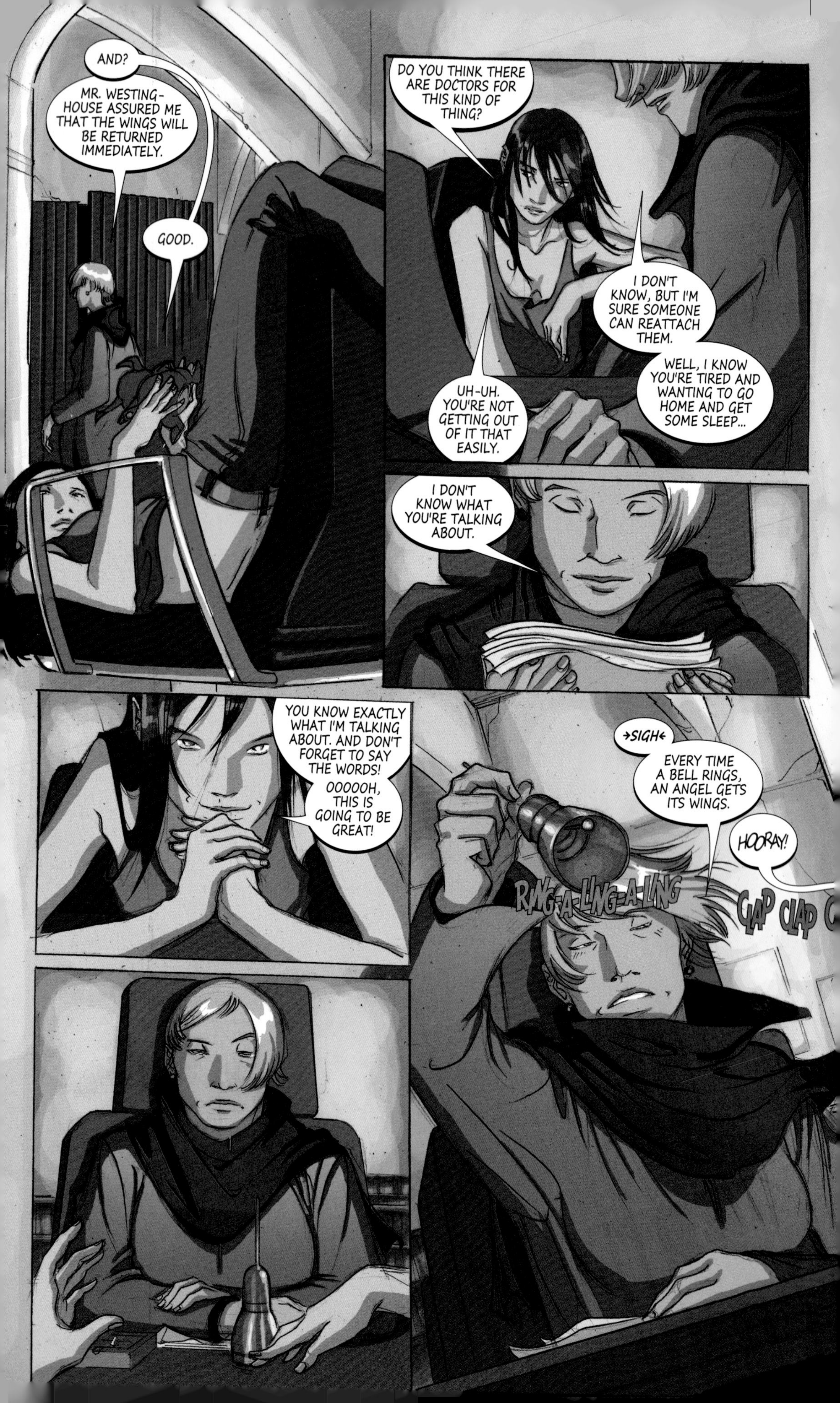
AND?
MR. WESTING-HOUSE ASSURED ME THAT THE WINGS WILL BE RETURNED IMMEDIATELY.
GOOD.
DO YOU THINK THERE ARE DOCTORS FOR THIS KIND OF THING?
I DON'T KNOW, BUT I'M SURE SOMEONE CAN REATTACH THEM.
WELL, I KNOW YOU'RE TIRED AND WANTING TO GO HOME AND GET SOME SLEEP...
UH-UH. YOU'RE NOT GETTING OUT OF IT THAT EASILY.
I DON'T KNOW WHAT YOU'RE TALKING ABOUT.
YOU KNOW EXACTLY WHAT I'M TALKING ABOUT. AND DON'T FORGET TO SAY THE WORDS!
OOOOOH, THIS IS GOING TO BE GREAT!
>SIGH<
EVERY TIME A BELL RINGS, AN ANGEL GETS ITS WINGS.
RING-A-LING-A-LING
HOORAY!
CLAP CLAP

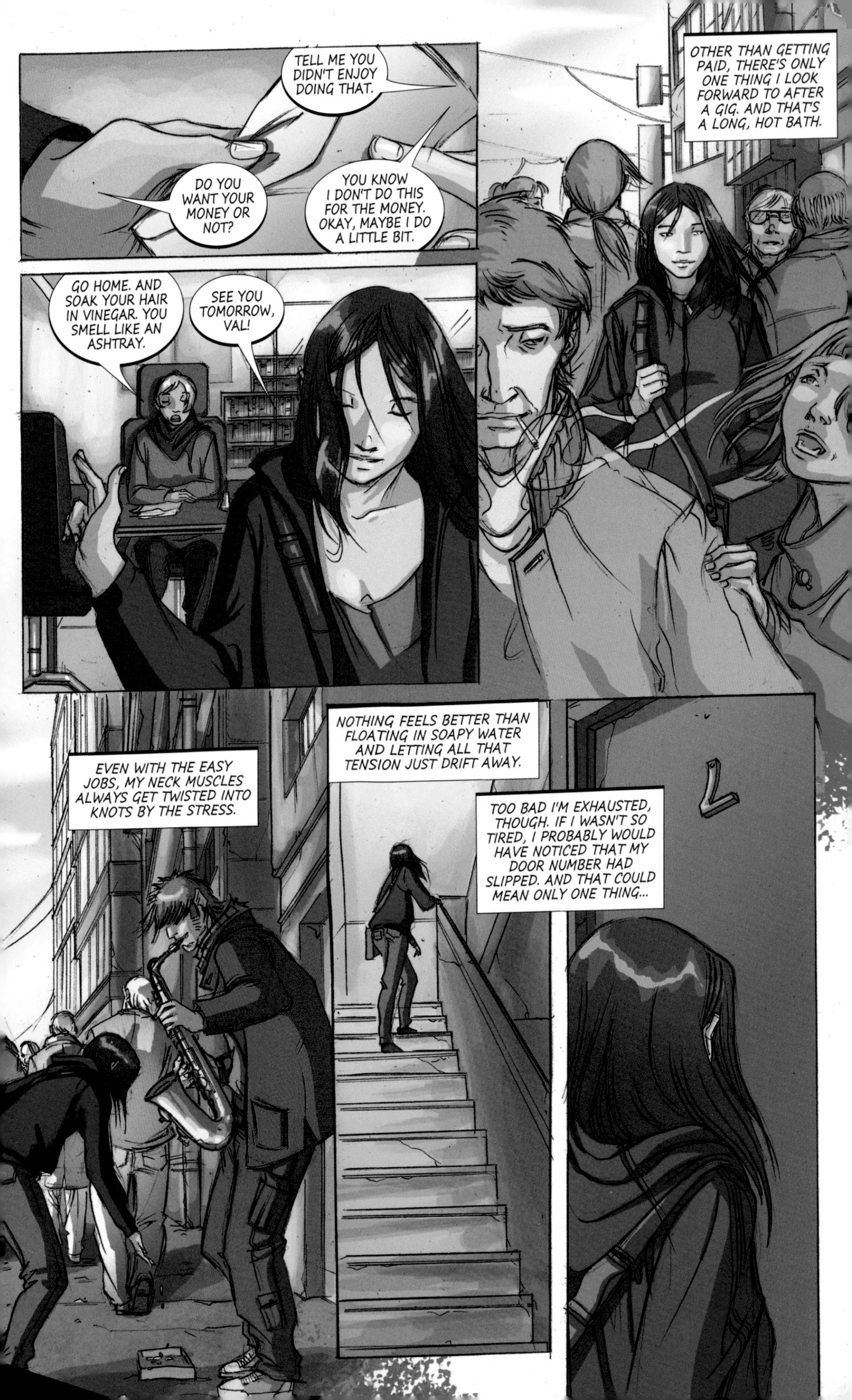
TELL ME YOU DIDN'T ENJOY DOING THAT.
DO YOU WANT YOUR MONEY OR NOT?
YOU KNOW I DON'T DO THIS FOR THE MONEY. OKAY, MAYBE I DO A LITTLE BIT.
OTHER THAN GETTING PAID, THERE'S ONLY ONE THING I LOOK FORWARD TO AFTER A GIG. AND THAT'S A LONG, HOT BATH.
GO HOME. AND SOAK YOUR HAIR IN VINEGAR. YOU SMELL LIKE AN ASHTRAY.
SEE YOU TOMORROW, VAL!
EVEN WITH THE EASY JOBS, MY NECK MUSCLES ALWAYS GET TWISTED INTO KNOTS BY THE STRESS.
NOTHING FEELS BETTER THAN FLOATING IN SOAPY WATER AND LETTING ALL THAT TENSION JUST DRIFT AWAY.
TOO BAD I'M EXHAUSTED, THOUGH. IF I WASN'T SO TIRED, I PROBABLY WOULD HAVE NOTICED THAT MY DOOR NUMBER HAD SLIPPED. AND THAT COULD MEAN ONLY ONE THING...

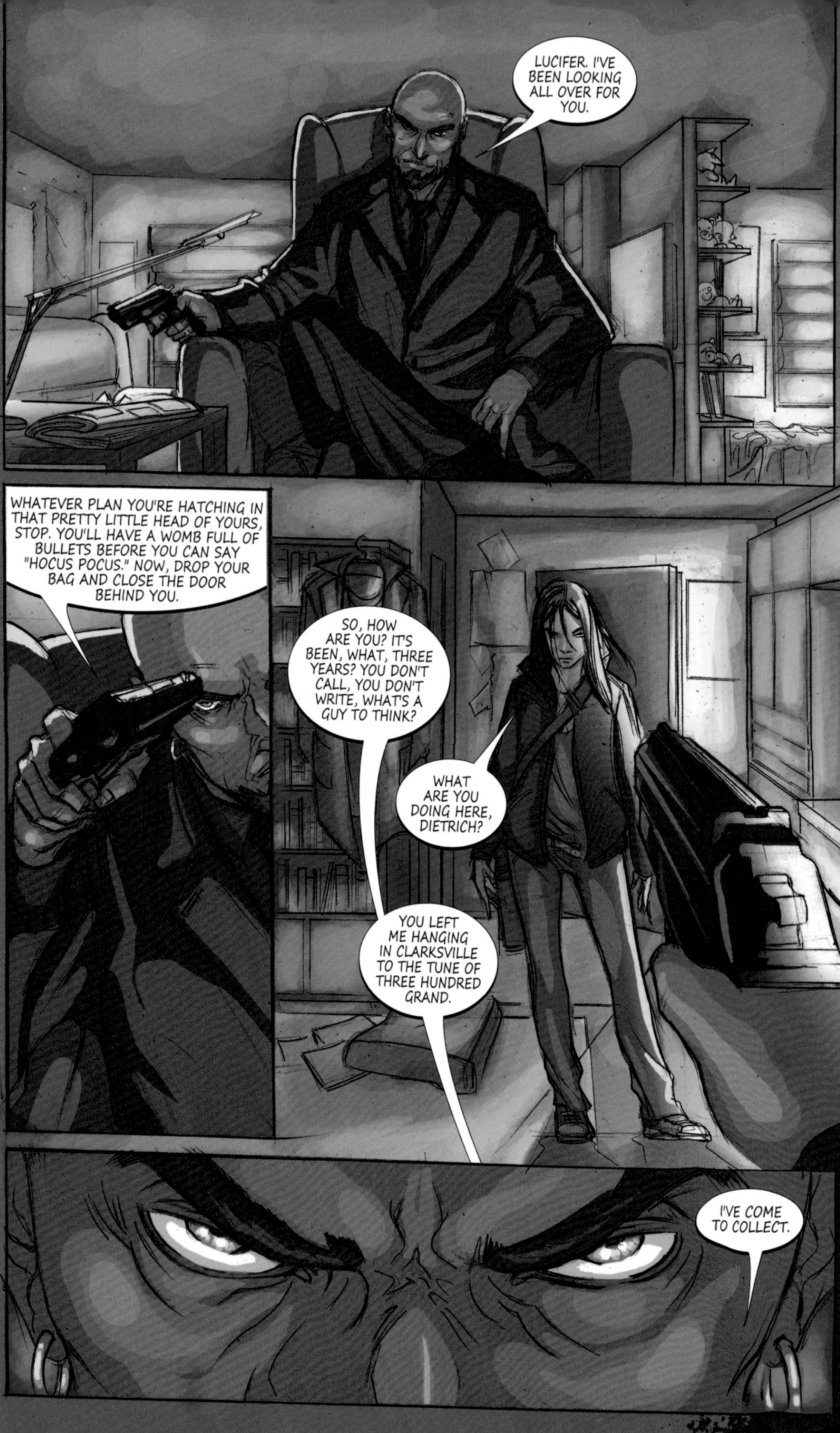
LUCIFER. I'VE BEEN LOOKING ALL OVER FOR YOU.
WHATEVER PLAN YOU'RE HATCHING IN THAT PRETTY LITTLE HEAD OF YOURS, STOP. YOU'LL HAVE A WOMB FULL OF BULLETS BEFORE YOU CAN SAY "HOCUS POCUS." NOW, DROP YOUR BAG AND CLOSE THE DOOR BEHIND YOU.
SO, HOW ARE YOU? IT'S BEEN, WHAT, THREE YEARS? YOU DON'T CALL, YOU DON'T WRITE, WHAT'S A GUY TO THINK?
WHAT ARE YOU DOING HERE, DIETRICH?
YOU LEFT ME HANGING IN CLARKSVILLE TO THE TUNE OF THREE HUNDRED GRAND.
I'VE COME TO COLLECT.

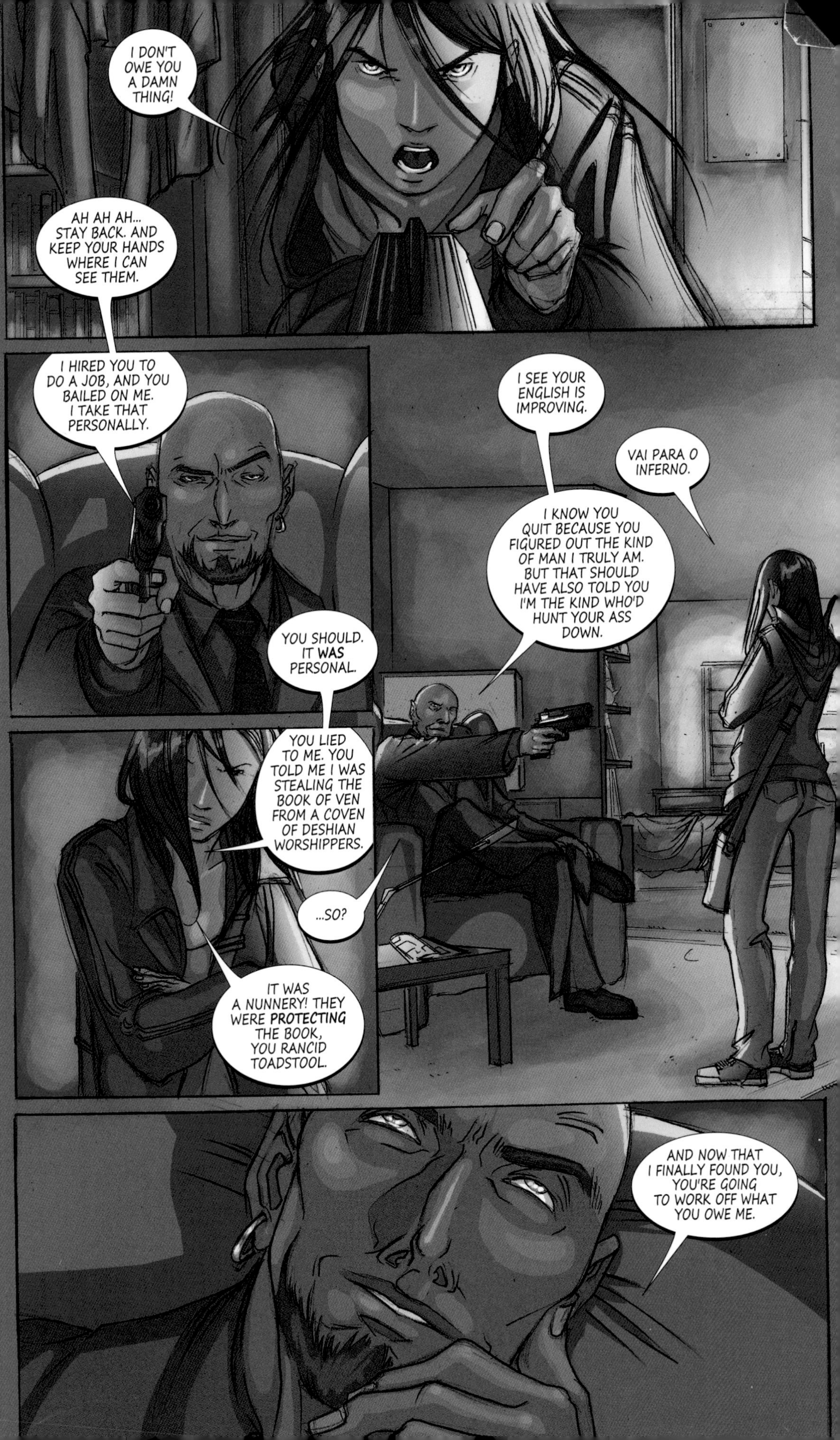
I DON'T OWE YOU A DAMN THING!
AH AH AH... STAY BACK. AND KEEP YOUR HANDS WHERE I CAN SEE THEM.
I HIRED YOU TO DO A JOB, AND YOU BAILED ON ME. I TAKE THAT PERSONALLY.
I SEE YOUR ENGLISH IS IMPROVING.
VAI PARA O INFERNO.
I KNOW YOU QUIT BECAUSE YOU FIGURED OUT THE KIND OF MAN I TRULY AM. BUT THAT SHOULD HAVE ALSO TOLD YOU I'M THE KIND WHO'D HUNT YOUR ASS DOWN.
YOU SHOULD. IT **WAS** PERSONAL.
YOU LIED TO ME. YOU TOLD ME I WAS STEALING THE BOOK OF VEN FROM A COVEN OF DESHIAN WORSHIPPERS.
...SO?
IT WAS A NUNNERY! THEY WERE **PROTECTING** THE BOOK, YOU RANCID TOADSTOOL.
AND NOW THAT I FINALLY FOUND YOU, YOU'RE GOING TO WORK OFF WHAT YOU OWE ME.

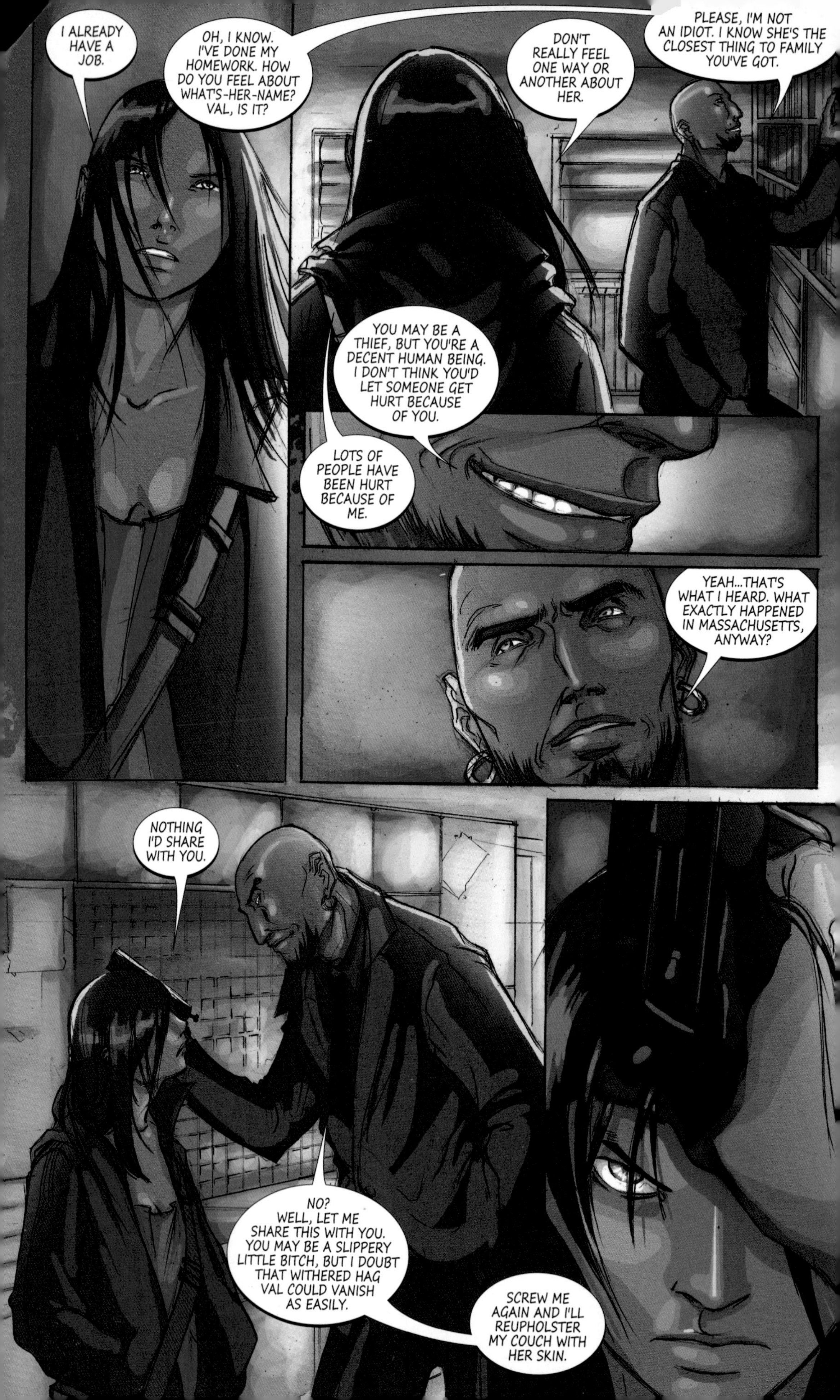
I ALREADY HAVE A JOB.
OH, I KNOW. I'VE DONE MY HOMEWORK. HOW DO YOU FEEL ABOUT WHAT'S-HER-NAME? VAL, IS IT?
DON'T REALLY FEEL ONE WAY OR ANOTHER ABOUT HER.
PLEASE, I'M NOT AN IDIOT. I KNOW SHE'S THE CLOSEST THING TO FAMILY YOU'VE GOT.
YOU MAY BE A THIEF, BUT YOU'RE A DECENT HUMAN BEING. I DON'T THINK YOU'D LET SOMEONE GET HURT BECAUSE OF YOU.
LOTS OF PEOPLE HAVE BEEN HURT BECAUSE OF ME.
YEAH...THAT'S WHAT I HEARD. WHAT EXACTLY HAPPENED IN MASSACHUSETTS, ANYWAY?
NOTHING I'D SHARE WITH YOU.
NO? WELL, LET ME SHARE THIS WITH YOU. YOU MAY BE A SLIPPERY LITTLE BITCH, BUT I DOUBT THAT WITHERED HAG VAL COULD VANISH AS EASILY.
SCREW ME AGAIN AND I'LL REUPHOLSTER MY COUCH WITH HER SKIN.

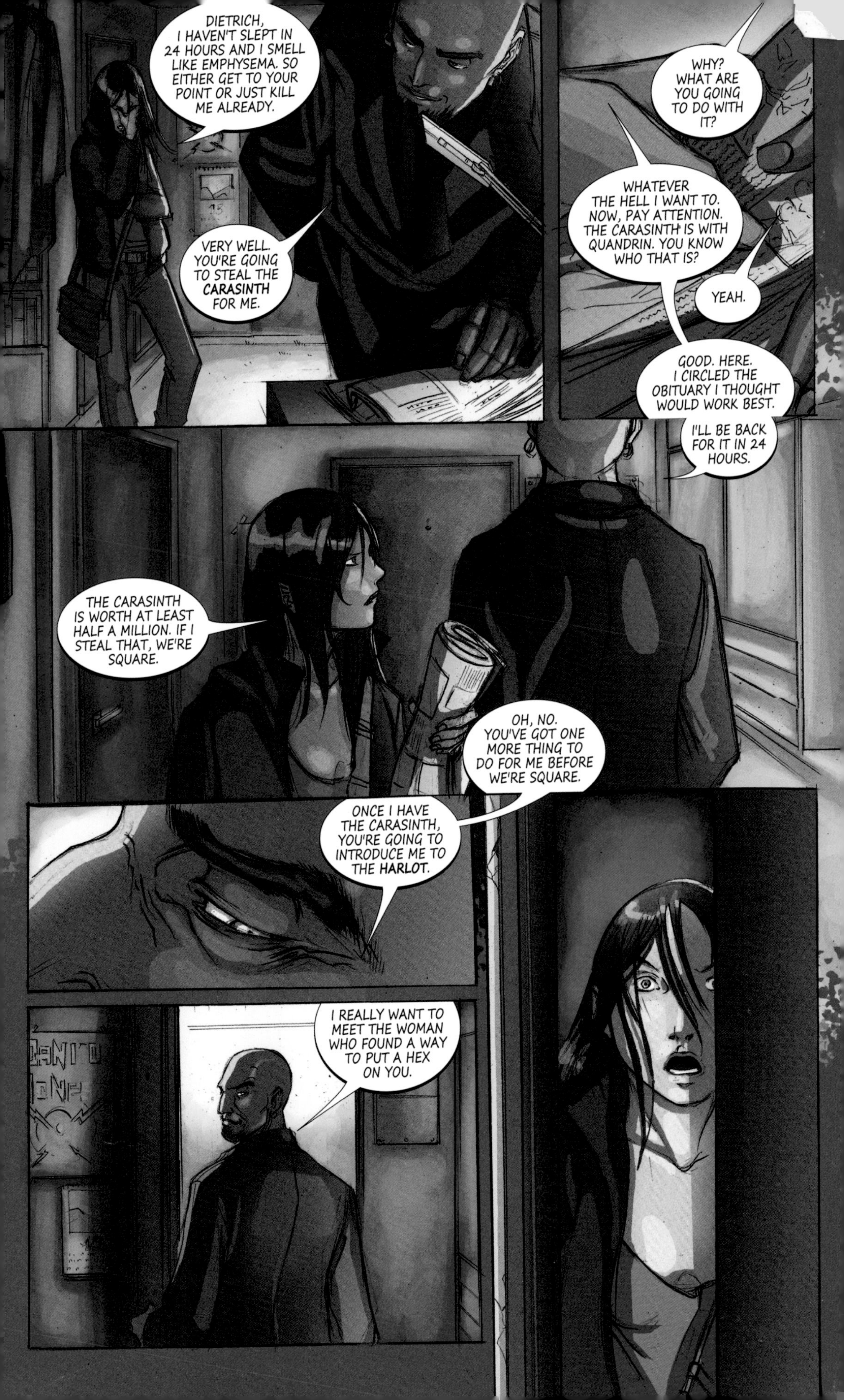
DIETRICH, I HAVEN'T SLEPT IN 24 HOURS AND I SMELL LIKE EMPHYSEMA. SO EITHER GET TO YOUR POINT OR JUST KILL ME ALREADY.
VERY WELL. YOU'RE GOING TO STEAL THE **CARASINTH** FOR ME.
WHY? WHAT ARE YOU GOING TO DO WITH IT?
WHATEVER THE HELL I WANT TO. NOW, PAY ATTENTION. THE CARASINTH IS WITH QUANDRIN. YOU KNOW WHO THAT IS?
YEAH.
GOOD. HERE. I CIRCLED THE OBITUARY I THOUGHT WOULD WORK BEST.
I'LL BE BACK FOR IT IN 24 HOURS.
THE CARASINTH IS WORTH AT LEAST HALF A MILLION. IF I STEAL THAT, WE'RE SQUARE.
OH, NO. YOU'VE GOT ONE MORE THING TO DO FOR ME BEFORE WE'RE SQUARE.
ONCE I HAVE THE CARASINTH, YOU'RE GOING TO INTRODUCE ME TO THE **HARLOT**.
I REALLY WANT TO MEET THE WOMAN WHO FOUND A WAY TO PUT A HEX ON YOU.

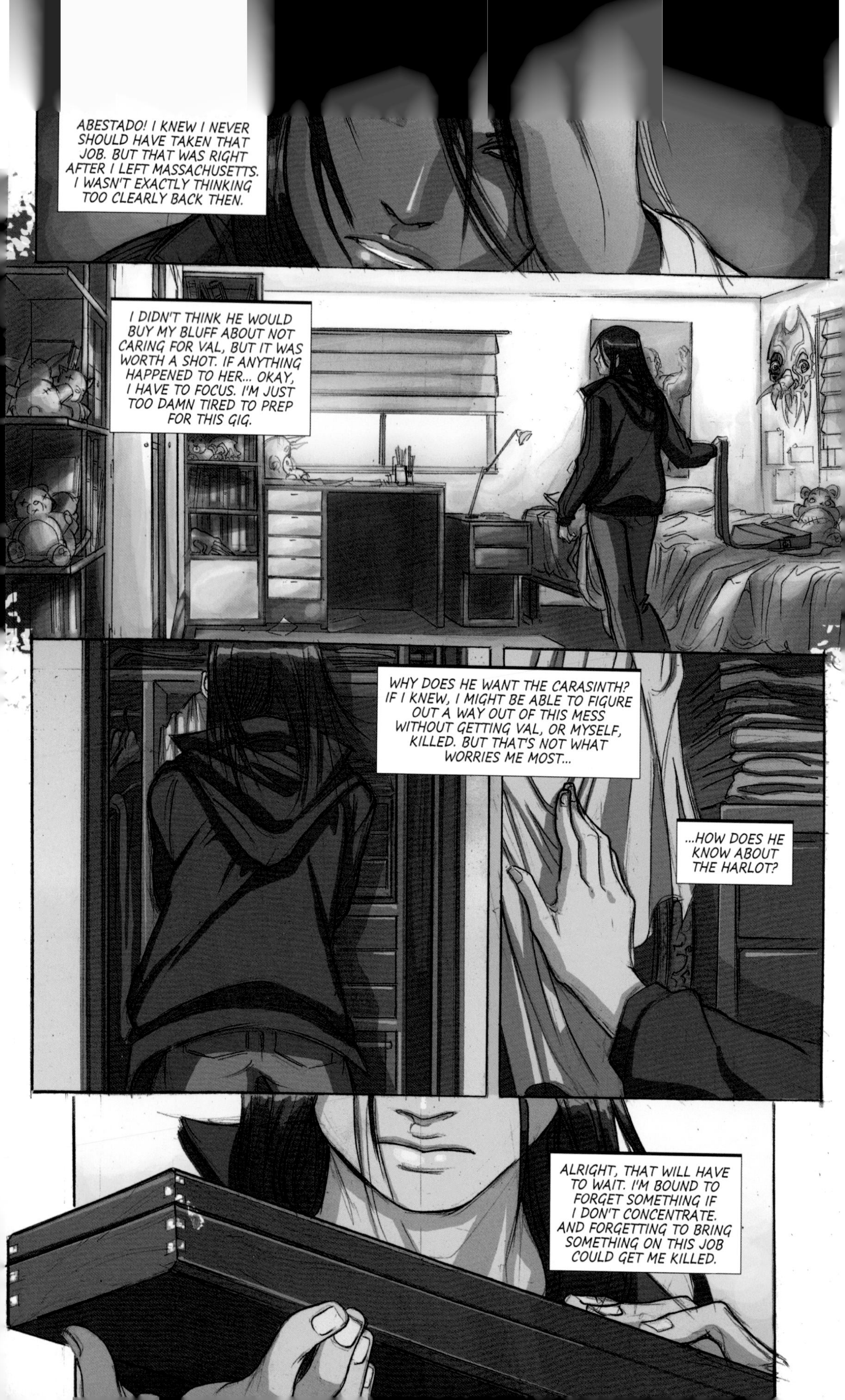
ABESTADO! I KNEW I NEVER SHOULD HAVE TAKEN THAT JOB. BUT THAT WAS RIGHT AFTER I LEFT MASSACHUSETTS. I WASN'T EXACTLY THINKING TOO CLEARLY BACK THEN.
I DIDN'T THINK HE WOULD BUY MY BLUFF ABOUT NOT CARING FOR VAL, BUT IT WAS WORTH A SHOT. IF ANYTHING HAPPENED TO HER... OKAY, I HAVE TO FOCUS. I'M JUST TOO DAMN TIRED TO PREP FOR THIS GIG.
WHY DOES HE WANT THE CARASINTH? IF I KNEW, I MIGHT BE ABLE TO FIGURE OUT A WAY OUT OF THIS MESS WITHOUT GETTING VAL, OR MYSELF, KILLED. BUT THAT'S NOT WHAT WORRIES ME MOST...
...HOW DOES HE KNOW ABOUT THE HARLOT?
ALRIGHT, THAT WILL HAVE TO WAIT. I'M BOUND TO FORGET SOMETHING IF I DON'T CONCENTRATE. AND FORGETTING TO BRING SOMETHING ON THIS JOB COULD GET ME KILLED.

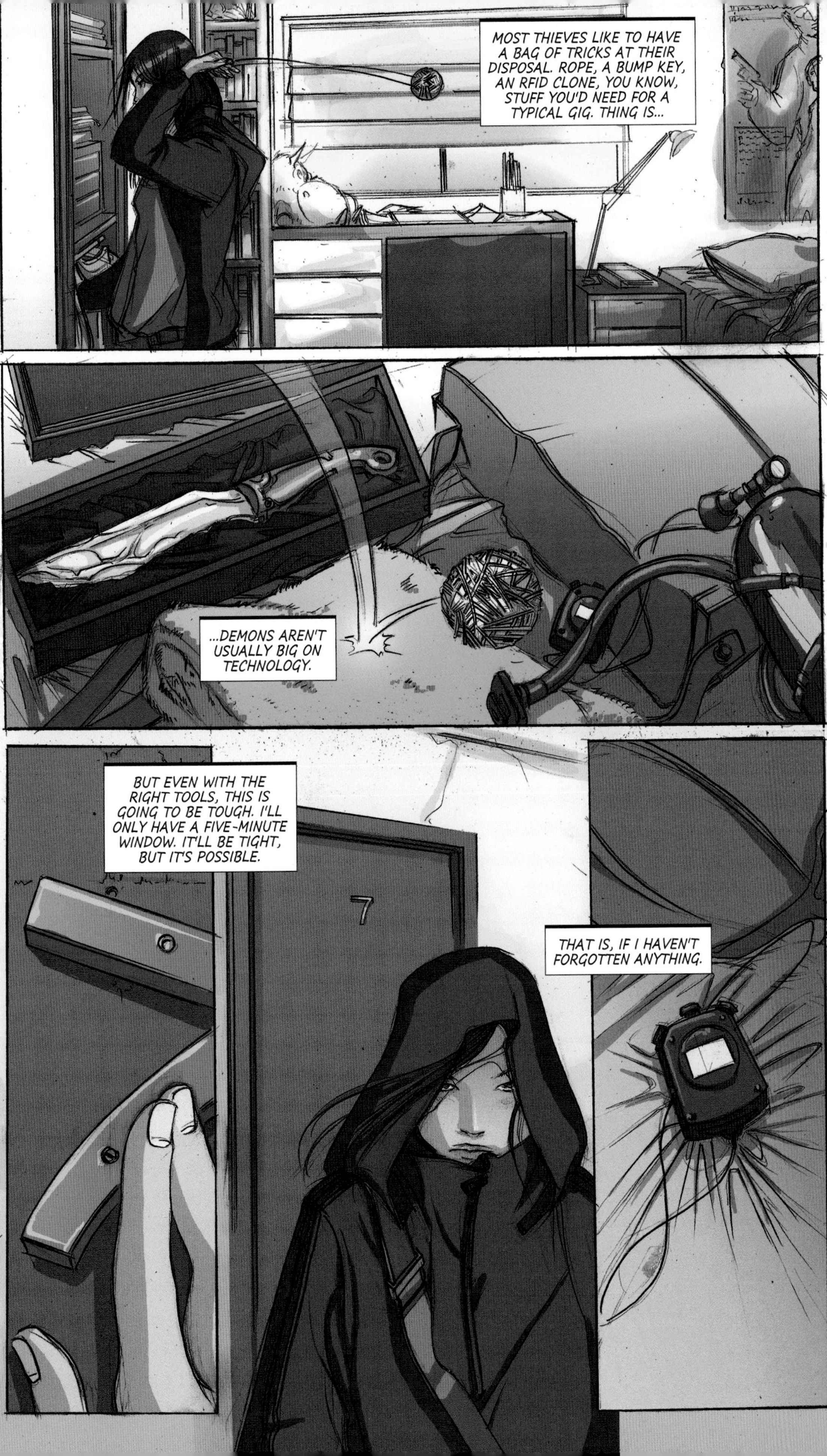
MOST THIEVES LIKE TO HAVE A BAG OF TRICKS AT THEIR DISPOSAL. ROPE, A BUMP KEY, AN RFID CLONE, YOU KNOW, STUFF YOU'D NEED FOR A TYPICAL GIG. THING IS...
...DEMONS AREN'T USUALLY BIG ON TECHNOLOGY.
BUT EVEN WITH THE RIGHT TOOLS, THIS IS GOING TO BE TOUGH. I'LL ONLY HAVE A FIVE-MINUTE WINDOW. IT'LL BE TIGHT, BUT IT'S POSSIBLE.
7
THAT IS, IF I HAVEN'T FORGOTTEN ANYTHING.

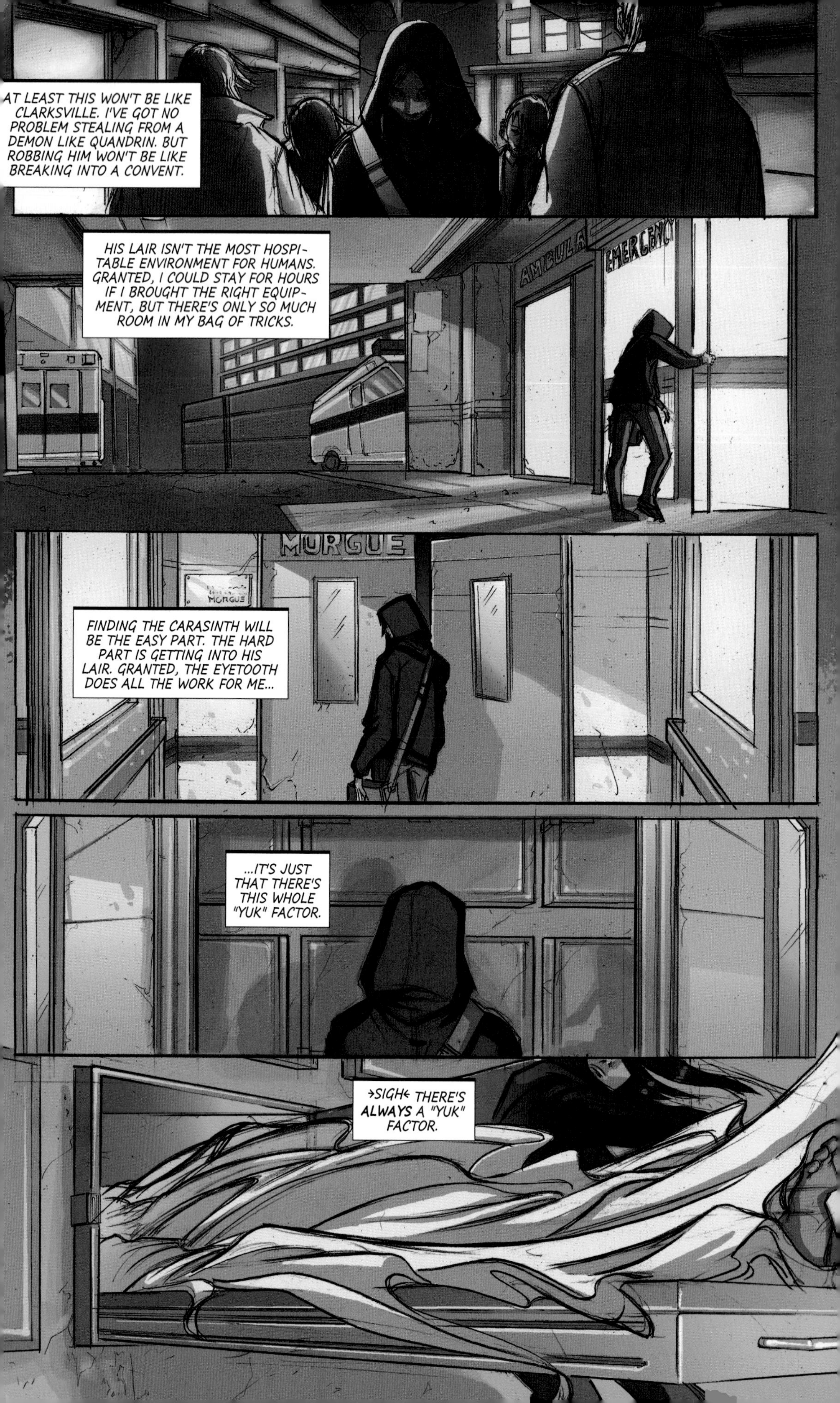
AT LEAST THIS WON'T BE LIKE CLARKSVILLE. I'VE GOT NO PROBLEM STEALING FROM A DEMON LIKE QUANDRIN. BUT ROBBING HIM WON'T BE LIKE BREAKING INTO A CONVENT.
HIS LAIR ISN'T THE MOST HOSPITABLE ENVIRONMENT FOR HUMANS. GRANTED, I COULD STAY FOR HOURS IF I BROUGHT THE RIGHT EQUIPMENT, BUT THERE'S ONLY SO MUCH ROOM IN MY BAG OF TRICKS.
AMBULA
EMERGENCY
MORGUE
MORGUE
FINDING THE CARASINTH WILL BE THE EASY PART. THE HARD PART IS GETTING INTO HIS LAIR. GRANTED, THE EYETOOTH DOES ALL THE WORK FOR ME...
...IT'S JUST THAT THERE'S THIS WHOLE "YUK" FACTOR.
>SIGH< THERE'S ALWAYS A "YUK" FACTOR.

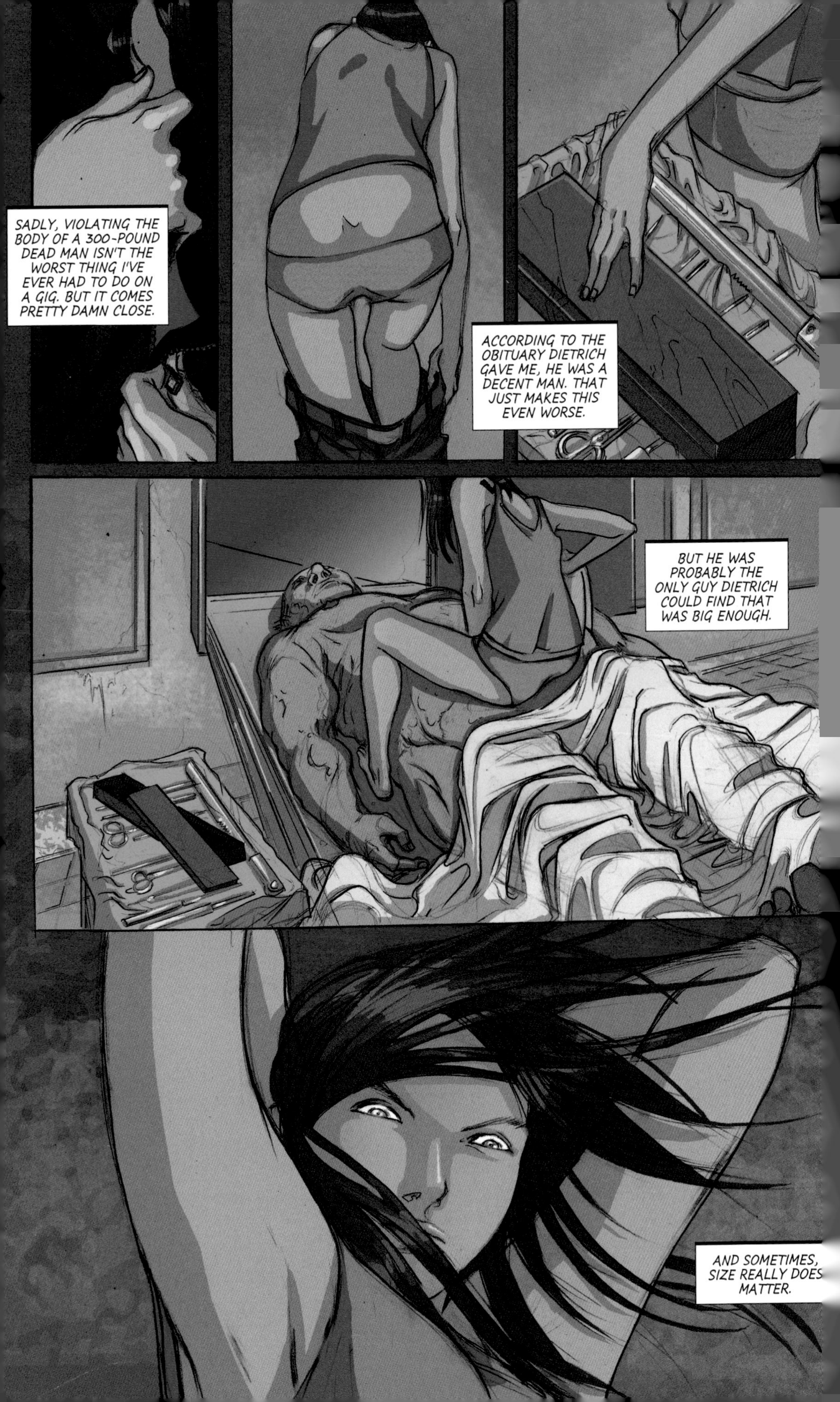
SADLY, VIOLATING THE BODY OF A 300-POUND DEAD MAN ISN'T THE WORST THING I'VE EVER HAD TO DO ON A GIG. BUT IT COMES PRETTY DAMN CLOSE.
ACCORDING TO THE OBITUARY DIETRICH GAVE ME, HE WAS A DECENT MAN. THAT JUST MAKES THIS EVEN WORSE.
BUT HE WAS PROBABLY THE ONLY GUY DIETRICH COULD FIND THAT WAS BIG ENOUGH.
AND SOMETIMES, SIZE REALLY DOES MATTER.

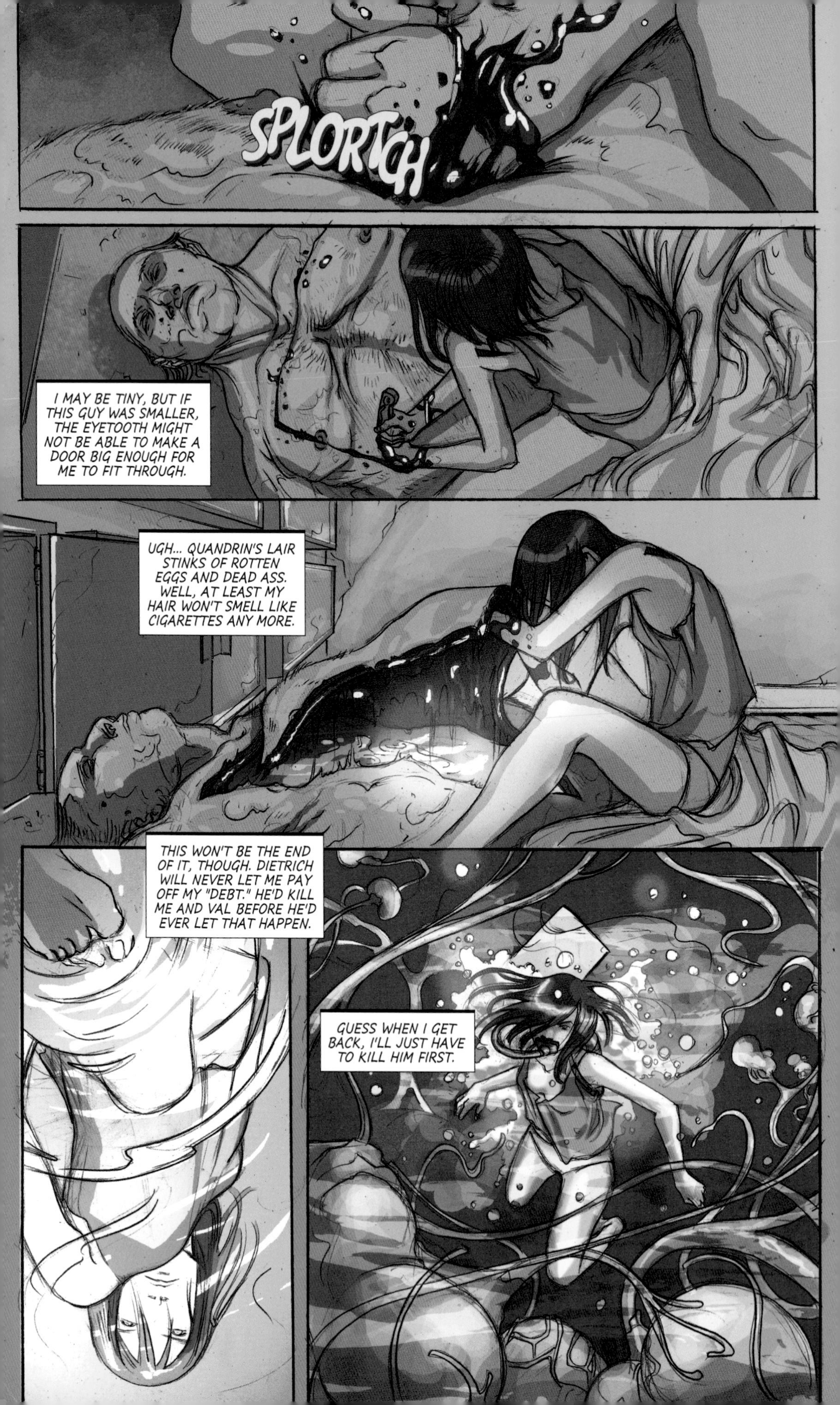
SPLORTCH
I MAY BE TINY, BUT IF THIS GUY WAS SMALLER, THE EYETOOTH MIGHT NOT BE ABLE TO MAKE A DOOR BIG ENOUGH FOR ME TO FIT THROUGH.
UGH... QUANDRIN'S LAIR STINKS OF ROTTEN EGGS AND DEAD ASS. WELL, AT LEAST MY HAIR WON'T SMELL LIKE CIGARETTES ANY MORE.
THIS WON'T BE THE END OF IT, THOUGH. DIETRICH WILL NEVER LET ME PAY OFF MY "DEBT." HE'D KILL ME AND VAL BEFORE HE'D EVER LET THAT HAPPEN.
GUESS WHEN I GET BACK, I'LL JUST HAVE TO KILL HIM FIRST.

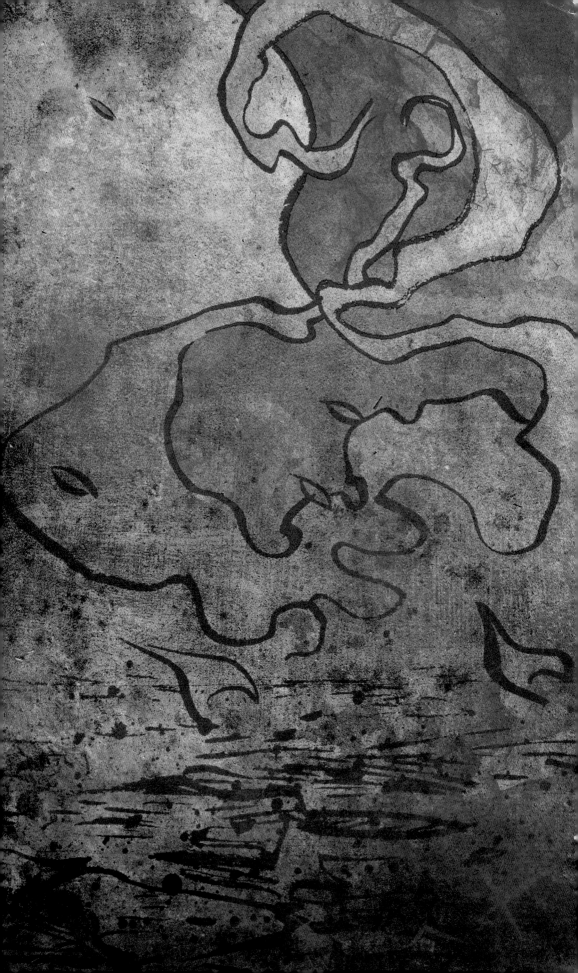

CHAPTER II

WHEREIN LUCIFER GETS UNEMPLOYMENT AND RECEIVES AN UNEXPECTED WAKE-UP CALL.

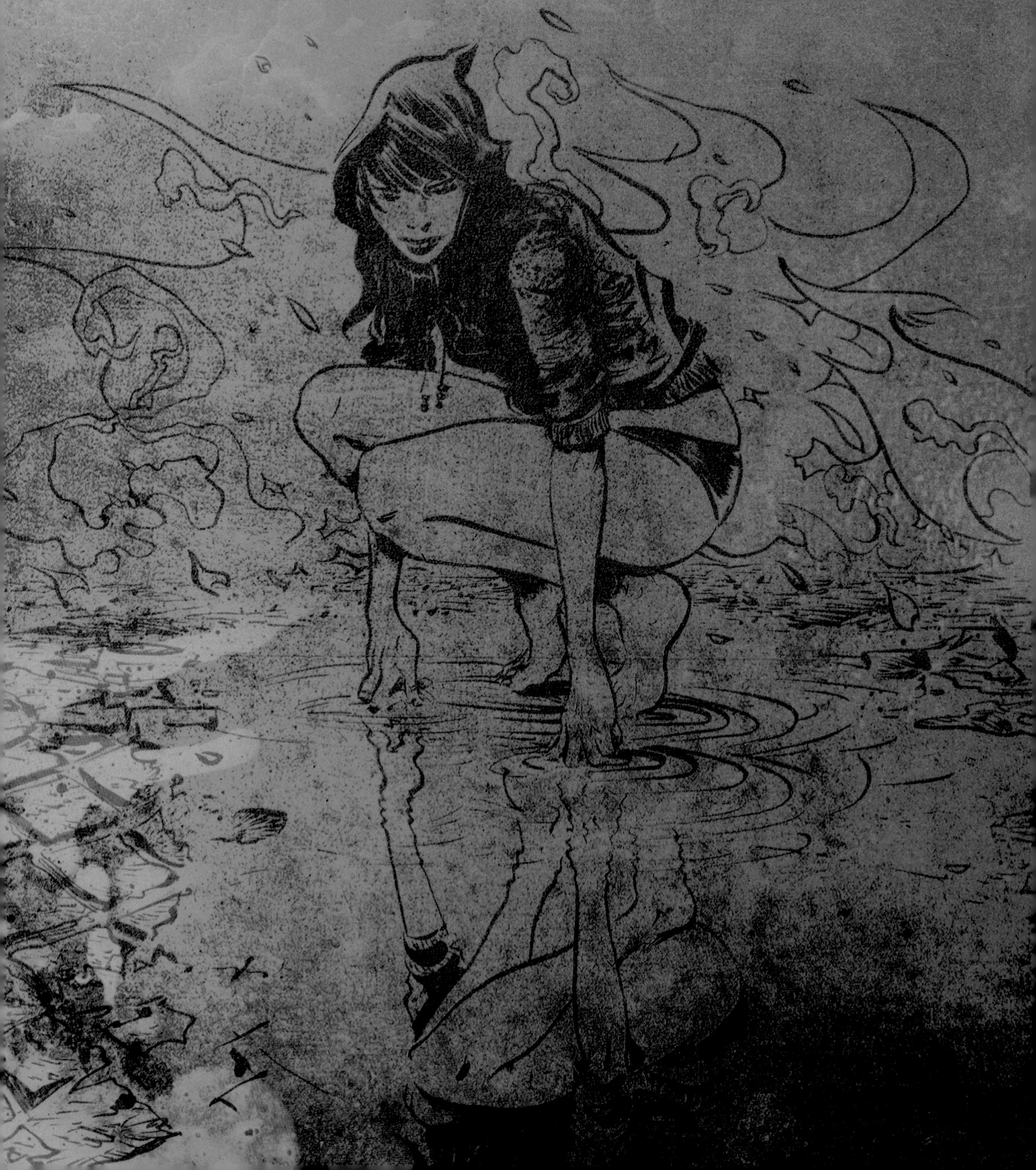

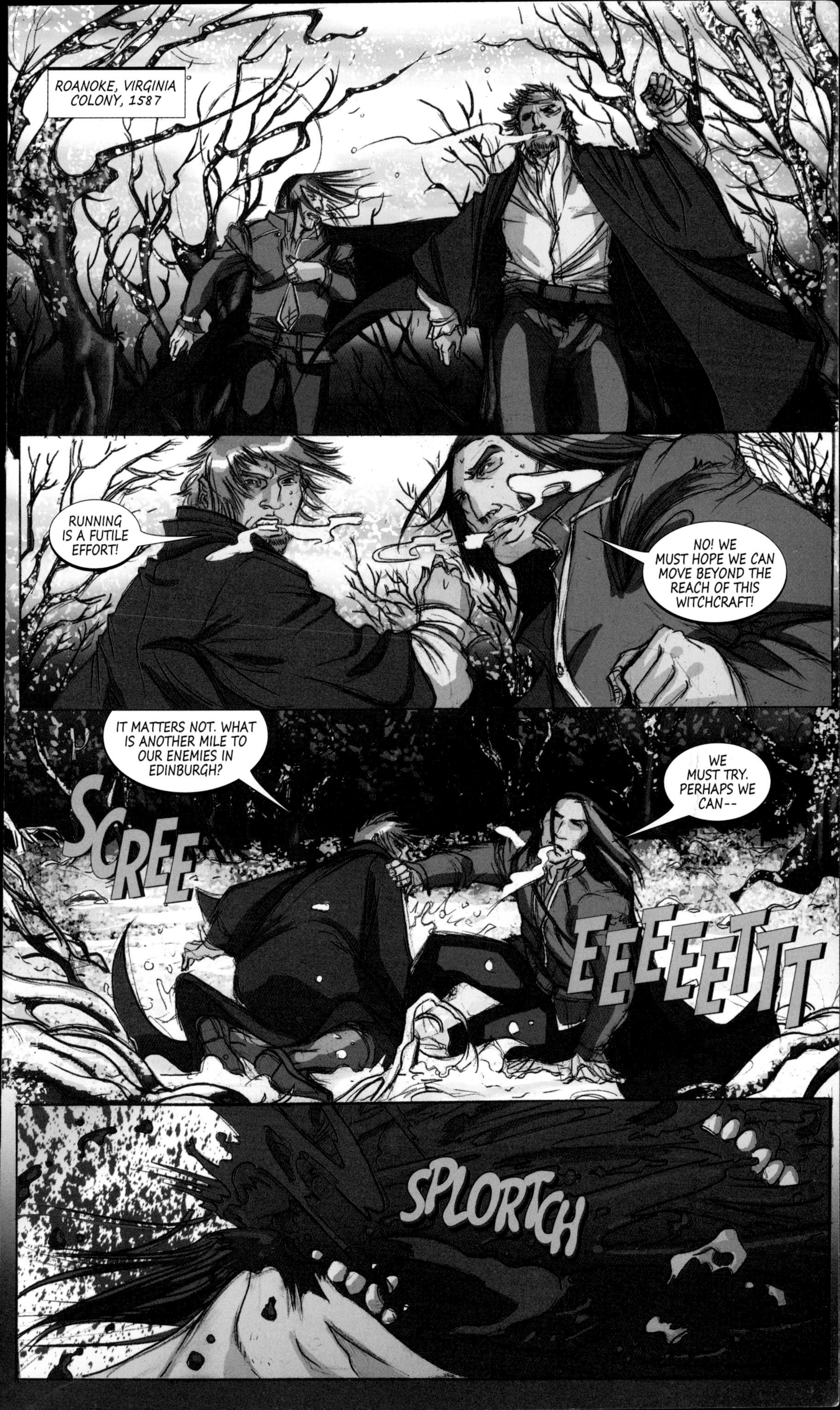
ROANOKE, VIRGINIA COLONY, 1587
RUNNING IS A FUTILE EFFORT!
NO! WE MUST HOPE WE CAN MOVE BEYOND THE REACH OF THIS WITCHCRAFT!
IT MATTERS NOT. WHAT IS ANOTHER MILE TO OUR ENEMIES IN EDINBURGH?
WE MUST TRY. PERHAPS WE CAN--
SCREE
EEEEETTT
SPLORTCH

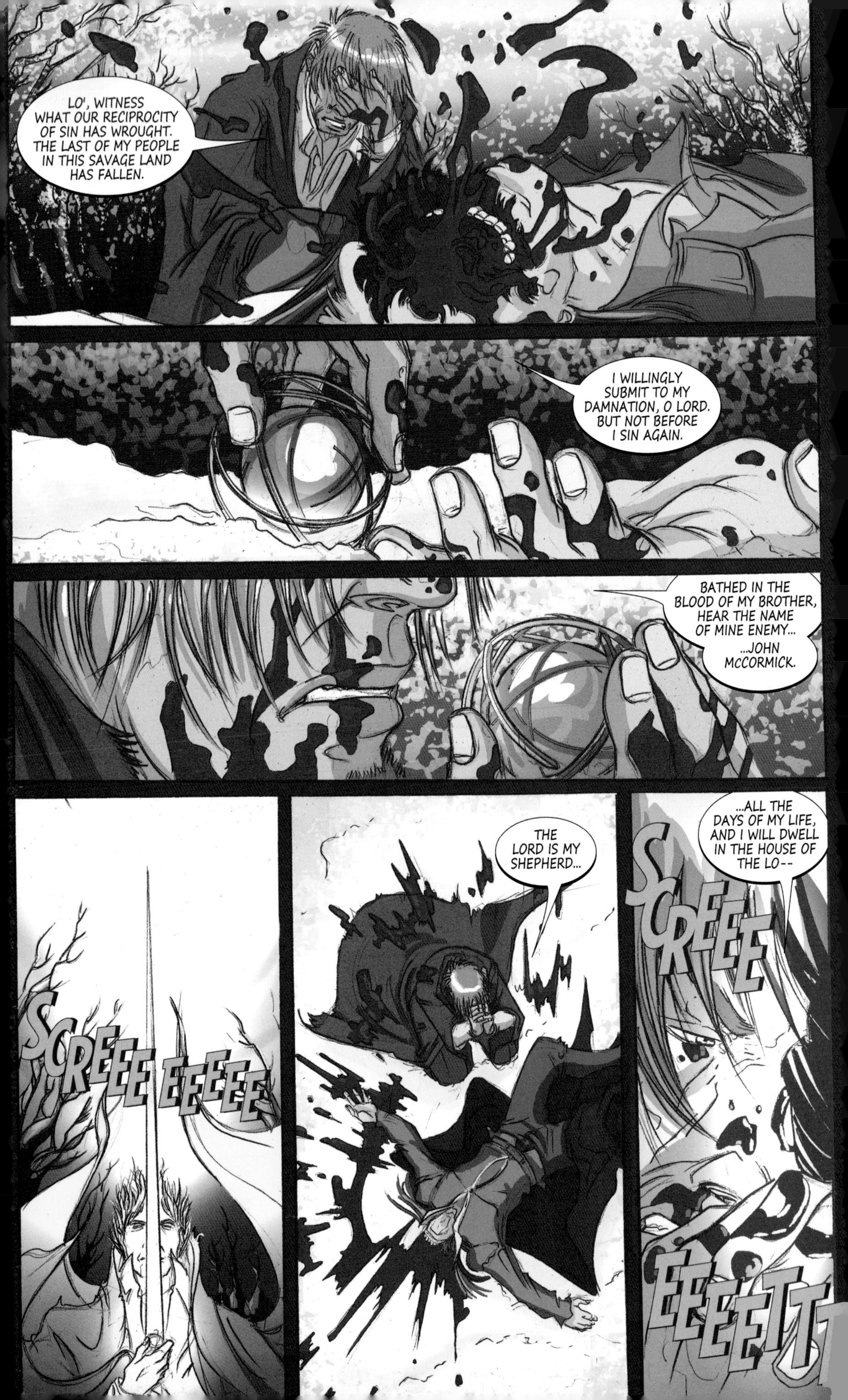
LO', WITNESS WHAT OUR RECIPROCITY OF SIN HAS WROUGHT. THE LAST OF MY PEOPLE IN THIS SAVAGE LAND HAS FALLEN.
I WILLINGLY SUBMIT TO MY DAMNATION, O LORD. BUT NOT BEFORE I SIN AGAIN.
BATHED IN THE BLOOD OF MY BROTHER, HEAR THE NAME OF MINE ENEMY...
...JOHN McCORMICK.
SCREEE EEEEEE
THE LORD IS MY SHEPHERD...
...ALL THE DAYS OF MY LIFE, AND I WILL DWELL IN THE HOUSE OF THE LO--
SCREEEEEEETTT

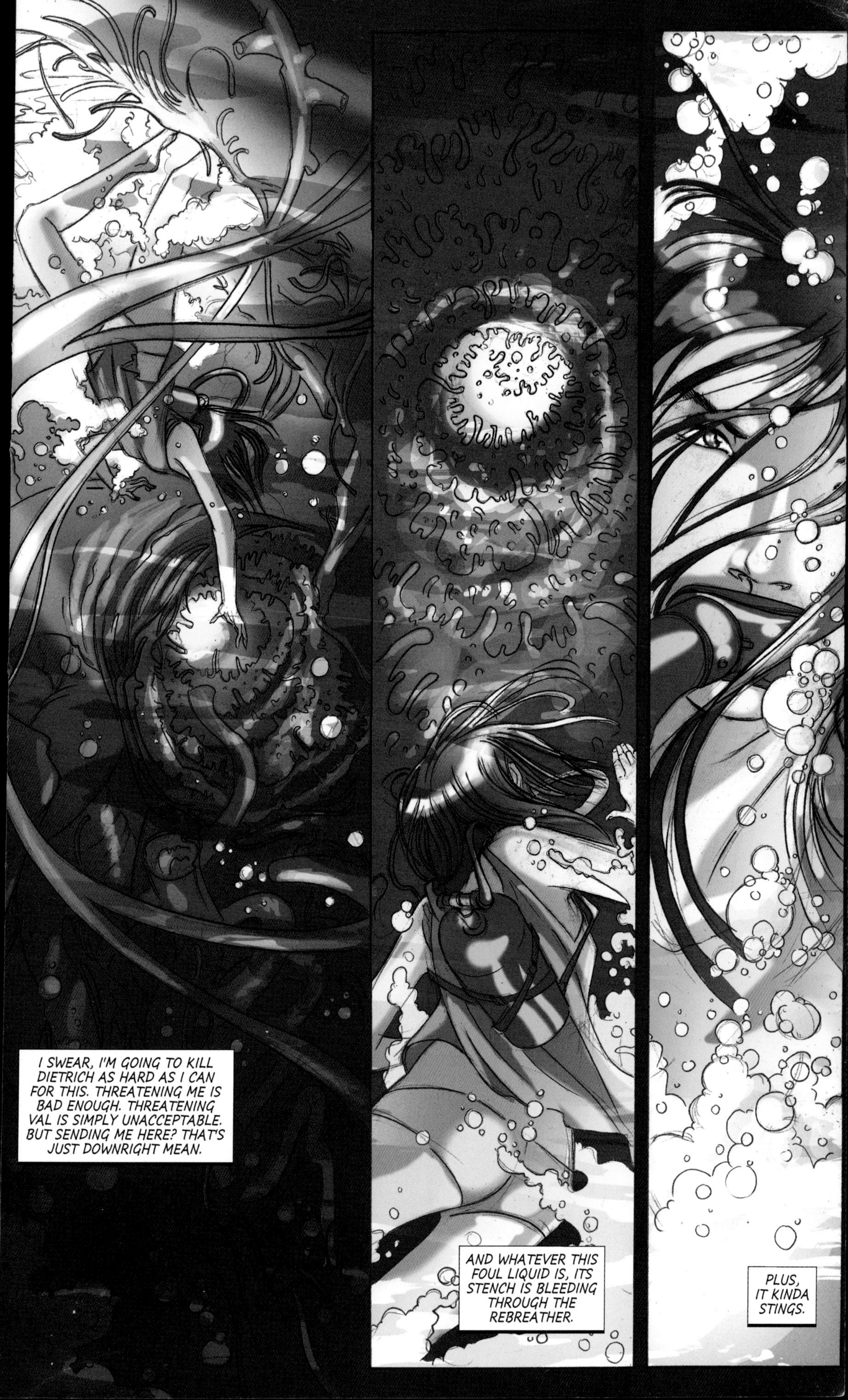
I SWEAR, I'M GOING TO KILL DIETRICH AS HARD AS I CAN FOR THIS. THREATENING ME IS BAD ENOUGH. THREATENING VAL IS SIMPLY UNACCEPTABLE. BUT SENDING ME HERE? THAT'S JUST DOWNRIGHT MEAN.
AND WHATEVER THIS FOUL LIQUID IS, ITS STENCH IS BLEEDING THROUGH THE REBREATHER.
PLUS, IT KINDA STINGS.

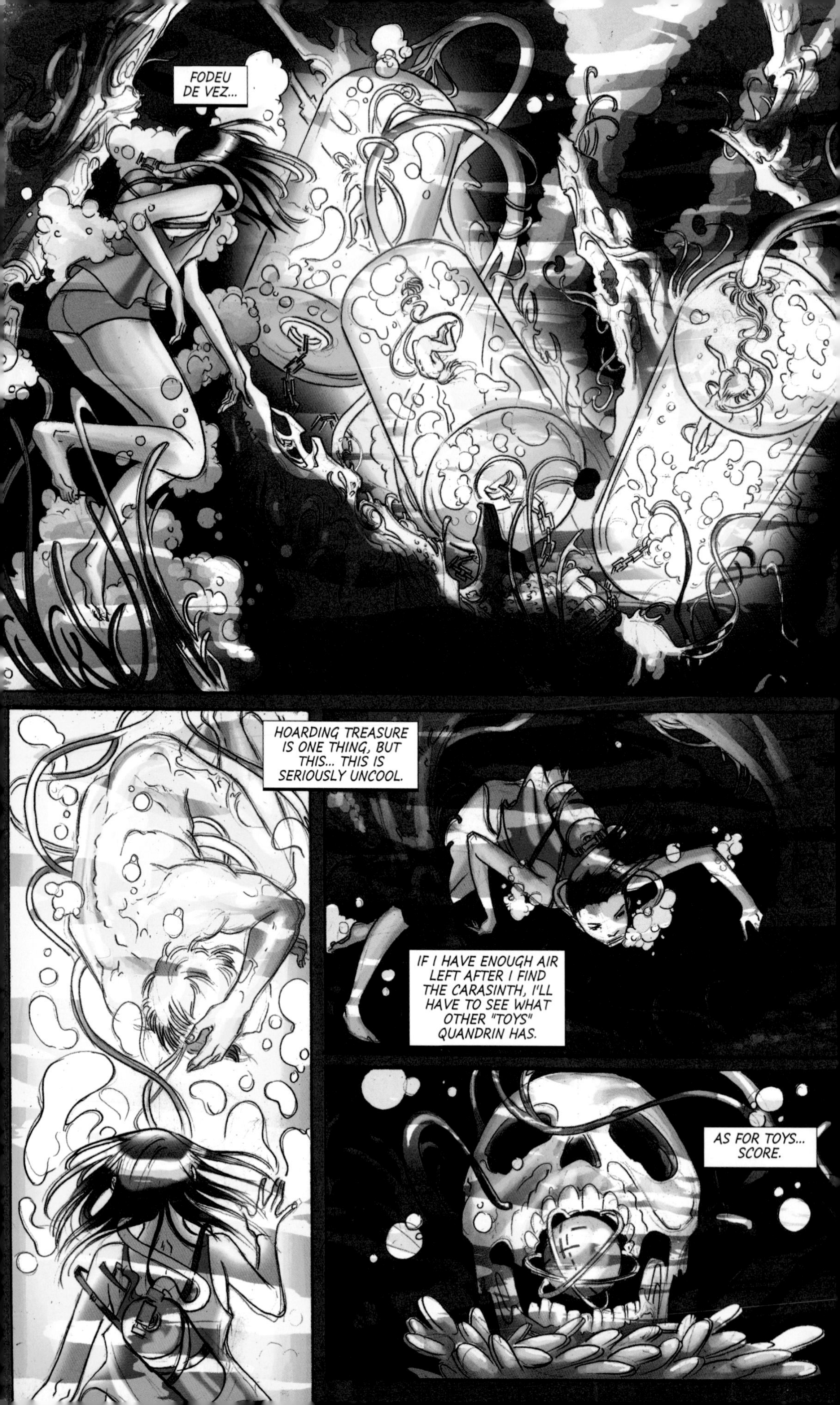
FODEU DE VEZ...
HOARDING TREASURE IS ONE THING, BUT THIS... THIS IS SERIOUSLY UNCOOL.
IF I HAVE ENOUGH AIR LEFT AFTER I FIND THE CARASINTH, I'LL HAVE TO SEE WHAT OTHER "TOYS" QUANDRIN HAS.
AS FOR TOYS... SCORE.

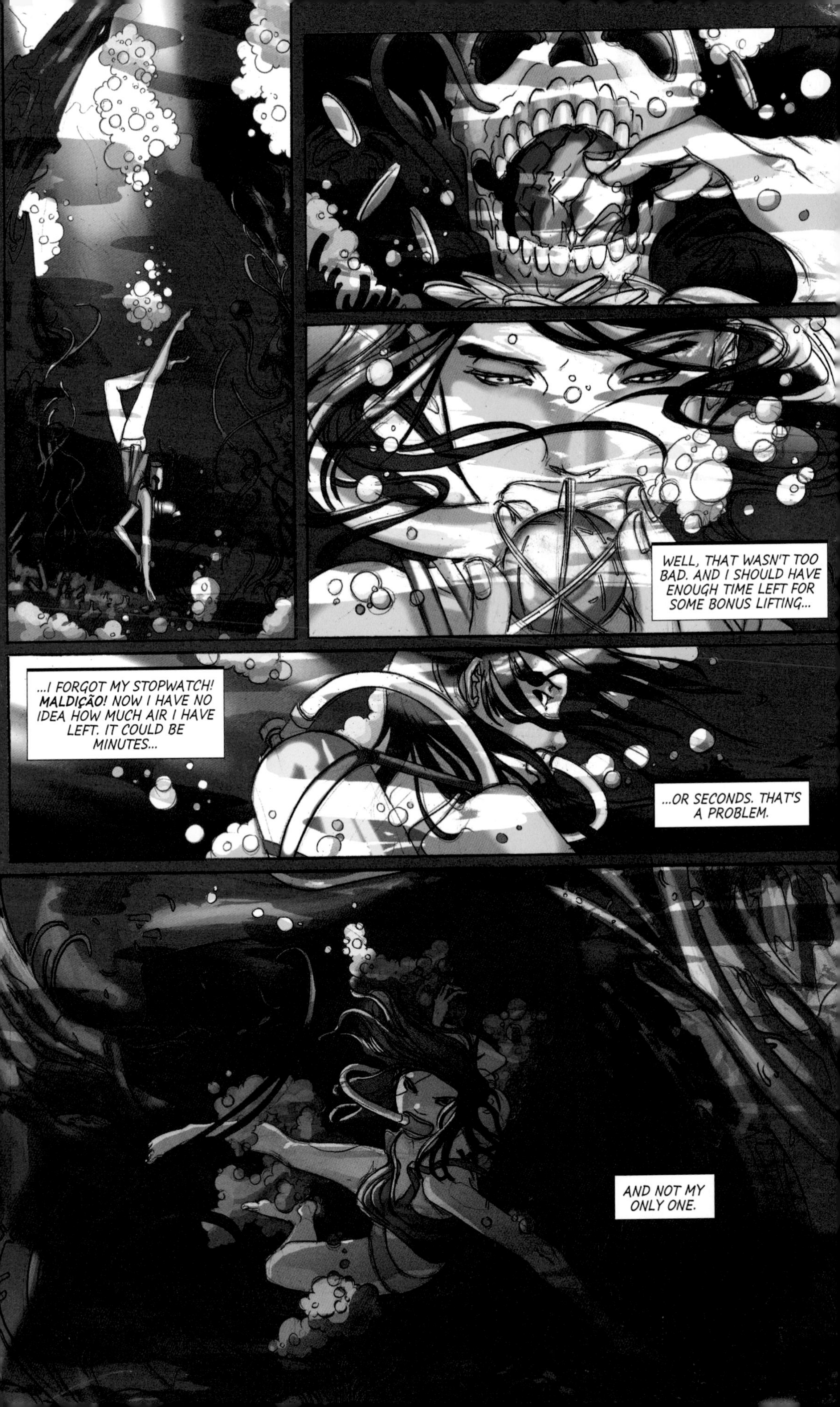
WELL, THAT WASN'T TOO BAD. AND I SHOULD HAVE ENOUGH TIME LEFT FOR SOME BONUS LIFTING...
...I FORGOT MY STOPWATCH! **MALDIÇÃO!** NOW I HAVE NO IDEA HOW MUCH AIR I HAVE LEFT. IT COULD BE MINUTES...
...OR SECONDS. THAT'S A PROBLEM.
AND NOT MY ONLY ONE.

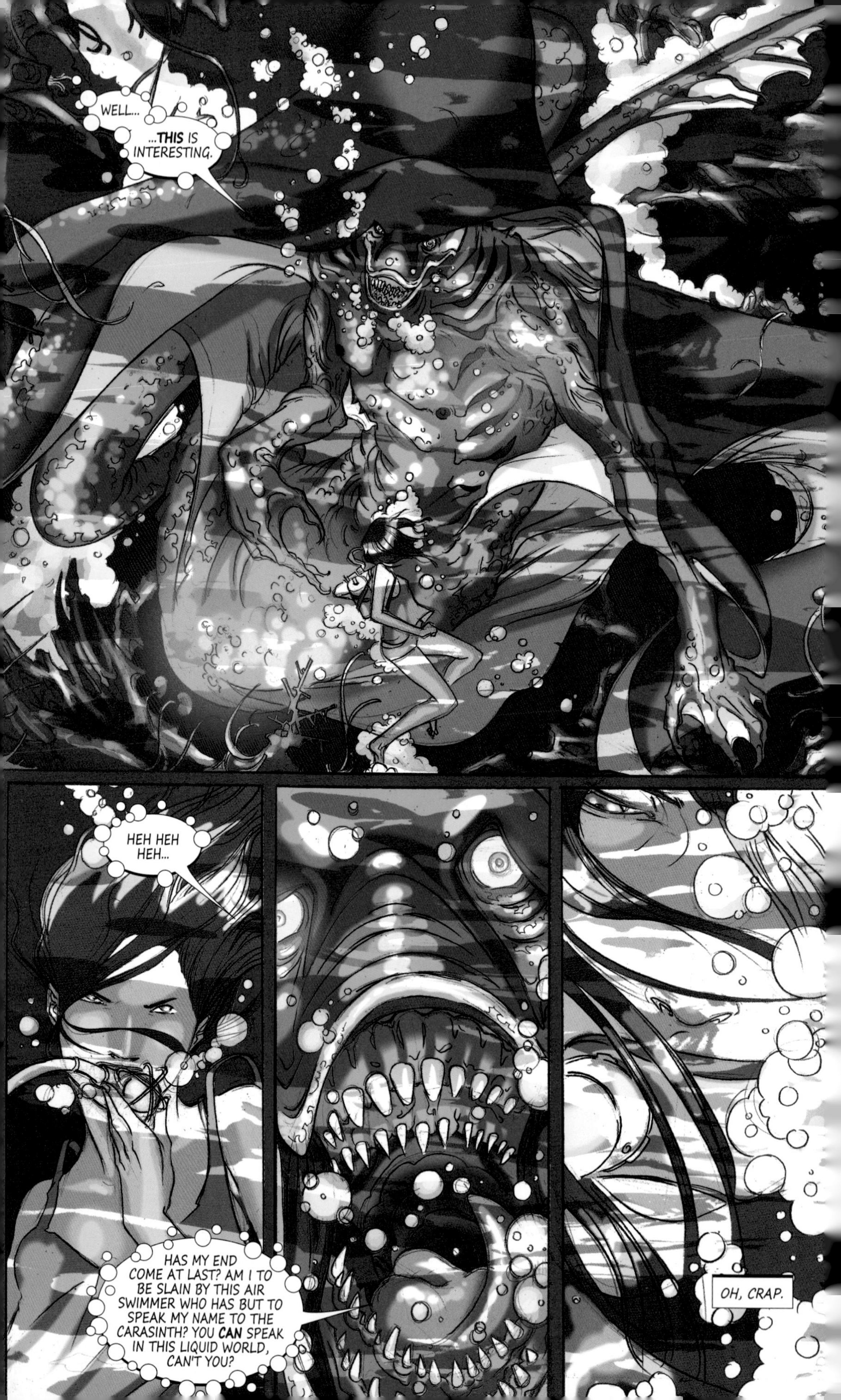
WELL...
...THIS IS INTERESTING.
HEH HEH HEH...
HAS MY END COME AT LAST? AM I TO BE SLAIN BY THIS AIR SWIMMER WHO HAS BUT TO SPEAK MY NAME TO THE CARASINTH? YOU CAN SPEAK IN THIS LIQUID WORLD, CAN'T YOU?
OH, CRAP.

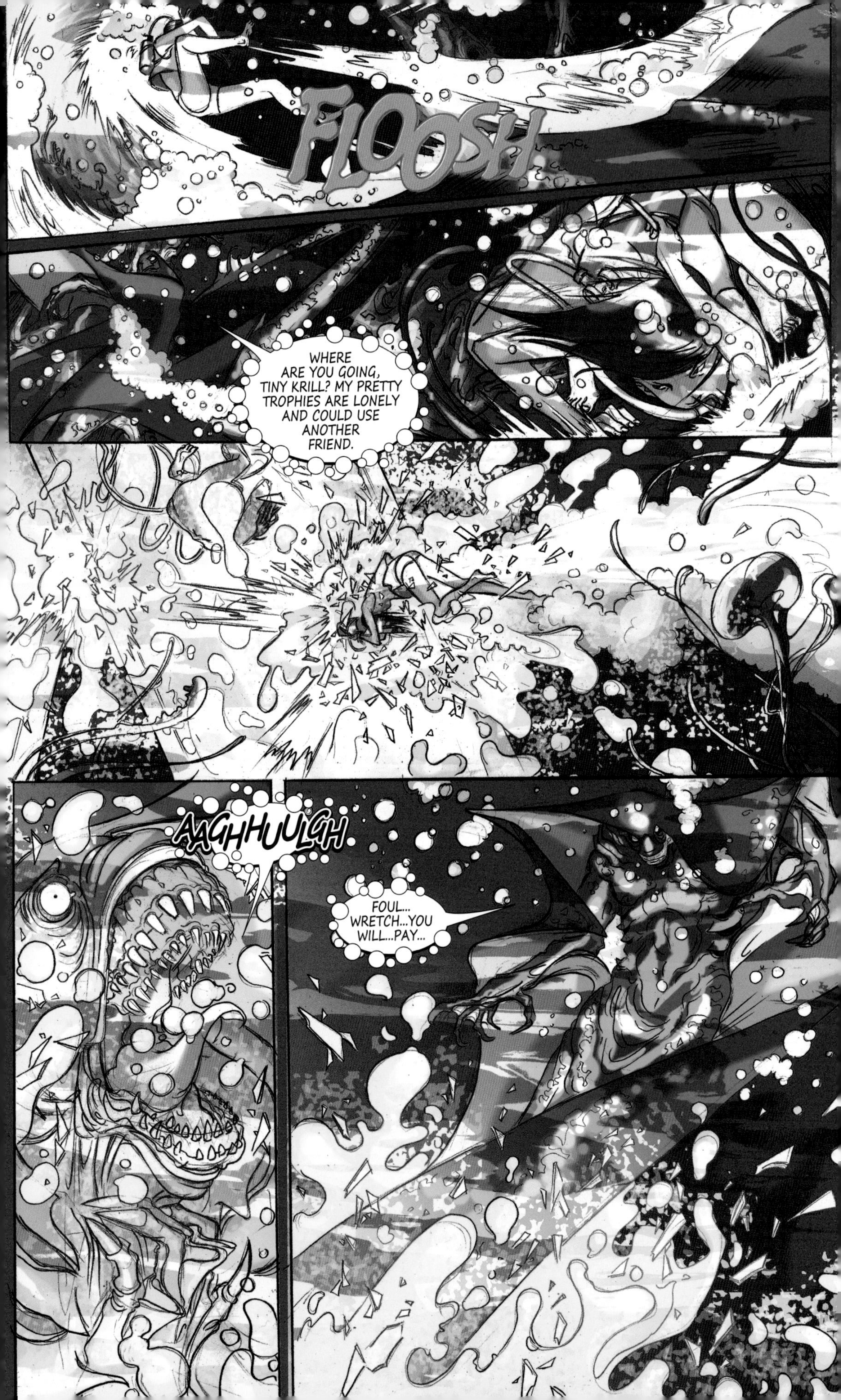
FLOOSH
WHERE ARE YOU GOING, TINY KRILL? MY PRETTY TROPHIES ARE LONELY AND COULD USE ANOTHER FRIEND.
AAGHHUULGH
FOUL... WRETCH...YOU WILL...PAY...

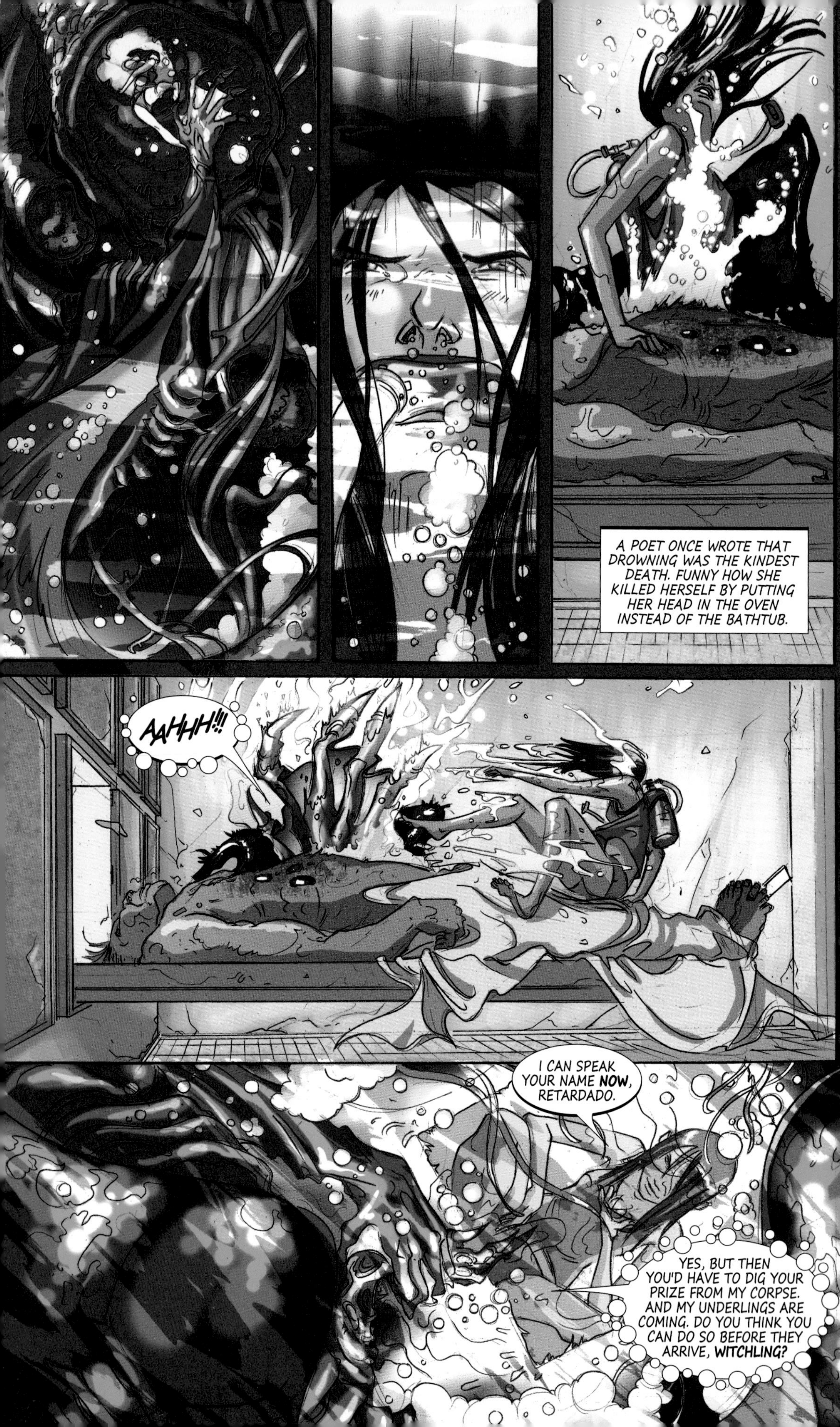
A POET ONCE WROTE THAT DROWNING WAS THE KINDEST DEATH. FUNNY HOW SHE KILLED HERSELF BY PUTTING HER HEAD IN THE OVEN INSTEAD OF THE BATHTUB.
AAHHH!!!
I CAN SPEAK YOUR NAME **NOW**, RETARDADO.
YES, BUT THEN YOU'D HAVE TO DIG YOUR PRIZE FROM MY CORPSE. AND MY UNDERLINGS ARE COMING. DO YOU THINK YOU CAN DO SO BEFORE THEY ARRIVE, **WITCHLING?**

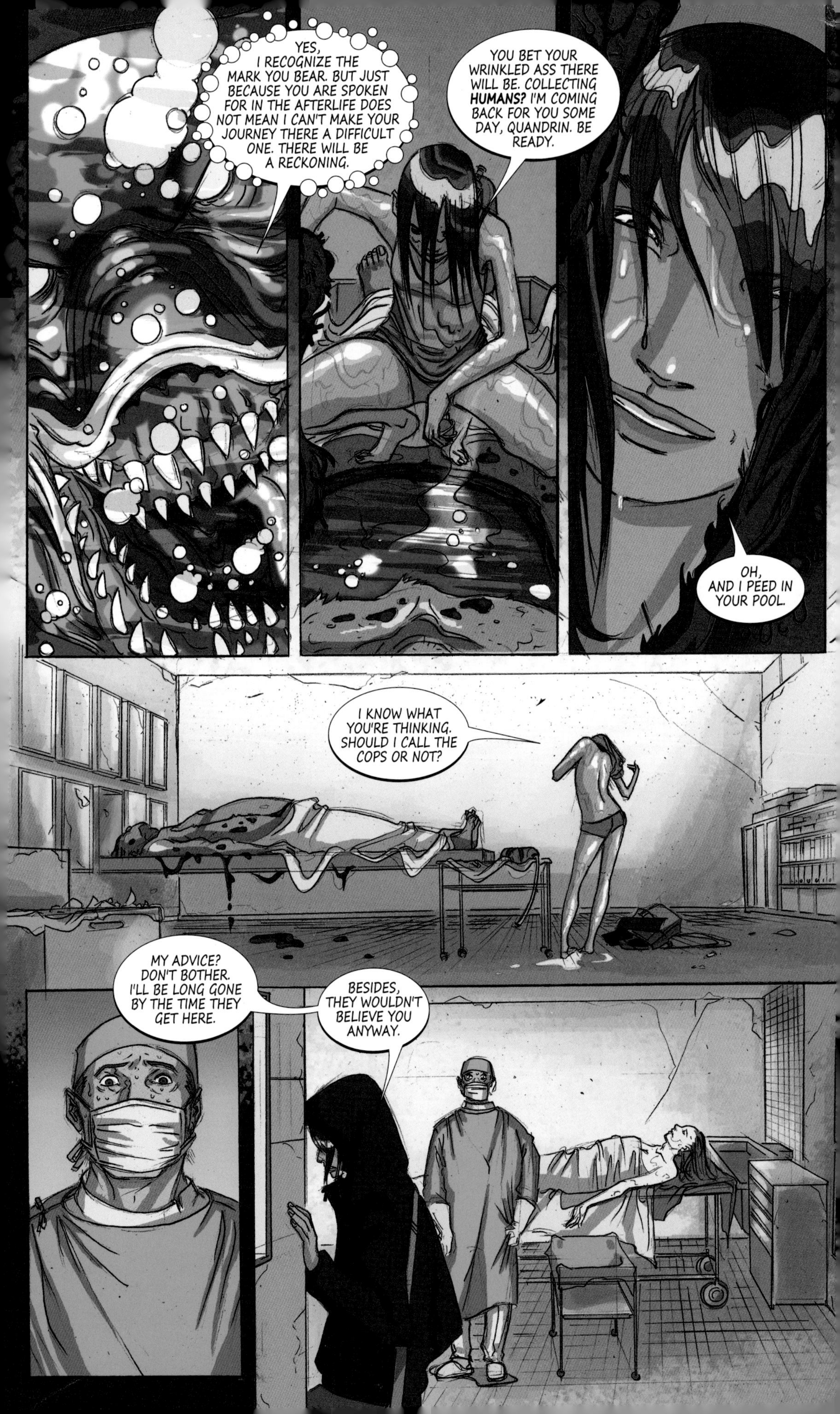
YES, I RECOGNIZE THE MARK YOU BEAR. BUT JUST BECAUSE YOU ARE SPOKEN FOR IN THE AFTERLIFE DOES NOT MEAN I CAN'T MAKE YOUR JOURNEY THERE A DIFFICULT ONE. THERE WILL BE A RECKONING.
YOU BET YOUR WRINKLED ASS THERE WILL BE. COLLECTING **HUMANS?** I'M COMING BACK FOR YOU SOME DAY, QUANDRIN. BE READY.
OH, AND I PEED IN YOUR POOL.
I KNOW WHAT YOU'RE THINKING. SHOULD I CALL THE COPS OR NOT?
MY ADVICE? DON'T BOTHER. I'LL BE LONG GONE BY THE TIME THEY GET HERE.
BESIDES, THEY WOULDN'T BELIEVE YOU ANYWAY.

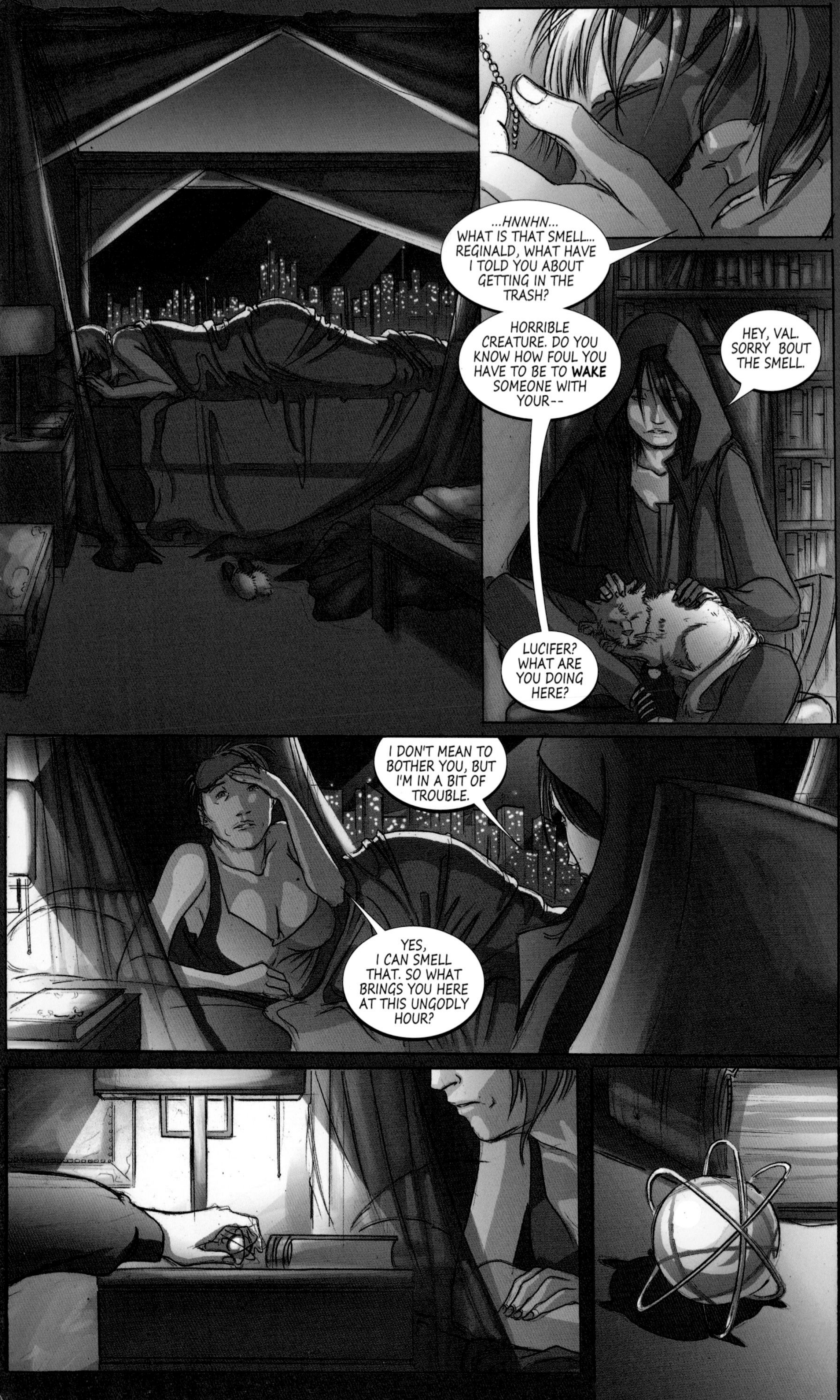

...HNNHN...
WHAT IS THAT SMELL...
REGINALD, WHAT HAVE I TOLD YOU ABOUT GETTING IN THE TRASH?
HORRIBLE CREATURE. DO YOU KNOW HOW FOUL YOU HAVE TO BE TO **WAKE** SOMEONE WITH YOUR--
HEY, VAL. SORRY BOUT THE SMELL.
LUCIFER? WHAT ARE YOU DOING HERE?
I DON'T MEAN TO BOTHER YOU, BUT I'M IN A BIT OF TROUBLE.
YES, I CAN SMELL THAT. SO WHAT BRINGS YOU HERE AT THIS UNGODLY HOUR?

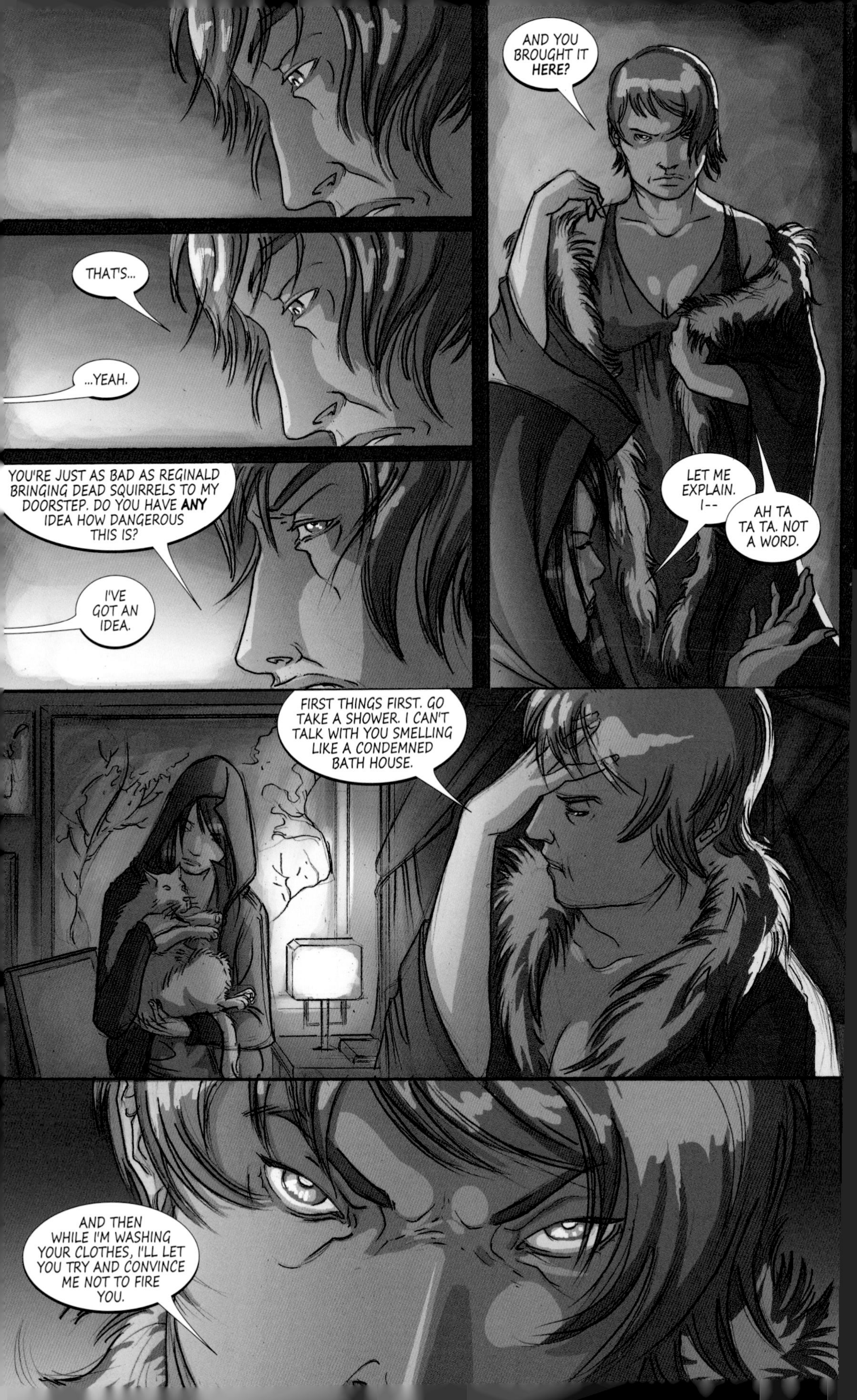
THAT'S...
...YEAH.
YOU'RE JUST AS BAD AS REGINALD BRINGING DEAD SQUIRRELS TO MY DOORSTEP. DO YOU HAVE **ANY** IDEA HOW DANGEROUS THIS IS?
I'VE GOT AN IDEA.
AND YOU BROUGHT IT **HERE?**
LET ME EXPLAIN. I--
AH TA TA TA. NOT A WORD.
FIRST THINGS FIRST. GO TAKE A SHOWER. I CAN'T TALK WITH YOU SMELLING LIKE A CONDEMNED BATH HOUSE.
AND THEN WHILE I'M WASHING YOUR CLOTHES, I'LL LET YOU TRY AND CONVINCE ME NOT TO FIRE YOU.

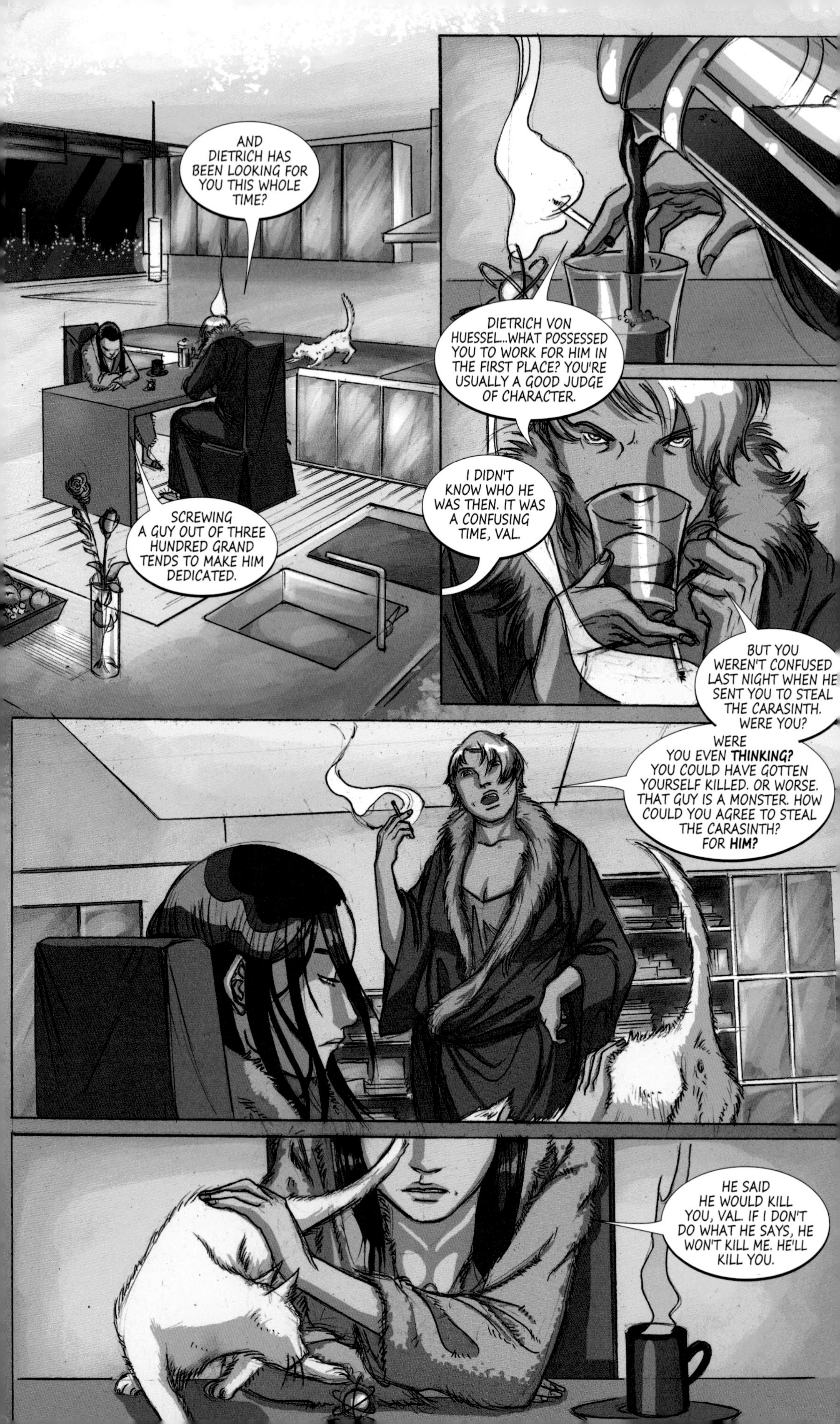
AND DIETRICH HAS BEEN LOOKING FOR YOU THIS WHOLE TIME?
SCREWING A GUY OUT OF THREE HUNDRED GRAND TENDS TO MAKE HIM DEDICATED.
DIETRICH VON HUESSEL...WHAT POSSESSED YOU TO WORK FOR HIM IN THE FIRST PLACE? YOU'RE USUALLY A GOOD JUDGE OF CHARACTER.
I DIDN'T KNOW WHO HE WAS THEN. IT WAS A CONFUSING TIME, VAL.
BUT YOU WEREN'T CONFUSED LAST NIGHT WHEN HE SENT YOU TO STEAL THE CARASINTH. WERE YOU?
WERE YOU EVEN **THINKING?** YOU COULD HAVE GOTTEN YOURSELF KILLED. OR WORSE. THAT GUY IS A MONSTER. HOW COULD YOU AGREE TO STEAL THE CARASINTH? FOR **HIM?**
HE SAID HE WOULD KILL YOU, VAL. IF I DON'T DO WHAT HE SAYS, HE WON'T KILL ME. HE'LL KILL YOU.

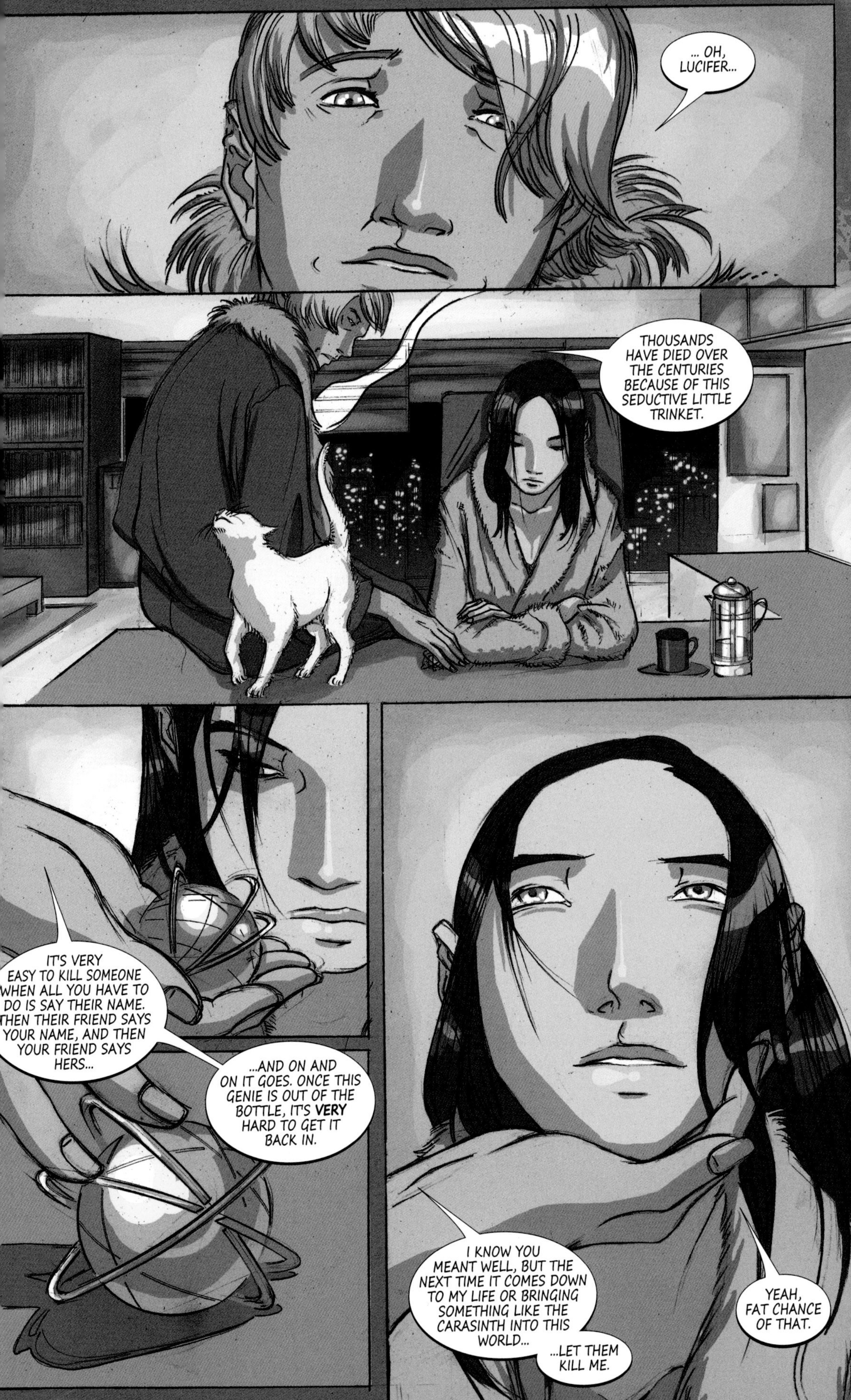

... OH, LUCIFER...
THOUSANDS HAVE DIED OVER THE CENTURIES BECAUSE OF THIS SEDUCTIVE LITTLE TRINKET.
IT'S VERY EASY TO KILL SOMEONE WHEN ALL YOU HAVE TO DO IS SAY THEIR NAME. THEN THEIR FRIEND SAYS YOUR NAME, AND THEN YOUR FRIEND SAYS HERS...
...AND ON AND ON IT GOES. ONCE THIS GENIE IS OUT OF THE BOTTLE, IT'S **VERY** HARD TO GET IT BACK IN.
I KNOW YOU MEANT WELL, BUT THE NEXT TIME IT COMES DOWN TO MY LIFE OR BRINGING SOMETHING LIKE THE CARASINTH INTO THIS WORLD...
...LET THEM KILL ME.
YEAH, FAT CHANCE OF THAT.

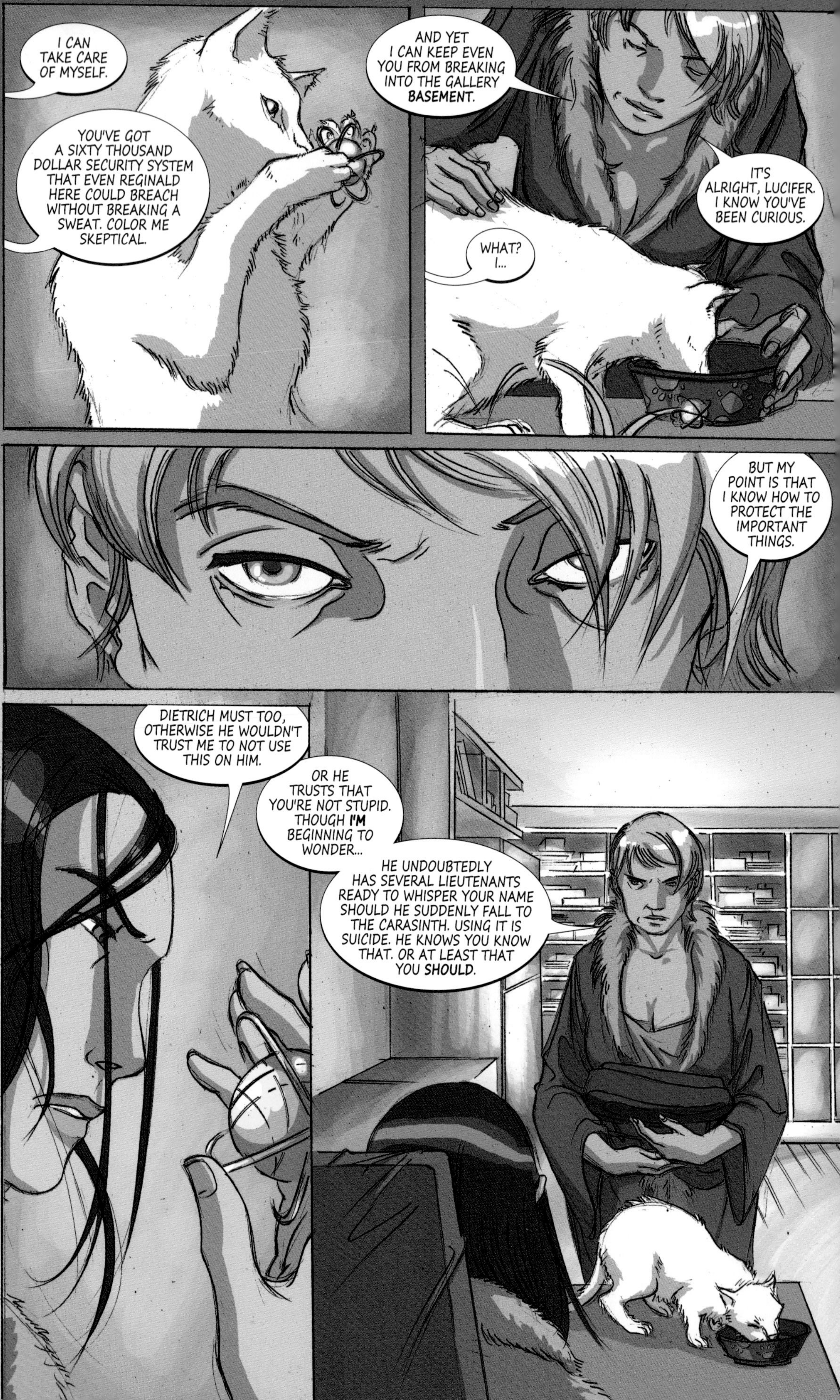
I CAN TAKE CARE OF MYSELF.
YOU'VE GOT A SIXTY THOUSAND DOLLAR SECURITY SYSTEM THAT EVEN REGINALD HERE COULD BREACH WITHOUT BREAKING A SWEAT. COLOR ME SKEPTICAL.
AND YET I CAN KEEP EVEN YOU FROM BREAKING INTO THE GALLERY **BASEMENT**.
IT'S ALRIGHT, LUCIFER. I KNOW YOU'VE BEEN CURIOUS.
WHAT? I...
BUT MY POINT IS THAT I KNOW HOW TO PROTECT THE IMPORTANT THINGS.
DIETRICH MUST TOO, OTHERWISE HE WOULDN'T TRUST ME TO NOT USE THIS ON HIM.
OR HE TRUSTS THAT YOU'RE NOT STUPID. THOUGH **I'M** BEGINNING TO WONDER...
HE UNDOUBTEDLY HAS SEVERAL LIEUTENANTS READY TO WHISPER YOUR NAME SHOULD HE SUDDENLY FALL TO THE CARASINTH. USING IT IS SUICIDE. HE KNOWS YOU KNOW THAT. OR AT LEAST THAT YOU **SHOULD**.

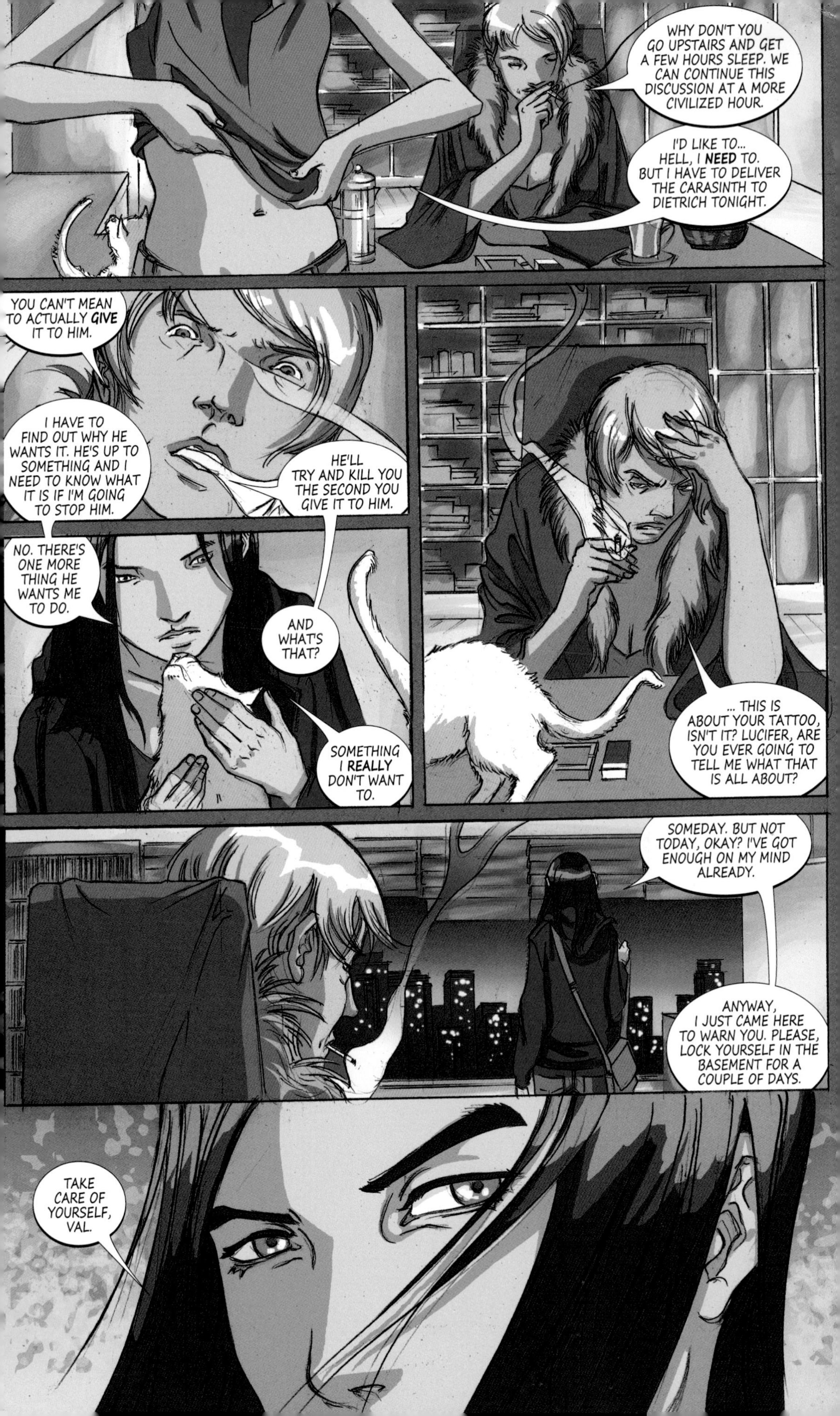
WHY DON'T YOU GO UPSTAIRS AND GET A FEW HOURS SLEEP. WE CAN CONTINUE THIS DISCUSSION AT A MORE CIVILIZED HOUR.
I'D LIKE TO... HELL, I **NEED** TO. BUT I HAVE TO DELIVER THE CARASINTH TO DIETRICH TONIGHT.
YOU CAN'T MEAN TO ACTUALLY **GIVE** IT TO HIM.
I HAVE TO FIND OUT WHY HE WANTS IT. HE'S UP TO SOMETHING AND I NEED TO KNOW WHAT IT IS IF I'M GOING TO STOP HIM.
HE'LL TRY AND KILL YOU THE SECOND YOU GIVE IT TO HIM.
NO. THERE'S ONE MORE THING HE WANTS ME TO DO.
AND WHAT'S THAT?
SOMETHING I **REALLY** DON'T WANT TO.
... THIS IS ABOUT YOUR TATTOO, ISN'T IT? LUCIFER, ARE YOU EVER GOING TO TELL ME WHAT THAT IS ALL ABOUT?
SOMEDAY. BUT NOT TODAY, OKAY? I'VE GOT ENOUGH ON MY MIND ALREADY.
ANYWAY, I JUST CAME HERE TO WARN YOU. PLEASE, LOCK YOURSELF IN THE BASEMENT FOR A COUPLE OF DAYS.
TAKE CARE OF YOURSELF, VAL.

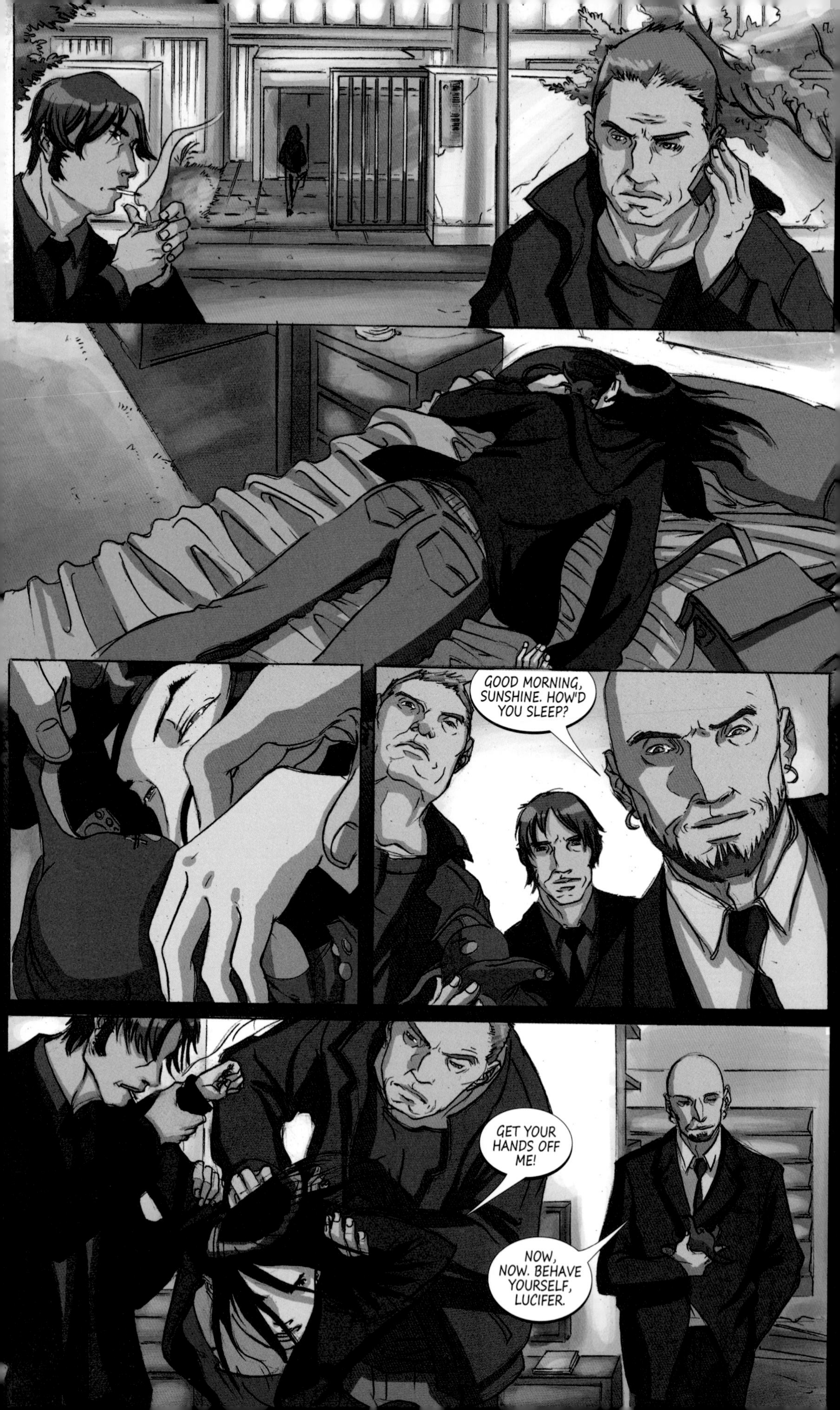
GOOD MORNING, SUNSHINE. HOW'D YOU SLEEP?
GET YOUR HANDS OFF ME!
NOW, NOW. BEHAVE YOURSELF, LUCIFER.

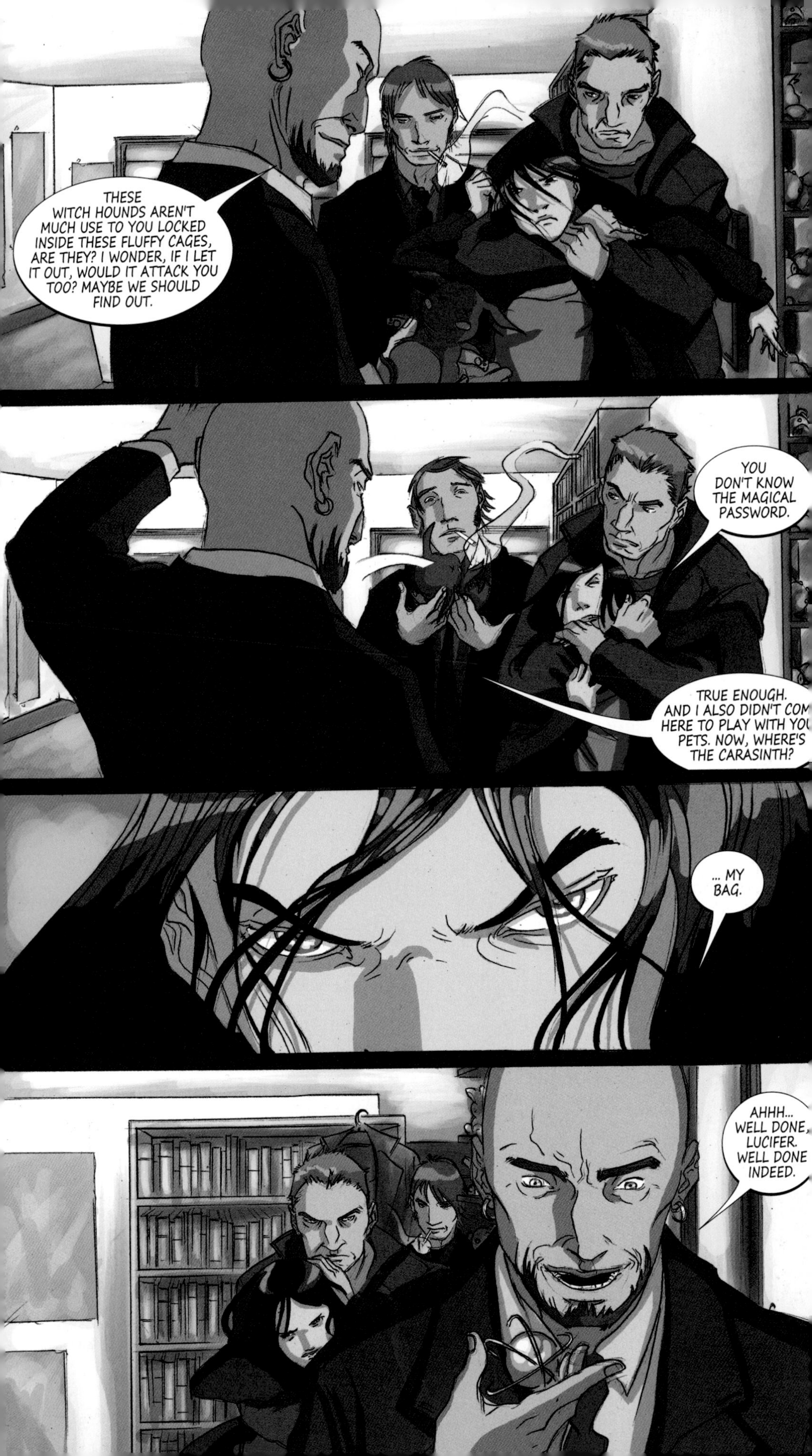
THESE WITCH HOUNDS AREN'T MUCH USE TO YOU LOCKED INSIDE THESE FLUFFY CAGES, ARE THEY? I WONDER, IF I LET IT OUT, WOULD IT ATTACK YOU TOO? MAYBE WE SHOULD FIND OUT.
YOU DON'T KNOW THE MAGICAL PASSWORD.
TRUE ENOUGH. AND I ALSO DIDN'T COM HERE TO PLAY WITH YOU PETS. NOW, WHERE'S THE CARASINTH?
... MY BAG.
AHHH... WELL DONE, LUCIFER. WELL DONE INDEED.

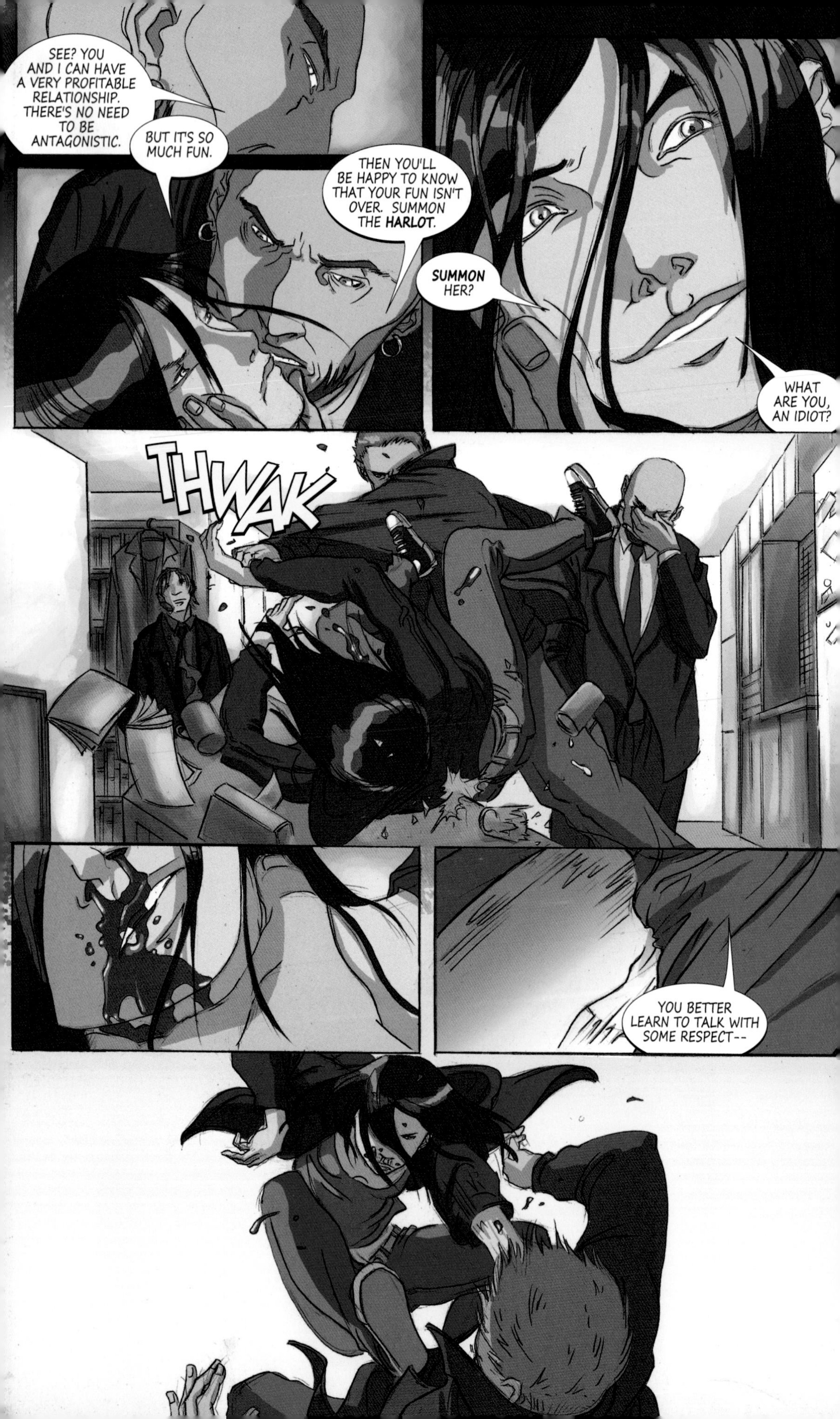
SEE? YOU AND I CAN HAVE A VERY PROFITABLE RELATIONSHIP. THERE'S NO NEED TO BE ANTAGONISTIC.
BUT IT'S SO MUCH FUN.
THEN YOU'LL BE HAPPY TO KNOW THAT YOUR FUN ISN'T OVER. SUMMON THE **HARLOT**.
SUMMON HER?
WHAT ARE YOU, AN IDIOT?
THWAK
YOU BETTER LEARN TO TALK WITH SOME RESPECT--

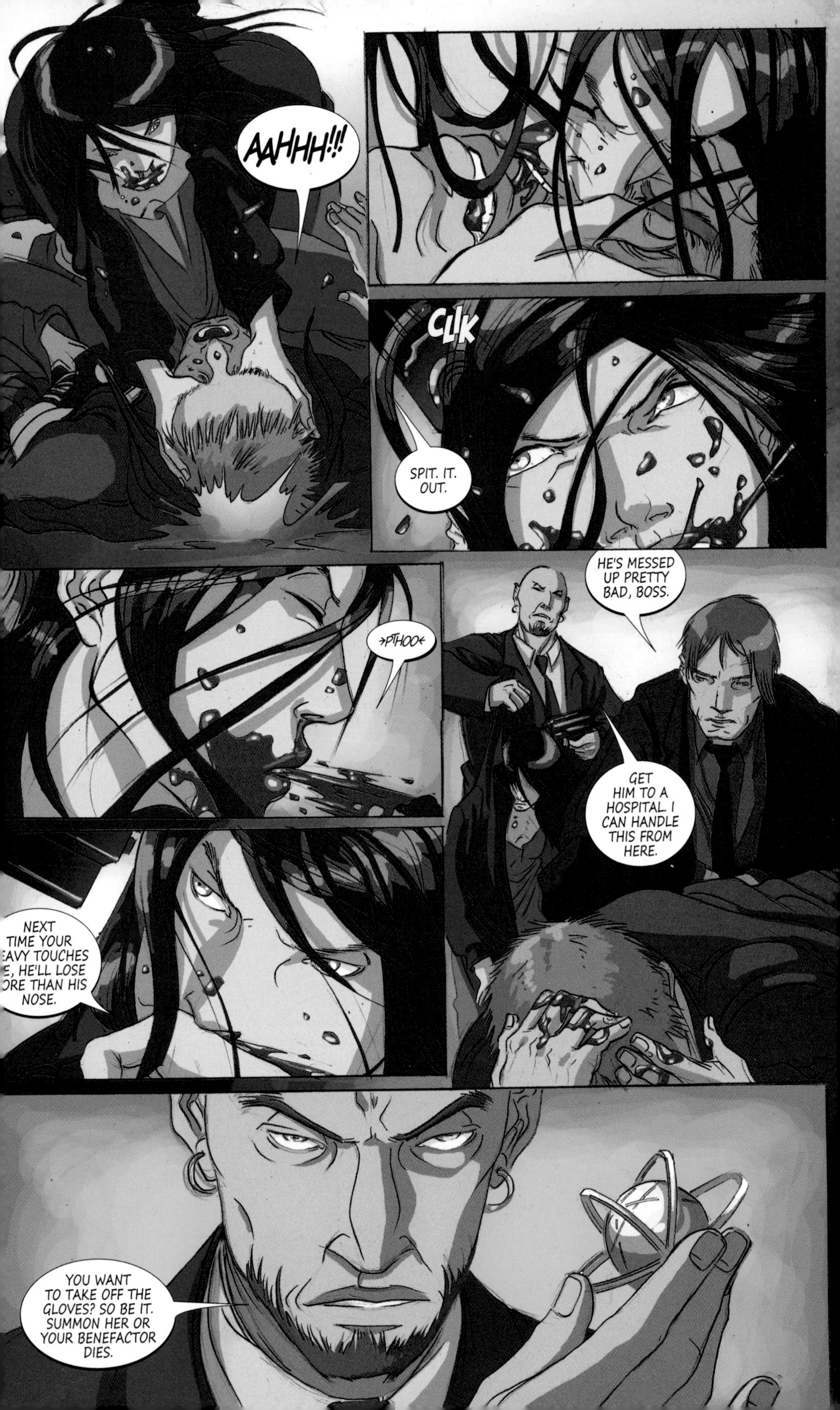

AAHHH!!!
CLIK
SPIT. IT. OUT.
>PTHOO<
HE'S MESSED UP PRETTY BAD, BOSS.
GET HIM TO A HOSPITAL. I CAN HANDLE THIS FROM HERE.
NEXT TIME YOUR EAVY TOUCHES E, HE'LL LOSE ORE THAN HIS NOSE.
YOU WANT TO TAKE OFF THE GLOVES? SO BE IT. SUMMON HER OR YOUR BENEFACTOR DIES.

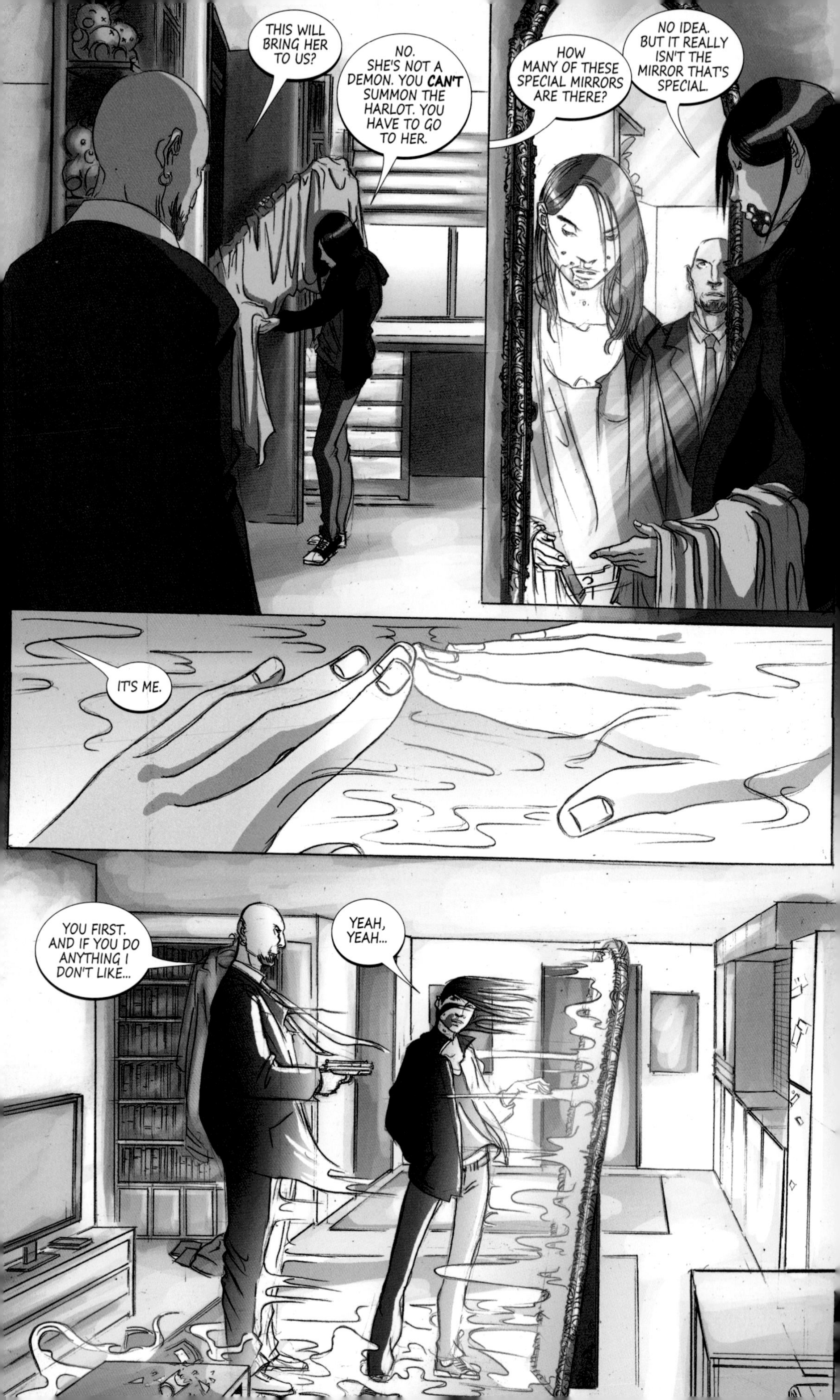
THIS WILL BRING HER TO US?
NO. SHE'S NOT A DEMON. YOU **CAN'T** SUMMON THE HARLOT. YOU HAVE TO GO TO HER.
HOW MANY OF THESE SPECIAL MIRRORS ARE THERE?
NO IDEA. BUT IT REALLY ISN'T THE MIRROR THAT'S SPECIAL.
IT'S ME.
YOU FIRST. AND IF YOU DO ANYTHING I DON'T LIKE...
YEAH, YEAH...

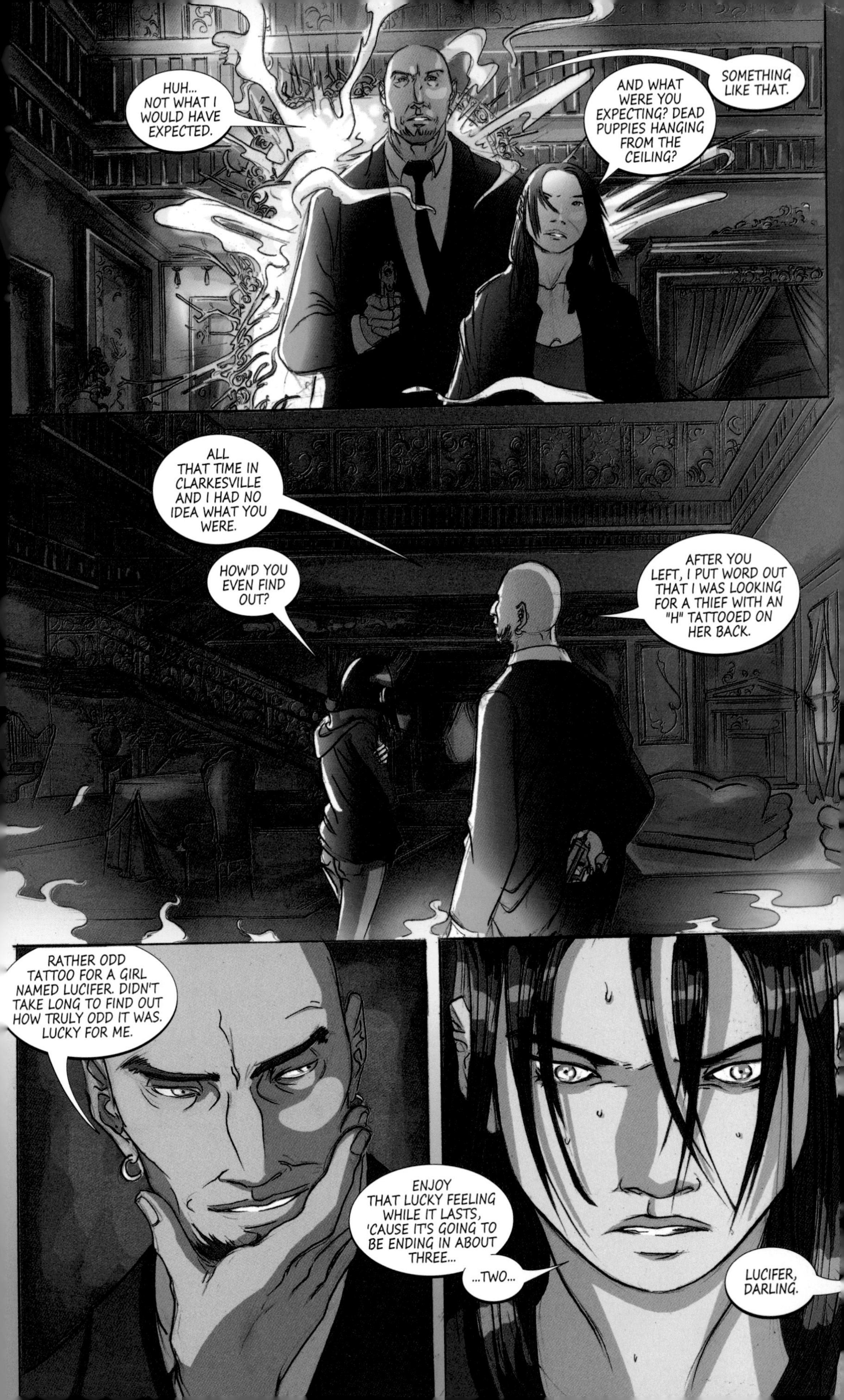
HUH... NOT WHAT I WOULD HAVE EXPECTED.
AND WHAT WERE YOU EXPECTING? DEAD PUPPIES HANGING FROM THE CEILING?
SOMETHING LIKE THAT.
ALL THAT TIME IN CLARKESVILLE AND I HAD NO IDEA WHAT YOU WERE.
HOW'D YOU EVEN FIND OUT?
AFTER YOU LEFT, I PUT WORD OUT THAT I WAS LOOKING FOR A THIEF WITH AN "H" TATTOOED ON HER BACK.
RATHER ODD TATTOO FOR A GIRL NAMED LUCIFER. DIDN'T TAKE LONG TO FIND OUT HOW TRULY ODD IT WAS. LUCKY FOR ME.
ENJOY THAT LUCKY FEELING WHILE IT LASTS, 'CAUSE IT'S GOING TO BE ENDING IN ABOUT THREE...
...TWO...
LUCIFER, DARLING.

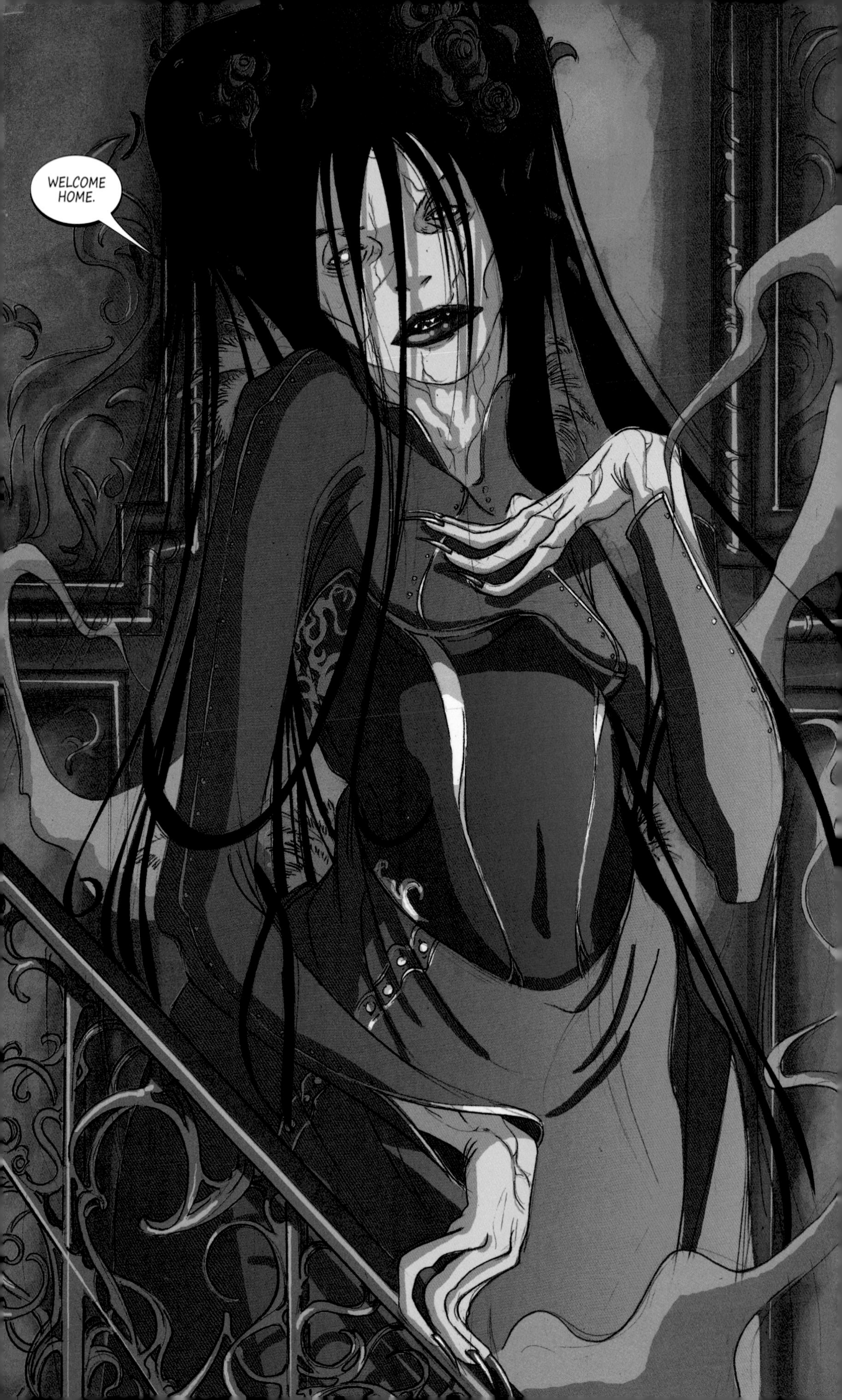
WELCOME HOME.

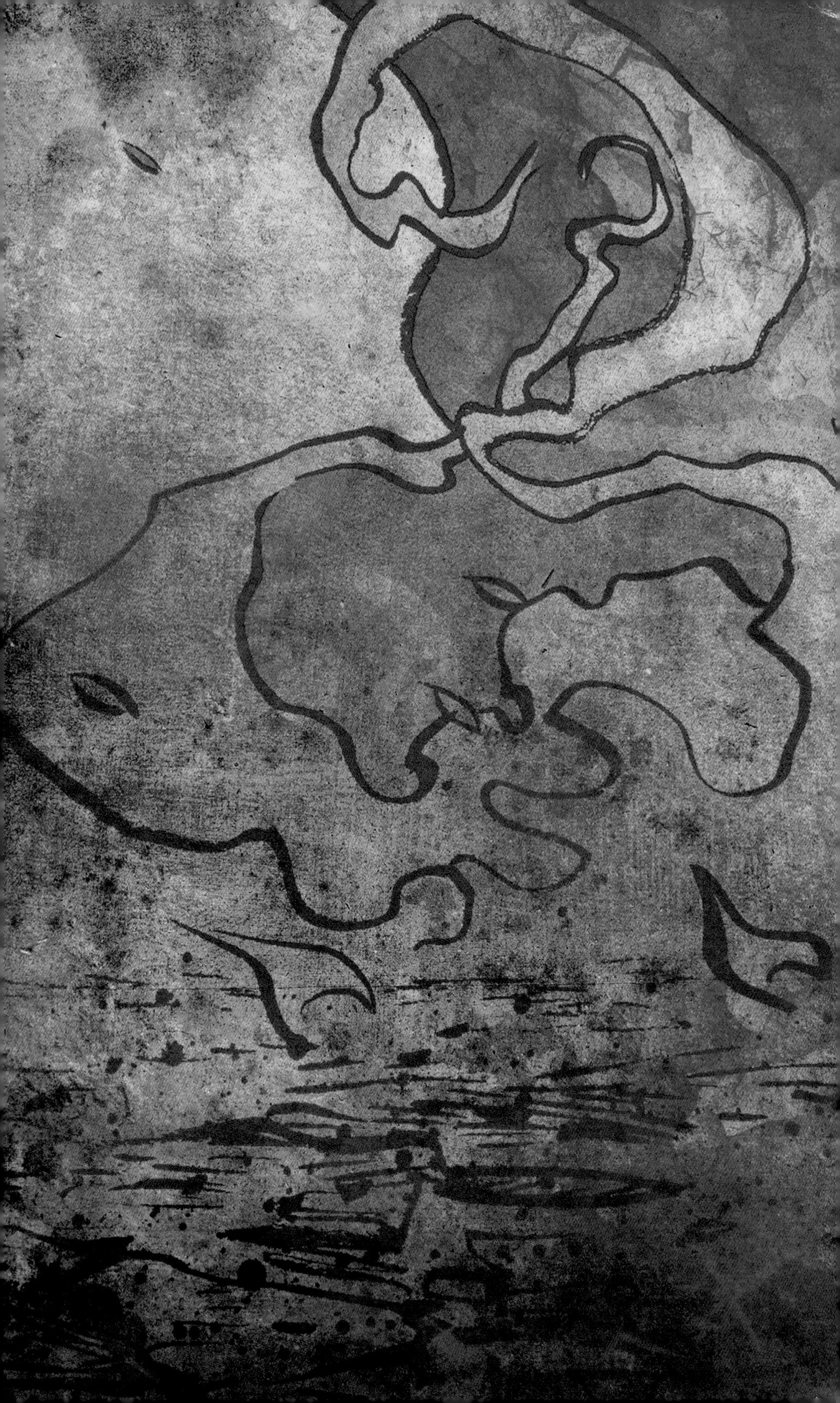

CHAPTER III

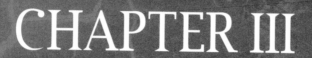

WHEREIN LUCIFER LEARNS TO DRIVE,
GETS HER PICTURE TAKEN,
AND CALLS IN A FAVOR
FROM A PEEPING TOM.

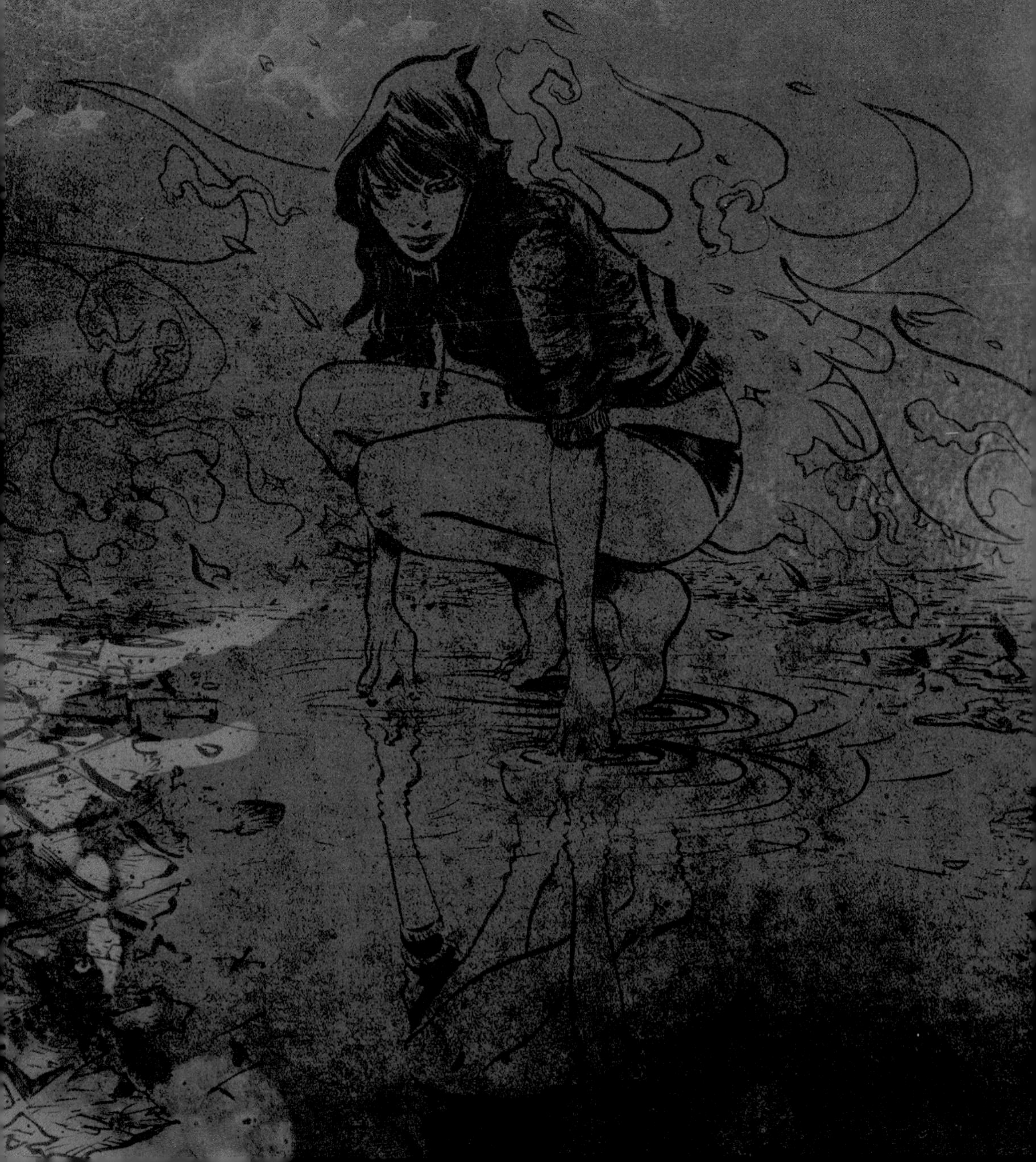

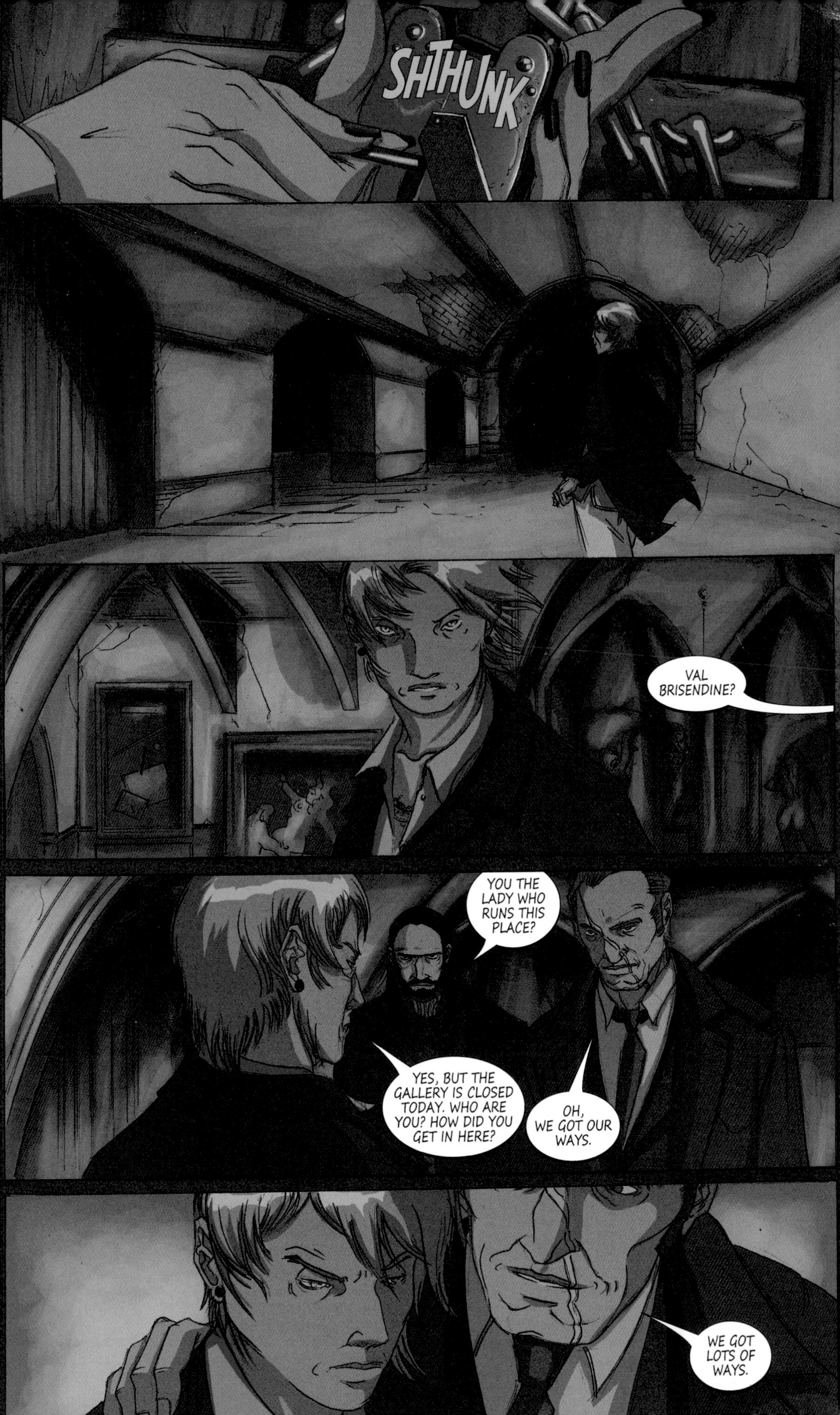
SHITHUNK
VAL BRISENDINE?
YOU THE LADY WHO RUNS THIS PLACE?
YES, BUT THE GALLERY IS CLOSED TODAY. WHO ARE YOU? HOW DID YOU GET IN HERE?
OH, WE GOT OUR WAYS.
WE GOT LOTS OF WAYS.

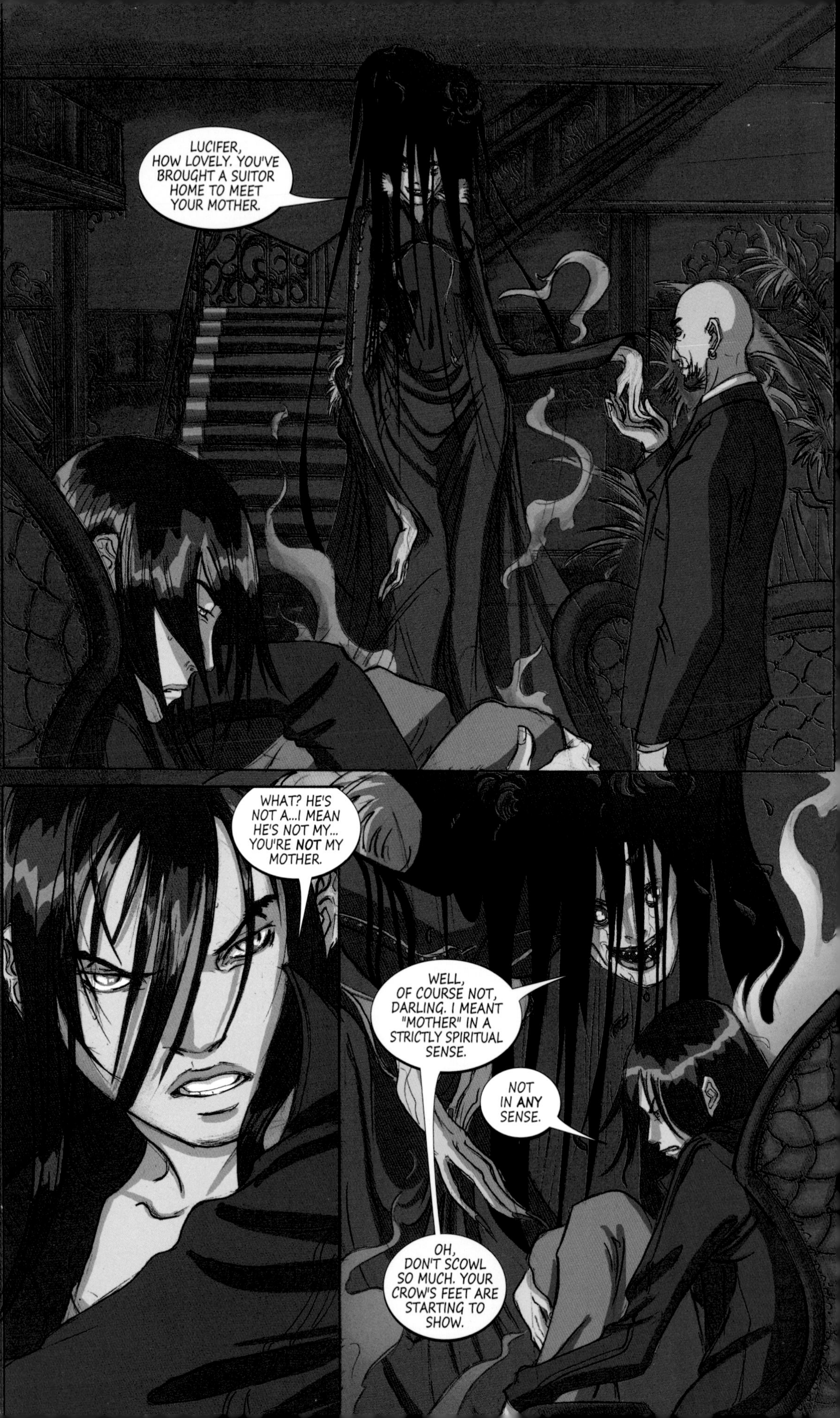

LUCIFER, HOW LOVELY. YOU'VE BROUGHT A SUITOR HOME TO MEET YOUR MOTHER.
WHAT? HE'S NOT A...I MEAN HE'S NOT MY... YOU'RE NOT MY MOTHER.
WELL, OF COURSE NOT, DARLING. I MEANT "MOTHER" IN A STRICTLY SPIRITUAL SENSE.
NOT IN ANY SENSE.
OH, DON'T SCOWL SO MUCH. YOUR CROW'S FEET ARE STARTING TO SHOW.

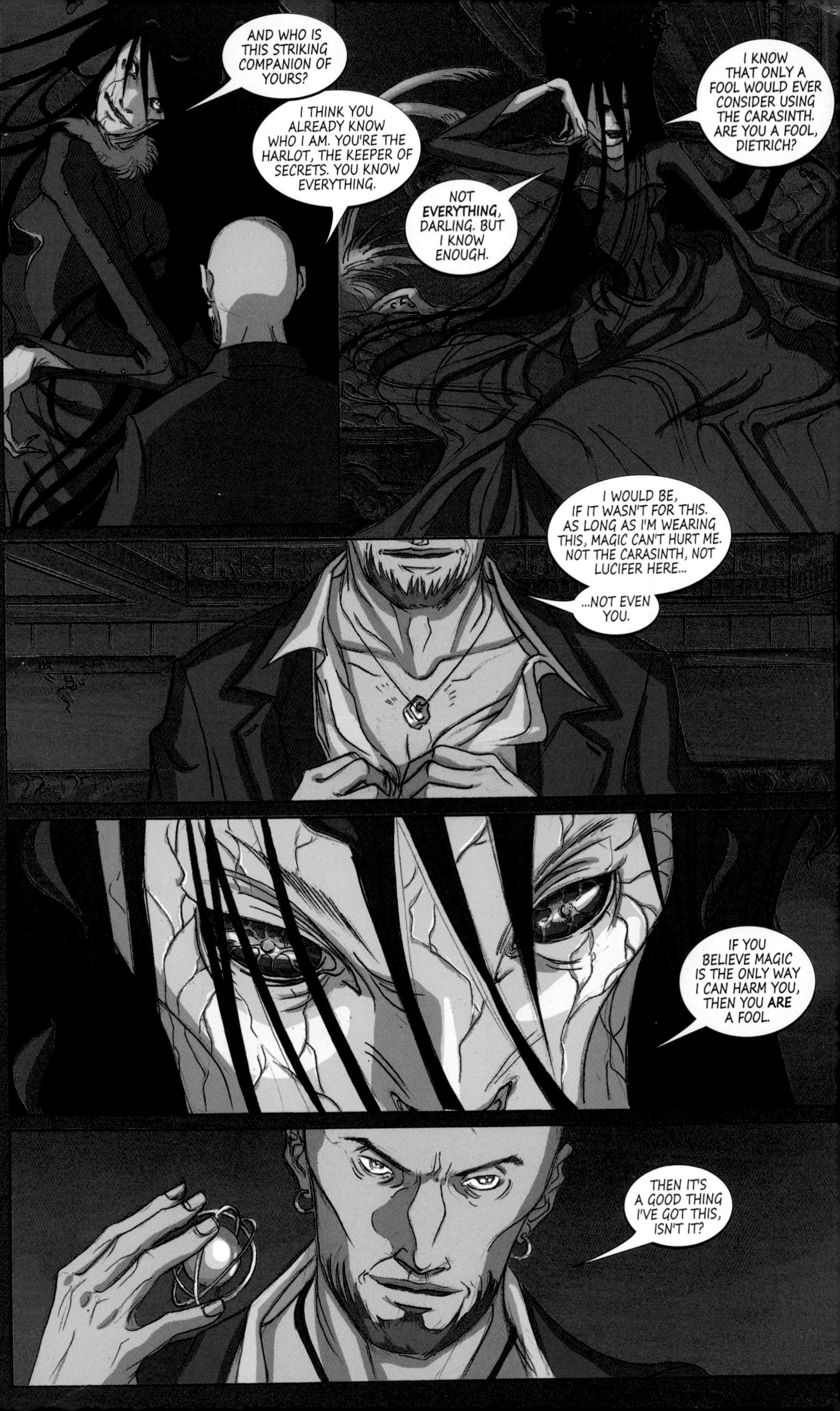
AND WHO IS THIS STRIKING COMPANION OF YOURS?
I THINK YOU ALREADY KNOW WHO I AM. YOU'RE THE HARLOT, THE KEEPER OF SECRETS. YOU KNOW EVERYTHING.
NOT **EVERYTHING**, DARLING. BUT I KNOW ENOUGH.
I KNOW THAT ONLY A FOOL WOULD EVER CONSIDER USING THE CARASINTH. ARE YOU A FOOL, DIETRICH?
I WOULD BE, IF IT WASN'T FOR THIS. AS LONG AS I'M WEARING THIS, MAGIC CAN'T HURT ME. NOT THE CARASINTH, NOT LUCIFER HERE...
...NOT EVEN YOU.
IF YOU BELIEVE MAGIC IS THE ONLY WAY I CAN HARM YOU, THEN YOU **ARE** A FOOL.
THEN IT'S A GOOD THING I'VE GOT THIS, ISN'T IT?

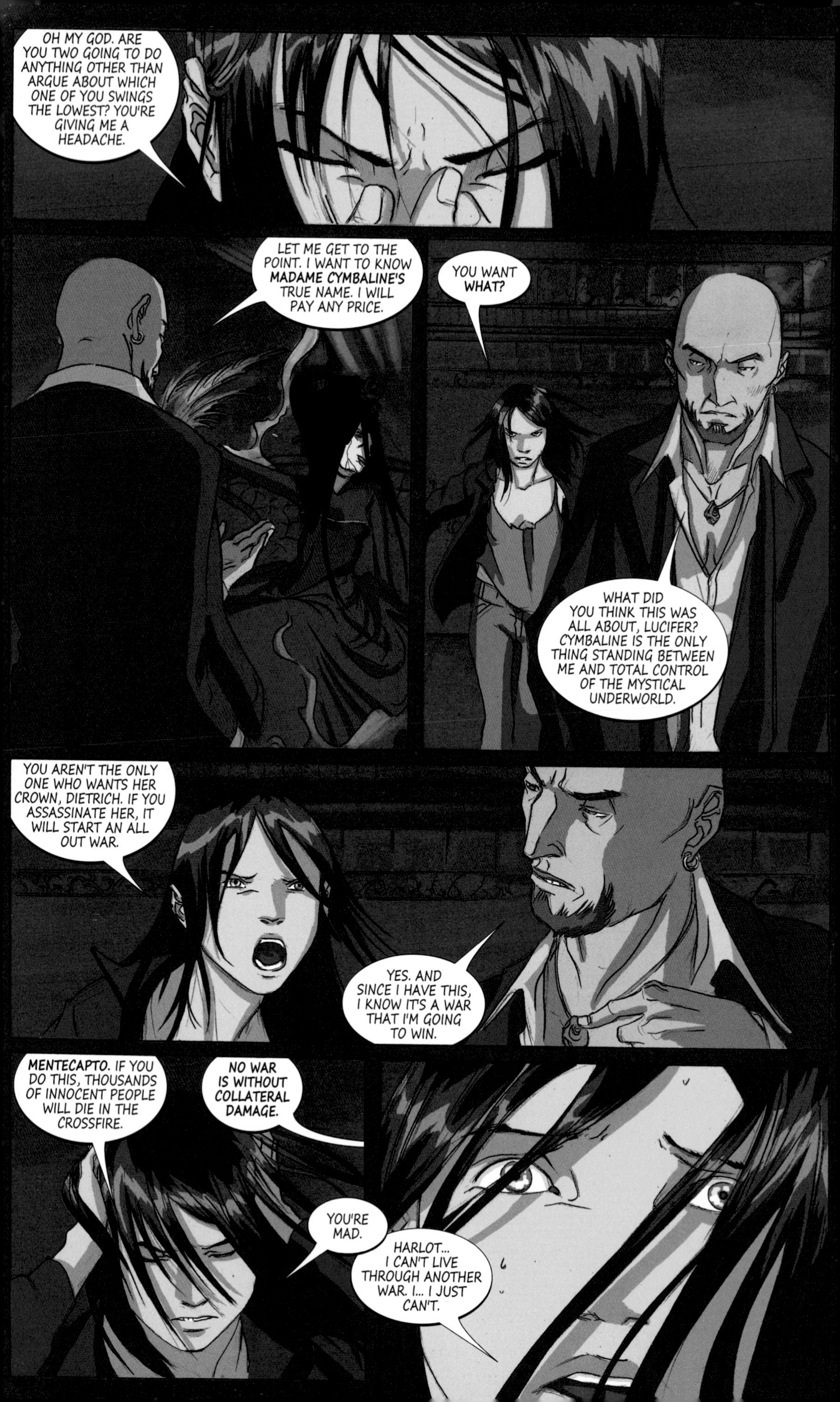

OH MY GOD. ARE YOU TWO GOING TO DO ANYTHING OTHER THAN ARGUE ABOUT WHICH ONE OF YOU SWINGS THE LOWEST? YOU'RE GIVING ME A HEADACHE.
LET ME GET TO THE POINT. I WANT TO KNOW **MADAME CYMBALINE'S** TRUE NAME. I WILL PAY ANY PRICE.
YOU WANT **WHAT?**
WHAT DID YOU THINK THIS WAS ALL ABOUT, LUCIFER? CYMBALINE IS THE ONLY THING STANDING BETWEEN ME AND TOTAL CONTROL OF THE MYSTICAL UNDERWORLD.
YOU AREN'T THE ONLY ONE WHO WANTS HER CROWN, DIETRICH. IF YOU ASSASSINATE HER, IT WILL START AN ALL OUT WAR.
YES. AND SINCE I HAVE THIS, I KNOW IT'S A WAR THAT I'M GOING TO WIN.
MENTECAPTO. IF YOU DO THIS, THOUSANDS OF INNOCENT PEOPLE WILL DIE IN THE CROSSFIRE.
NO WAR IS WITHOUT COLLATERAL DAMAGE.
YOU'RE MAD.
HARLOT... I CAN'T LIVE THROUGH ANOTHER WAR. I... I JUST CAN'T.

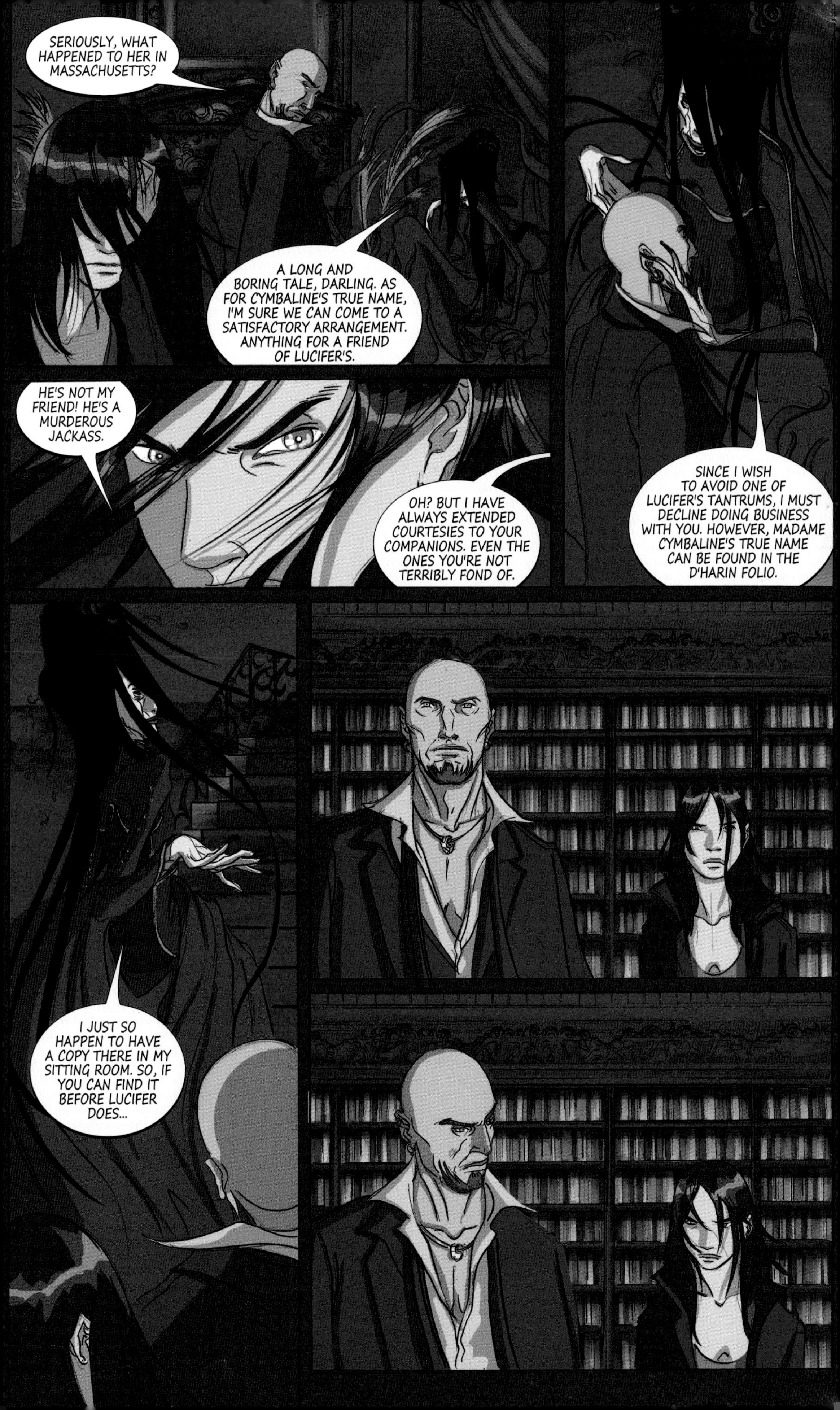
SERIOUSLY, WHAT HAPPENED TO HER IN MASSACHUSETTS?
A LONG AND BORING TALE, DARLING. AS FOR CYMBALINE'S TRUE NAME, I'M SURE WE CAN COME TO A SATISFACTORY ARRANGEMENT. ANYTHING FOR A FRIEND OF LUCIFER'S.
HE'S NOT MY FRIEND! HE'S A MURDEROUS JACKASS.
OH? BUT I HAVE ALWAYS EXTENDED COURTESIES TO YOUR COMPANIONS. EVEN THE ONES YOU'RE NOT TERRIBLY FOND OF.
SINCE I WISH TO AVOID ONE OF LUCIFER'S TANTRUMS, I MUST DECLINE DOING BUSINESS WITH YOU. HOWEVER, MADAME CYMBALINE'S TRUE NAME CAN BE FOUND IN THE D'HARIN FOLIO.
I JUST SO HAPPEN TO HAVE A COPY THERE IN MY SITTING ROOM. SO, IF YOU CAN FIND IT BEFORE LUCIFER DOES...

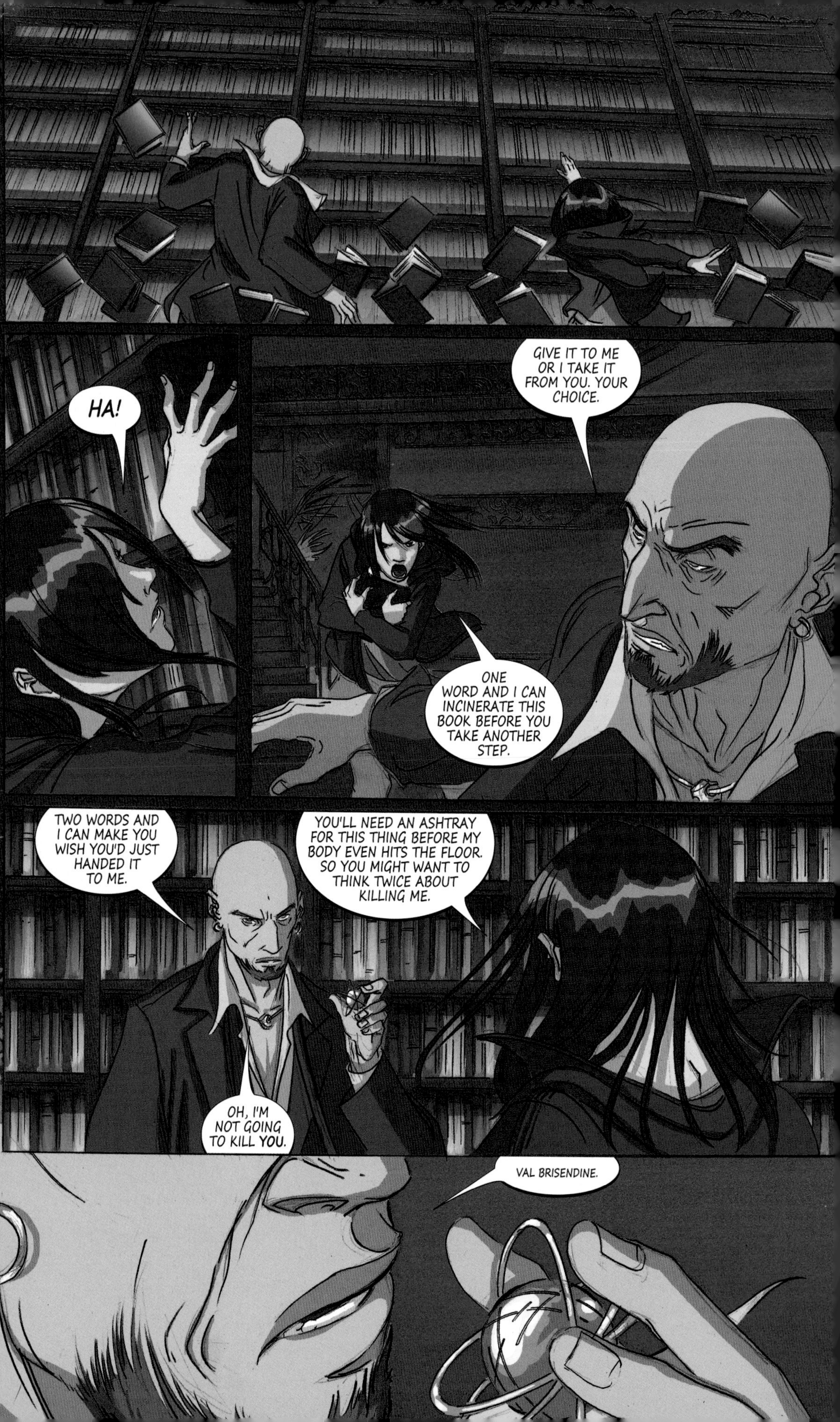
HA!
GIVE IT TO ME OR I TAKE IT FROM YOU. YOUR CHOICE.
ONE WORD AND I CAN INCINERATE THIS BOOK BEFORE YOU TAKE ANOTHER STEP.
TWO WORDS AND I CAN MAKE YOU WISH YOU'D JUST HANDED IT TO ME.
YOU'LL NEED AN ASHTRAY FOR THIS THING BEFORE MY BODY EVEN HITS THE FLOOR. SO YOU MIGHT WANT TO THINK TWICE ABOUT KILLING ME.
OH, I'M NOT GOING TO KILL YOU.
VAL BRISENDINE.

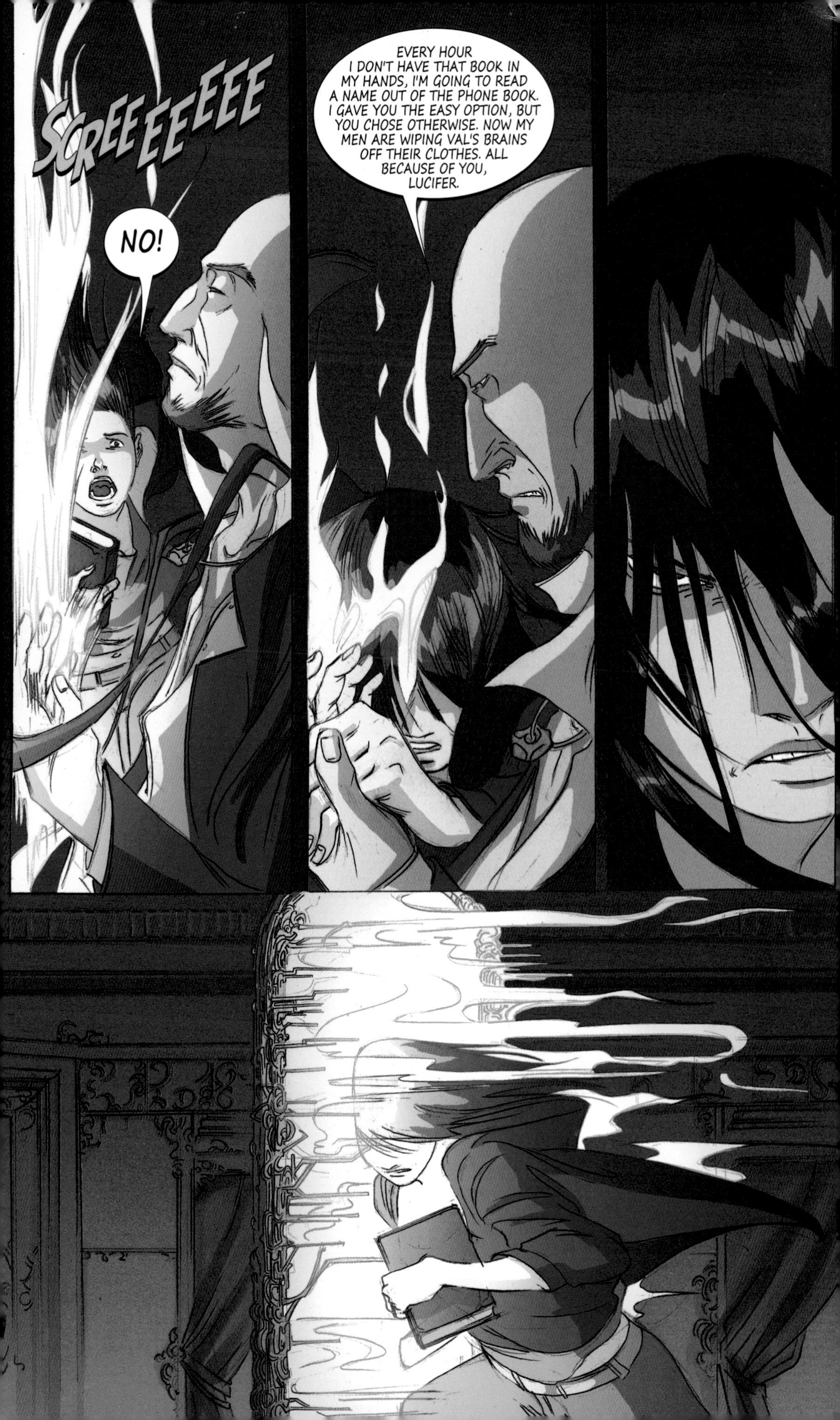
SCREEEEEEE
NO!
EVERY HOUR I DON'T HAVE THAT BOOK IN MY HANDS, I'M GOING TO READ A NAME OUT OF THE PHONE BOOK. I GAVE YOU THE EASY OPTION, BUT YOU CHOSE OTHERWISE. NOW MY MEN ARE WIPING VAL'S BRAINS OFF THEIR CLOTHES. ALL BECAUSE OF YOU, LUCIFER.

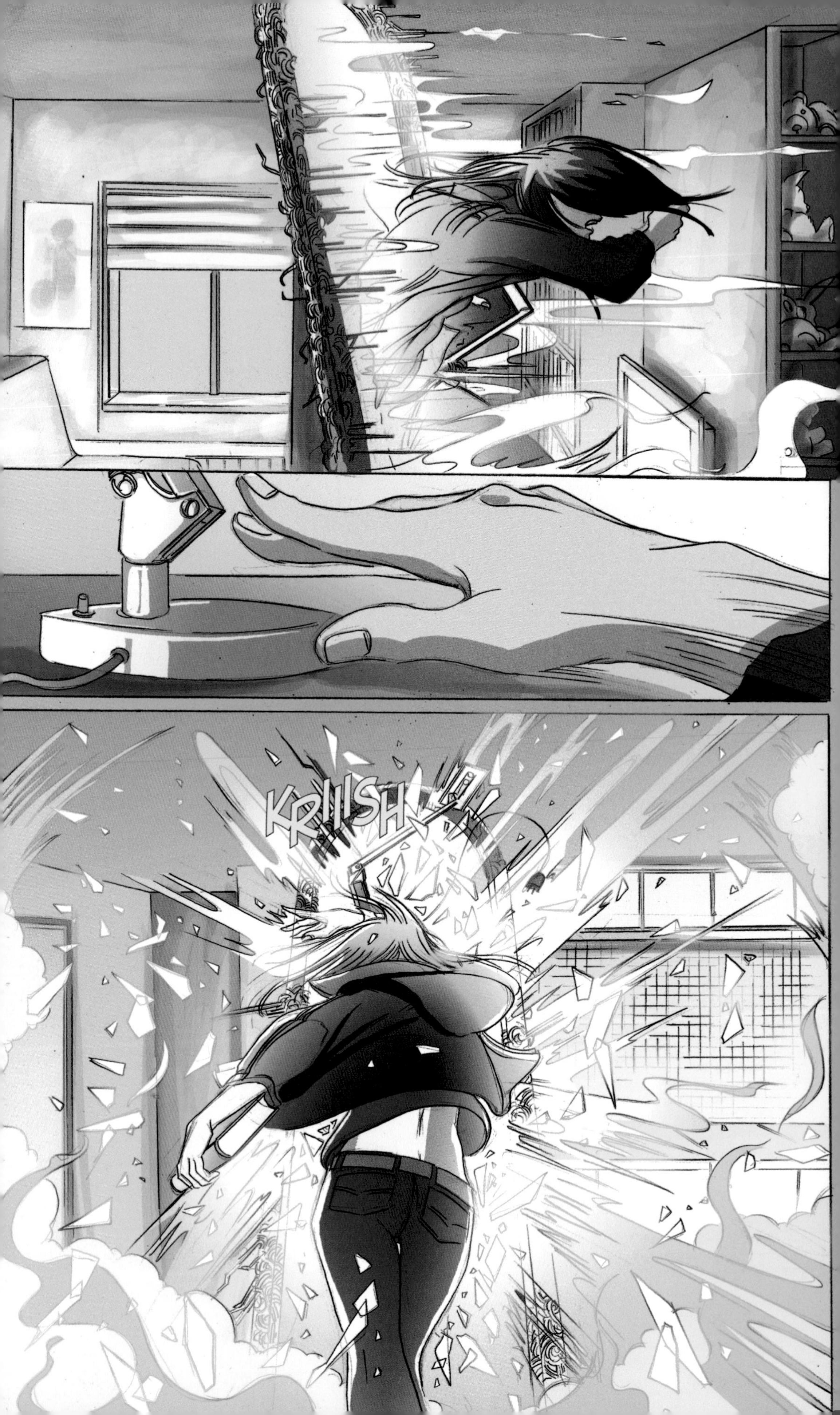
KRIISH

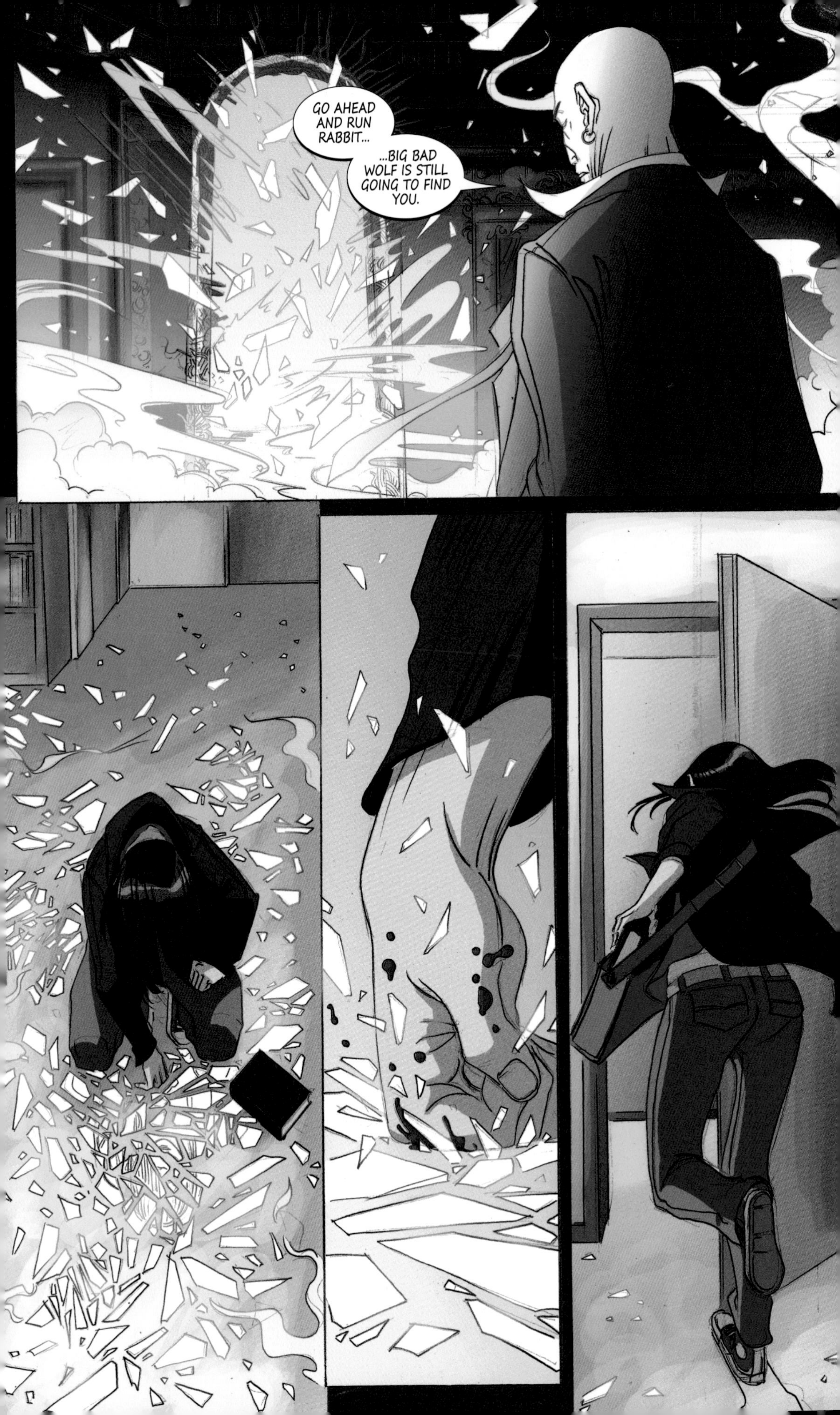
GO AHEAD AND RUN RABBIT...
...BIG BAD WOLF IS STILL GOING TO FIND YOU.

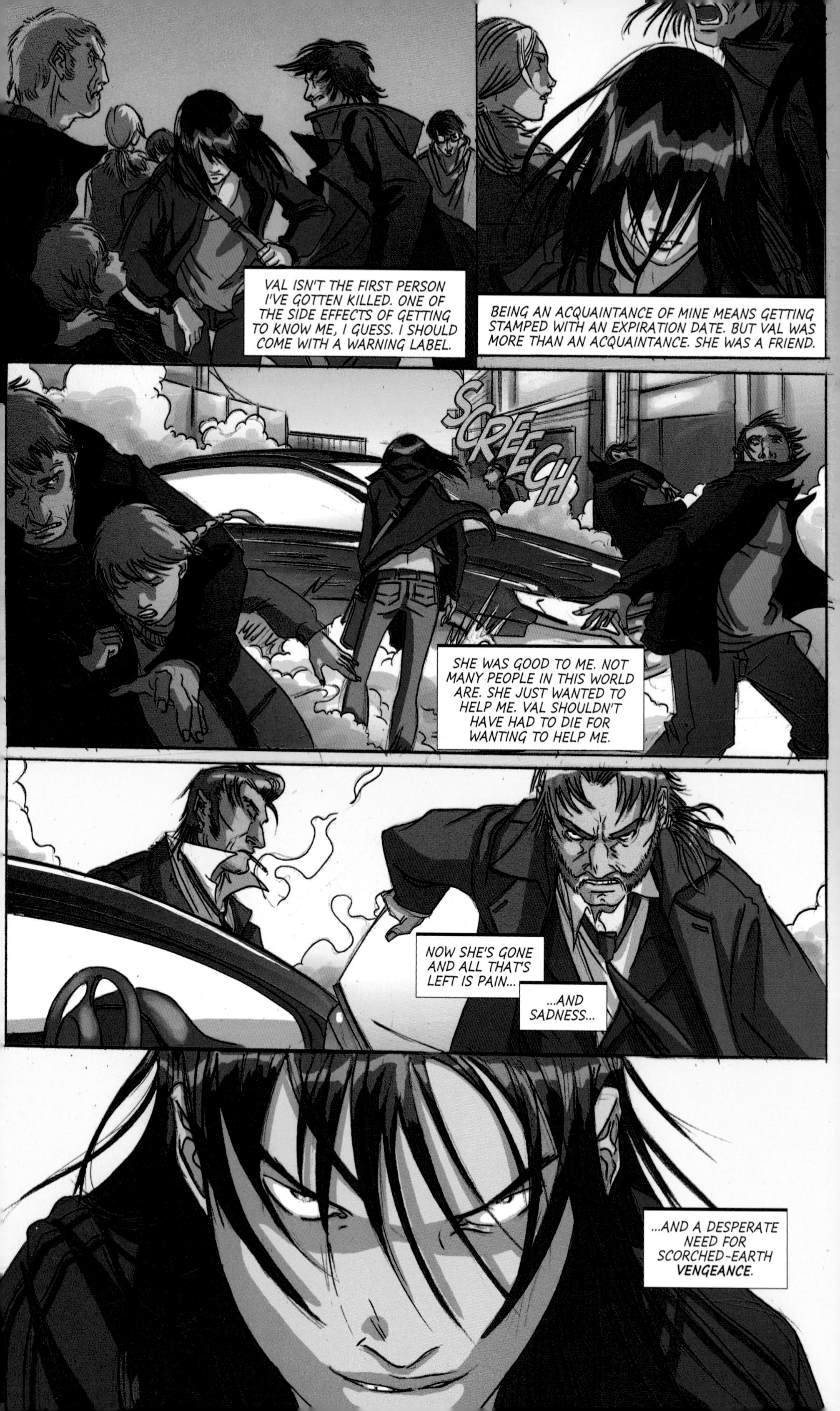

VAL ISN'T THE FIRST PERSON I'VE GOTTEN KILLED. ONE OF THE SIDE EFFECTS OF GETTING TO KNOW ME, I GUESS. I SHOULD COME WITH A WARNING LABEL.
BEING AN ACQUAINTANCE OF MINE MEANS GETTING STAMPED WITH AN EXPIRATION DATE. BUT VAL WAS MORE THAN AN ACQUAINTANCE. SHE WAS A FRIEND.
SCREECH
SHE WAS GOOD TO ME. NOT MANY PEOPLE IN THIS WORLD ARE. SHE JUST WANTED TO HELP ME. VAL SHOULDN'T HAVE HAD TO DIE FOR WANTING TO HELP ME.
NOW SHE'S GONE AND ALL THAT'S LEFT IS PAIN...
...AND SADNESS...
...AND A DESPERATE NEED FOR SCORCHED-EARTH **VENGEANCE**.

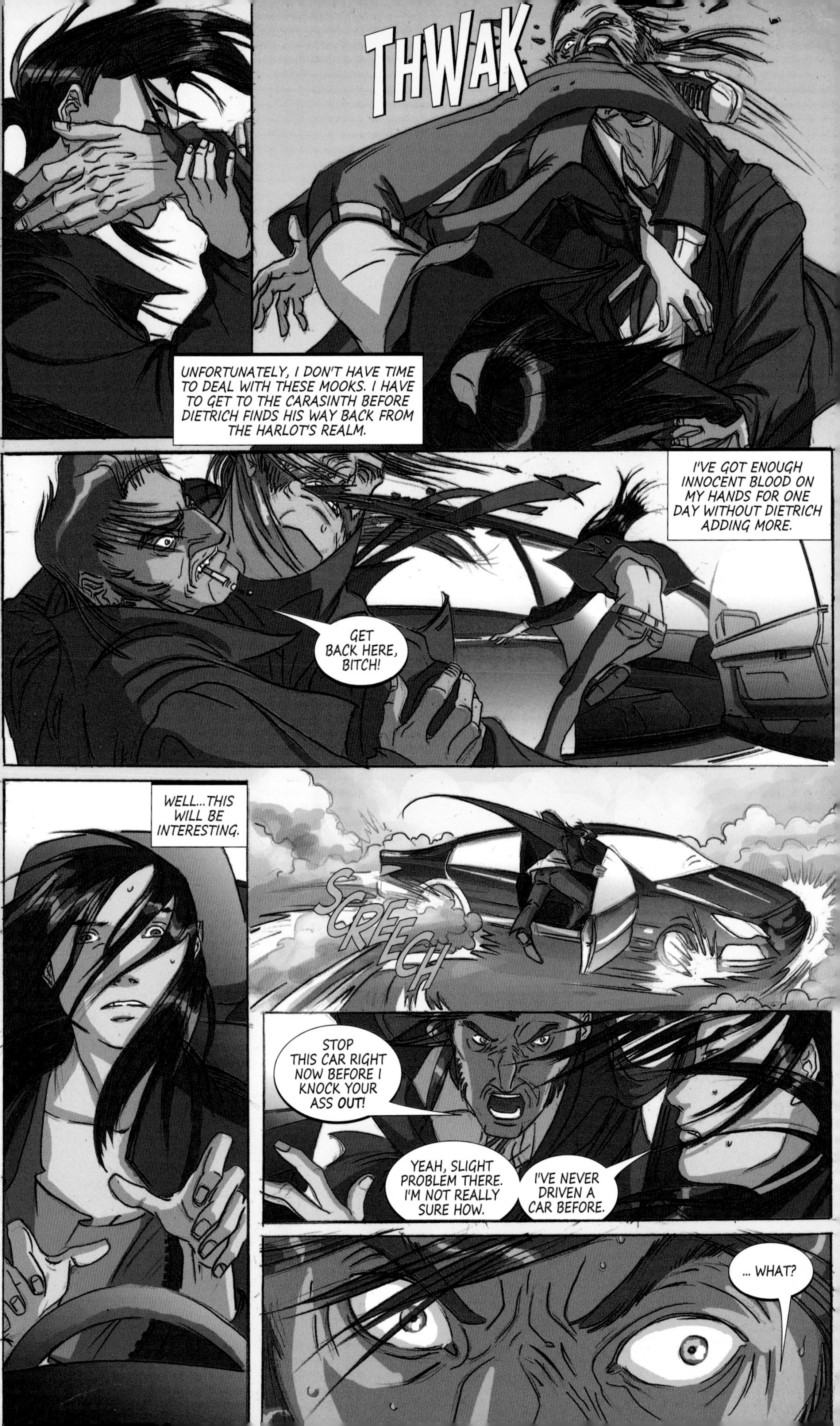
THWAK
UNFORTUNATELY, I DON'T HAVE TIME TO DEAL WITH THESE MOOKS. I HAVE TO GET TO THE CARASINTH BEFORE DIETRICH FINDS HIS WAY BACK FROM THE HARLOT'S REALM.
I'VE GOT ENOUGH INNOCENT BLOOD ON MY HANDS FOR ONE DAY WITHOUT DIETRICH ADDING MORE.
GET BACK HERE, BITCH!
WELL...THIS WILL BE INTERESTING.
SCREECH
STOP THIS CAR RIGHT NOW BEFORE I KNOCK YOUR ASS OUT!
YEAH, SLIGHT PROBLEM THERE. I'M NOT REALLY SURE HOW.
I'VE NEVER DRIVEN A CAR BEFORE.
... WHAT?

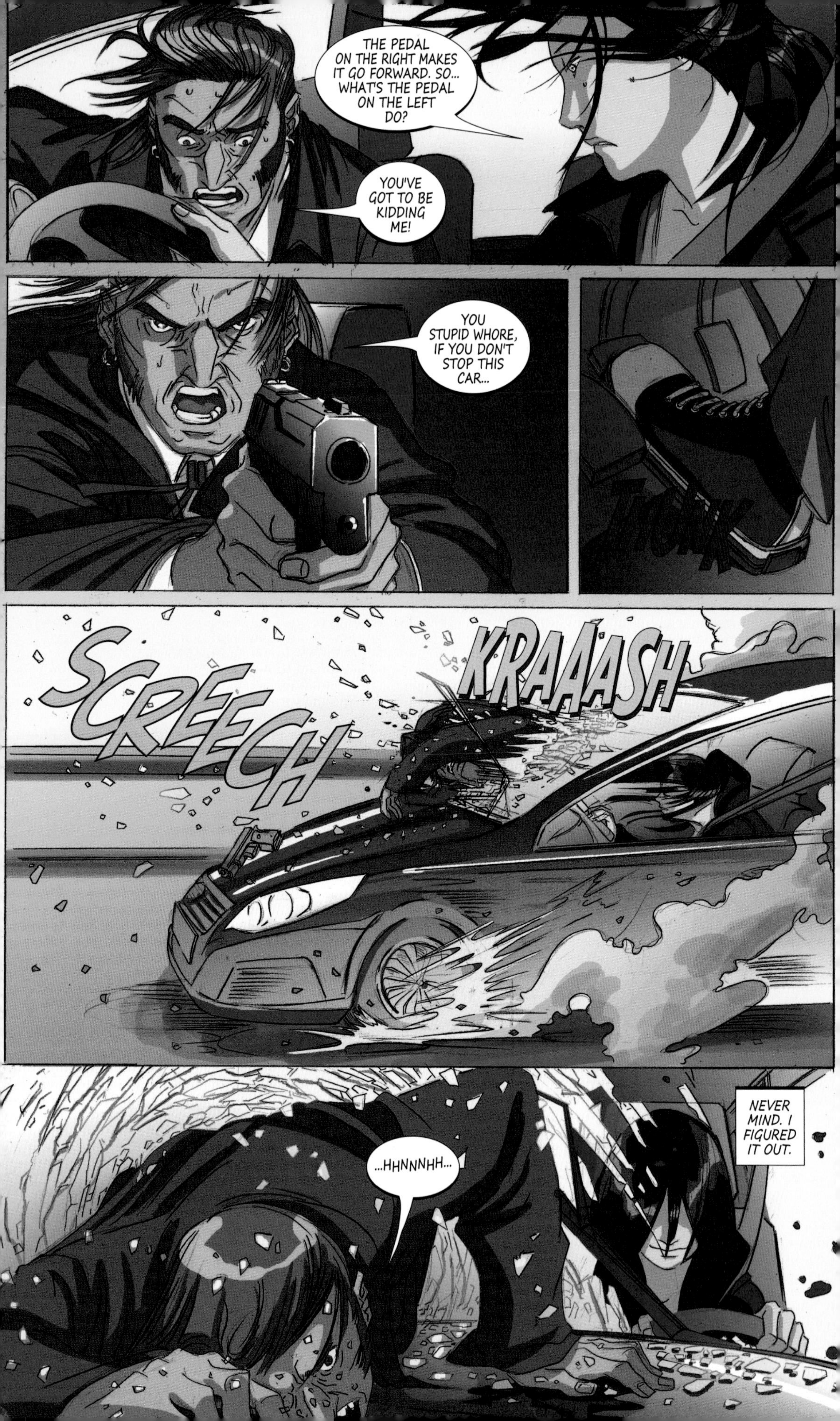
THE PEDAL ON THE RIGHT MAKES IT GO FORWARD. SO... WHAT'S THE PEDAL ON THE LEFT DO?
YOU'VE GOT TO BE KIDDING ME!
YOU STUPID WHORE, IF YOU DON'T STOP THIS CAR...
THONK
SCREECH
KRAAASH
NEVER MIND. I FIGURED IT OUT.
...HHNNNHH...

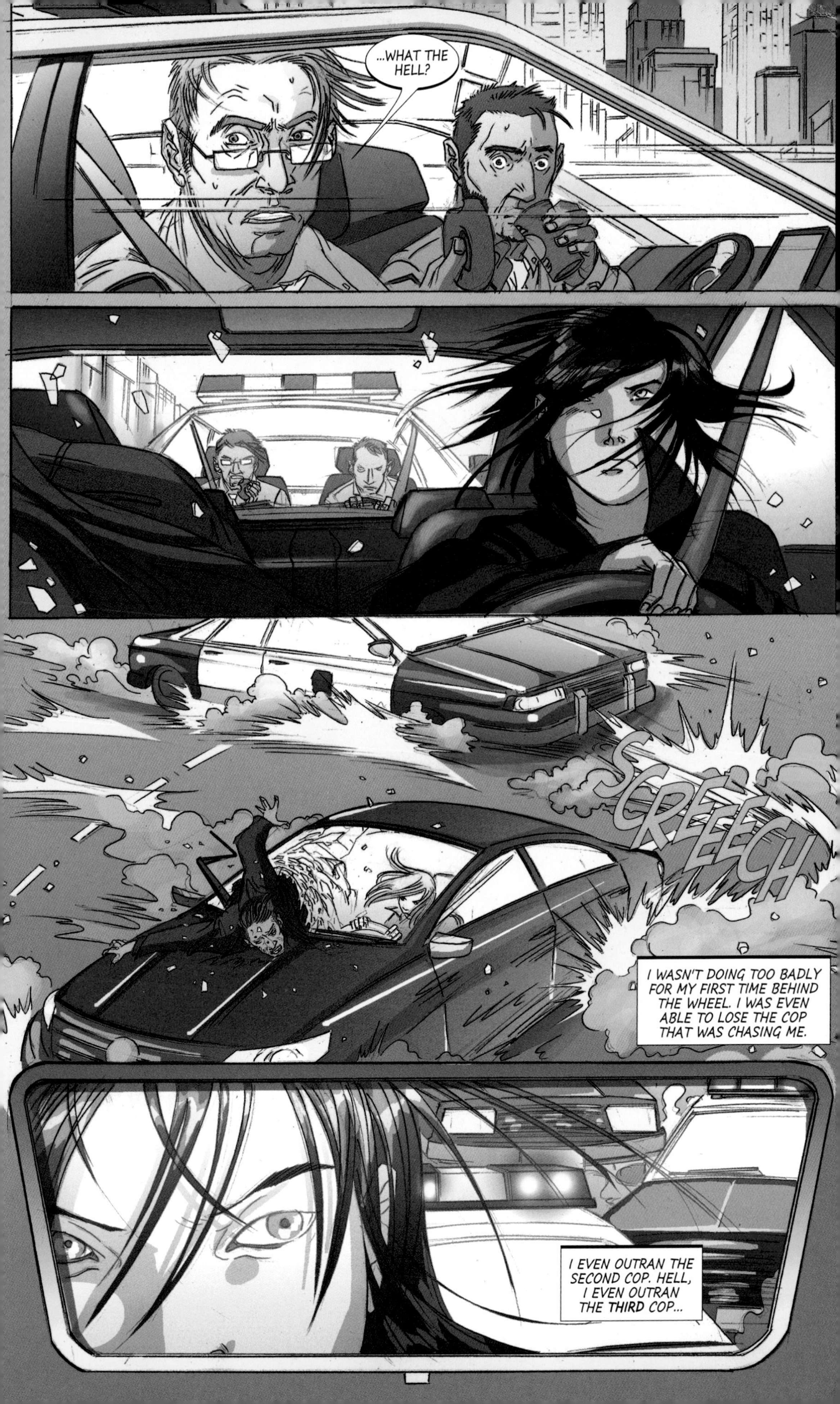
...WHAT THE HELL?
SCREEECH
I WASN'T DOING TOO BADLY FOR MY FIRST TIME BEHIND THE WHEEL. I WAS EVEN ABLE TO LOSE THE COP THAT WAS CHASING ME.
I EVEN OUTRAN THE SECOND COP. HELL, I EVEN OUTRAN THE **THIRD** COP...

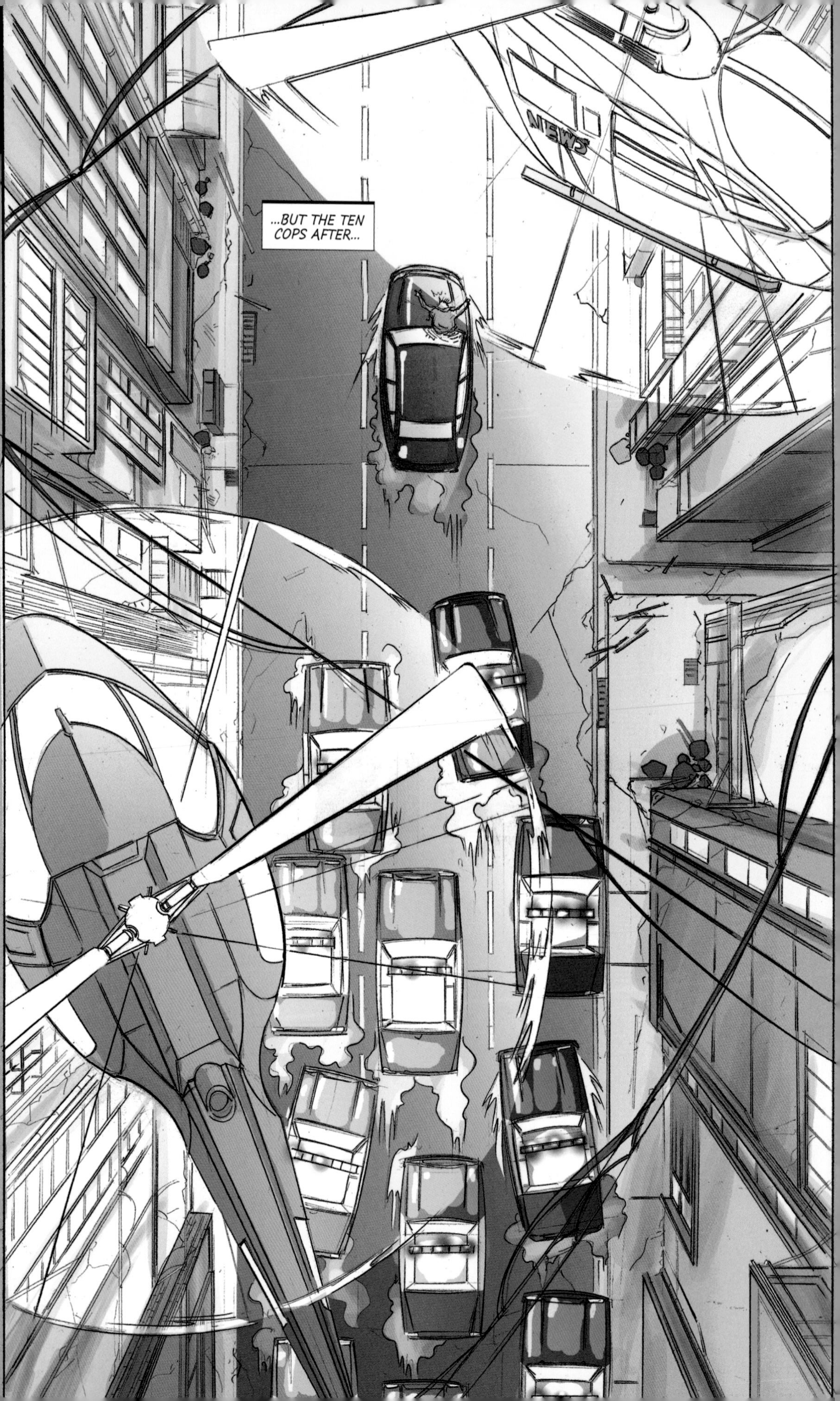
...BUT THE TEN COPS AFTER...
NEWS

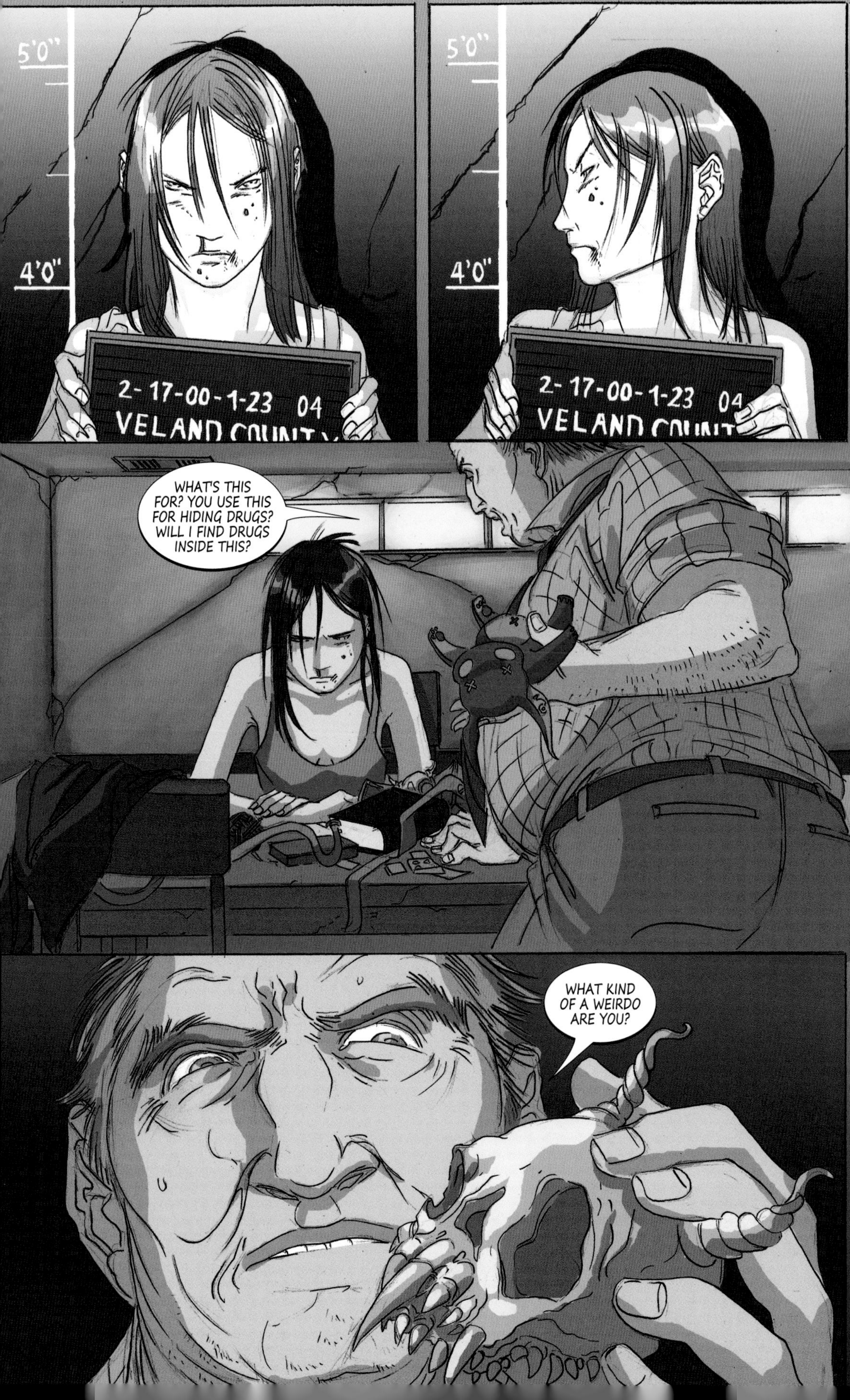
5'0"
4'0"
2-17-00-1-23 04
VELAND COUNTY
5'0"
4'0"
2-17-00-1-23 04
VELAND COUNT
WHAT'S THIS FOR? YOU USE THIS FOR HIDING DRUGS? WILL I FIND DRUGS INSIDE THIS?
WHAT KIND OF A WEIRDO ARE YOU?

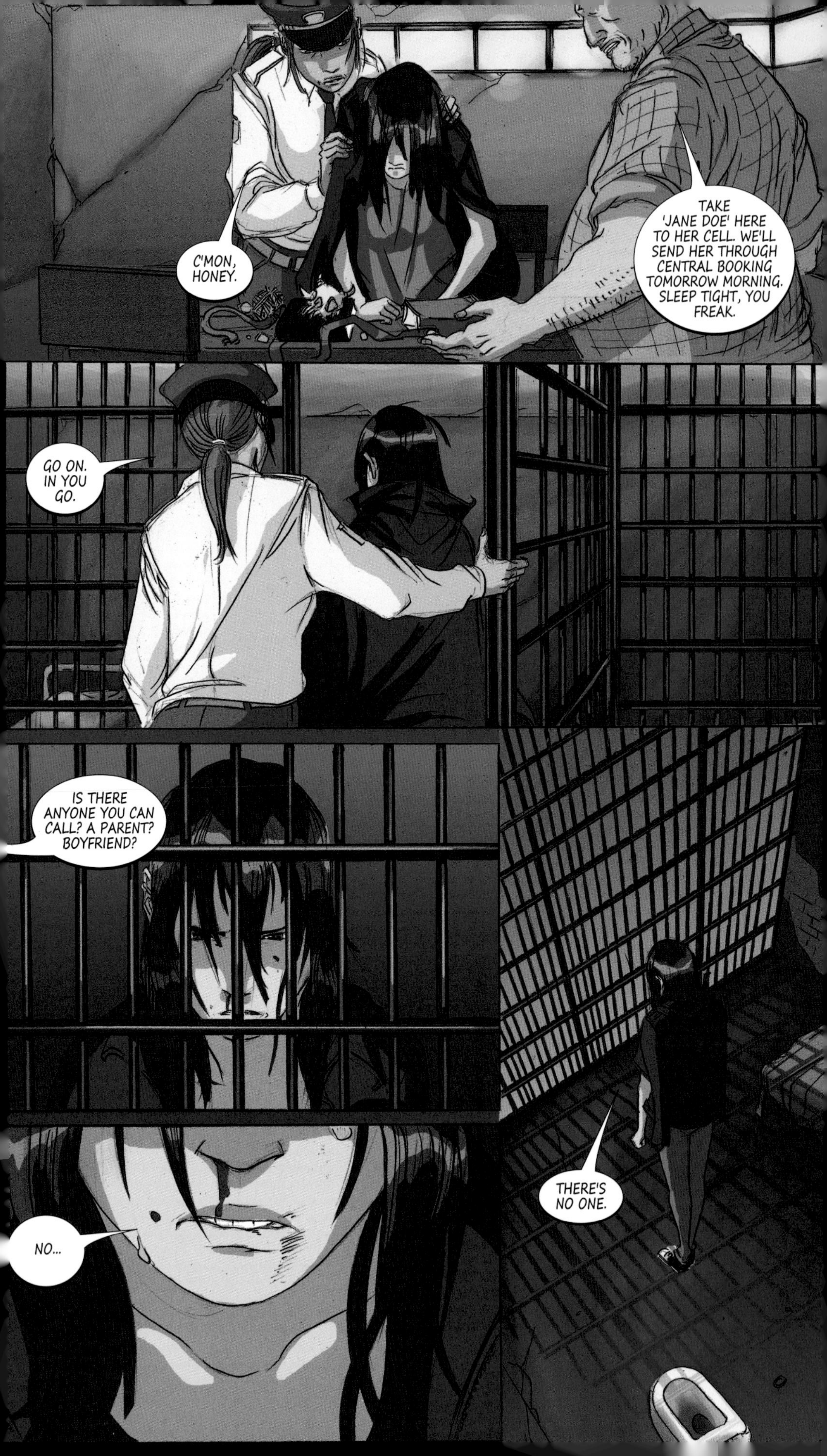
C'MON, HONEY.
TAKE 'JANE DOE' HERE TO HER CELL. WE'LL SEND HER THROUGH CENTRAL BOOKING TOMORROW MORNING. SLEEP TIGHT, YOU FREAK.
GO ON. IN YOU GO.
IS THERE ANYONE YOU CAN CALL? A PARENT? BOYFRIEND?
NO...
THERE'S NO ONE.

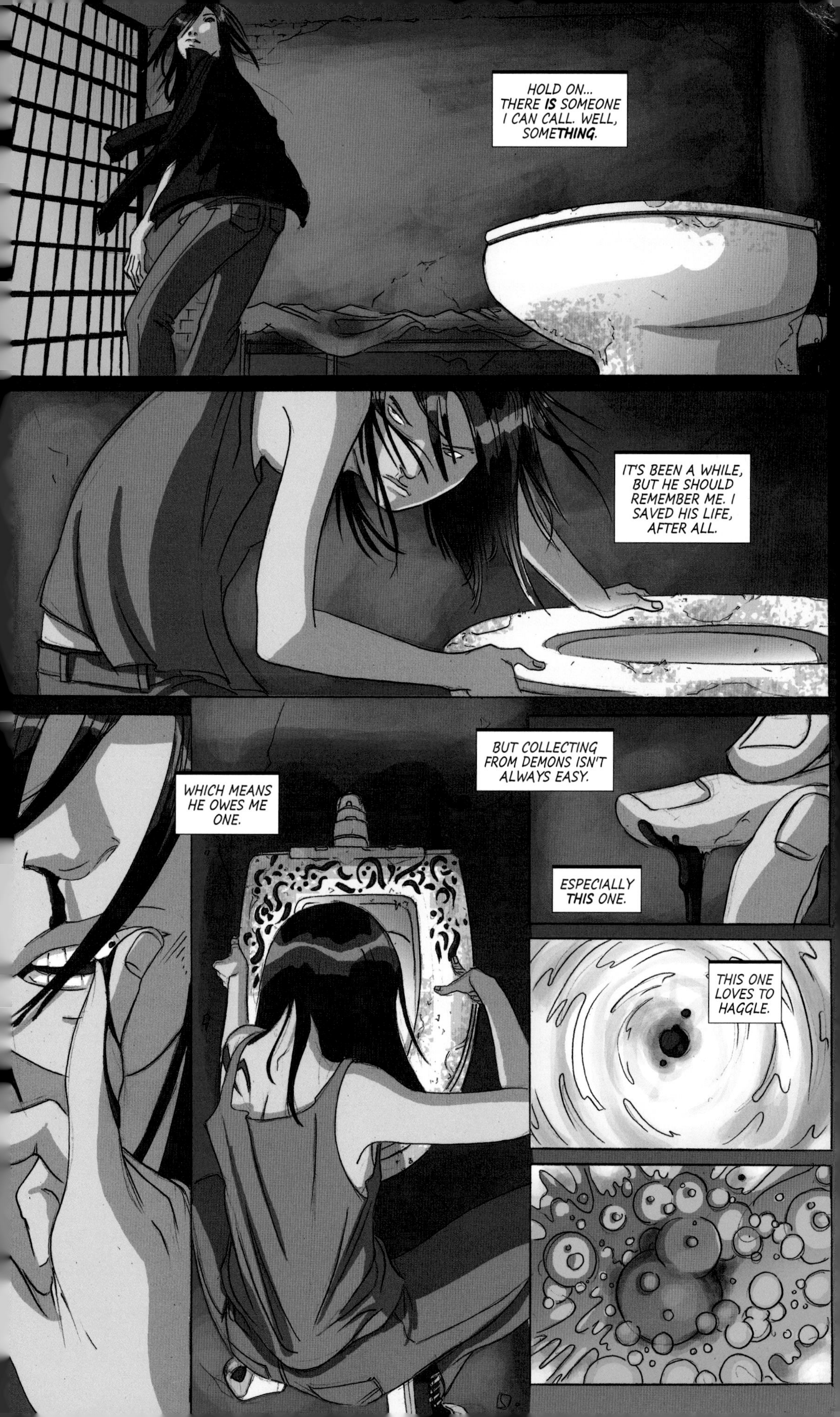
HOLD ON... THERE **IS** SOMEONE I CAN CALL. WELL, SOME**THING**.
IT'S BEEN A WHILE, BUT HE SHOULD REMEMBER ME. I SAVED HIS LIFE, AFTER ALL.
WHICH MEANS HE OWES ME ONE.
BUT COLLECTING FROM DEMONS ISN'T ALWAYS EASY.
ESPECIALLY THIS ONE.
THIS ONE LOVES TO HAGGLE.

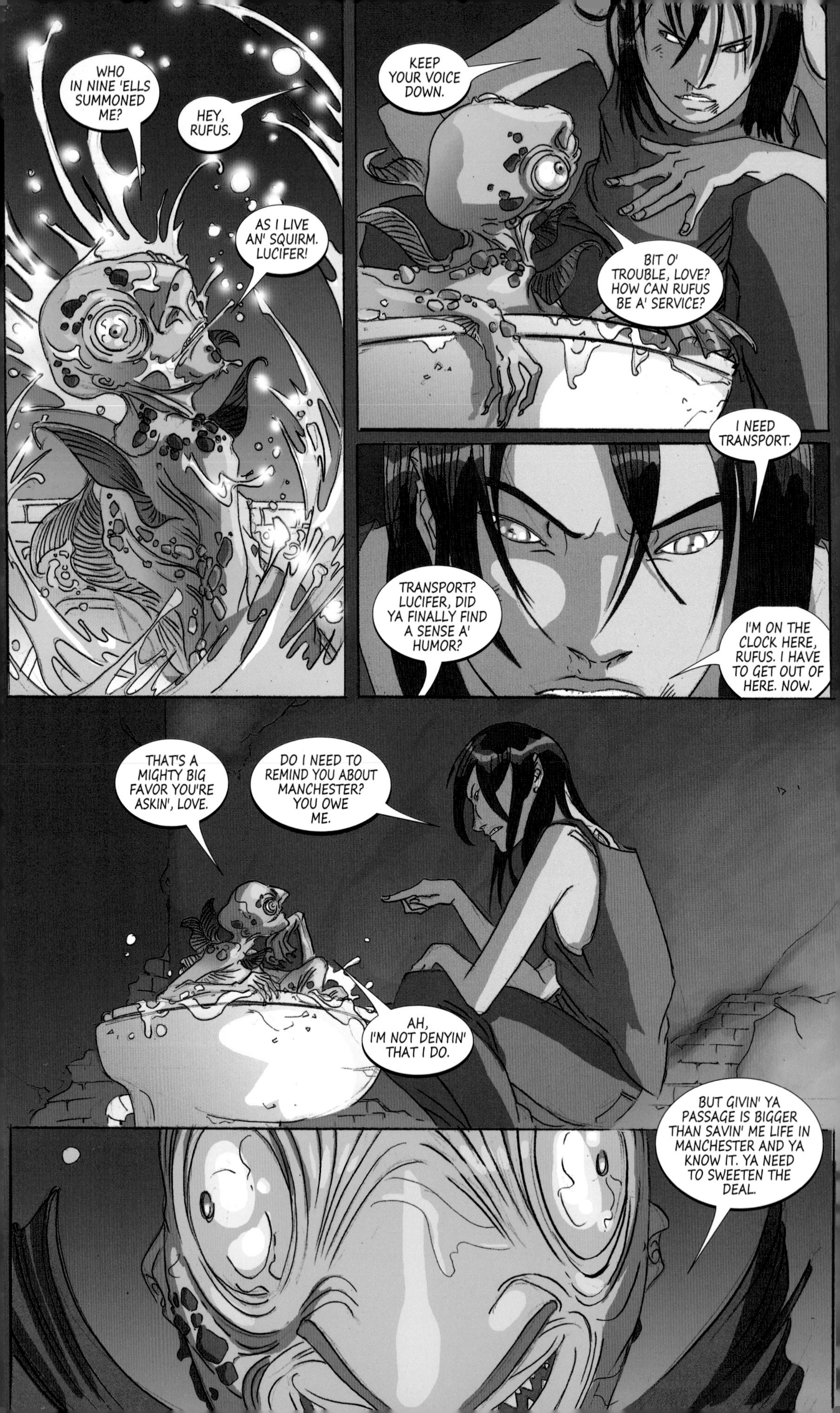
WHO IN NINE 'ELLS SUMMONED ME?
HEY, RUFUS.
AS I LIVE AN' SQUIRM. LUCIFER!
KEEP YOUR VOICE DOWN.
BIT O' TROUBLE, LOVE? HOW CAN RUFUS BE A' SERVICE?
I NEED TRANSPORT.
TRANSPORT? LUCIFER, DID YA FINALLY FIND A SENSE A' HUMOR?
I'M ON THE CLOCK HERE, RUFUS. I HAVE TO GET OUT OF HERE. NOW.
THAT'S A MIGHTY BIG FAVOR YOU'RE ASKIN', LOVE.
DO I NEED TO REMIND YOU ABOUT MANCHESTER? YOU OWE ME.
AH, I'M NOT DENYIN' THAT I DO.
BUT GIVIN' YA PASSAGE IS BIGGER THAN SAVIN' ME LIFE IN MANCHESTER AND YA KNOW IT. YA NEED TO SWEETEN THE DEAL.

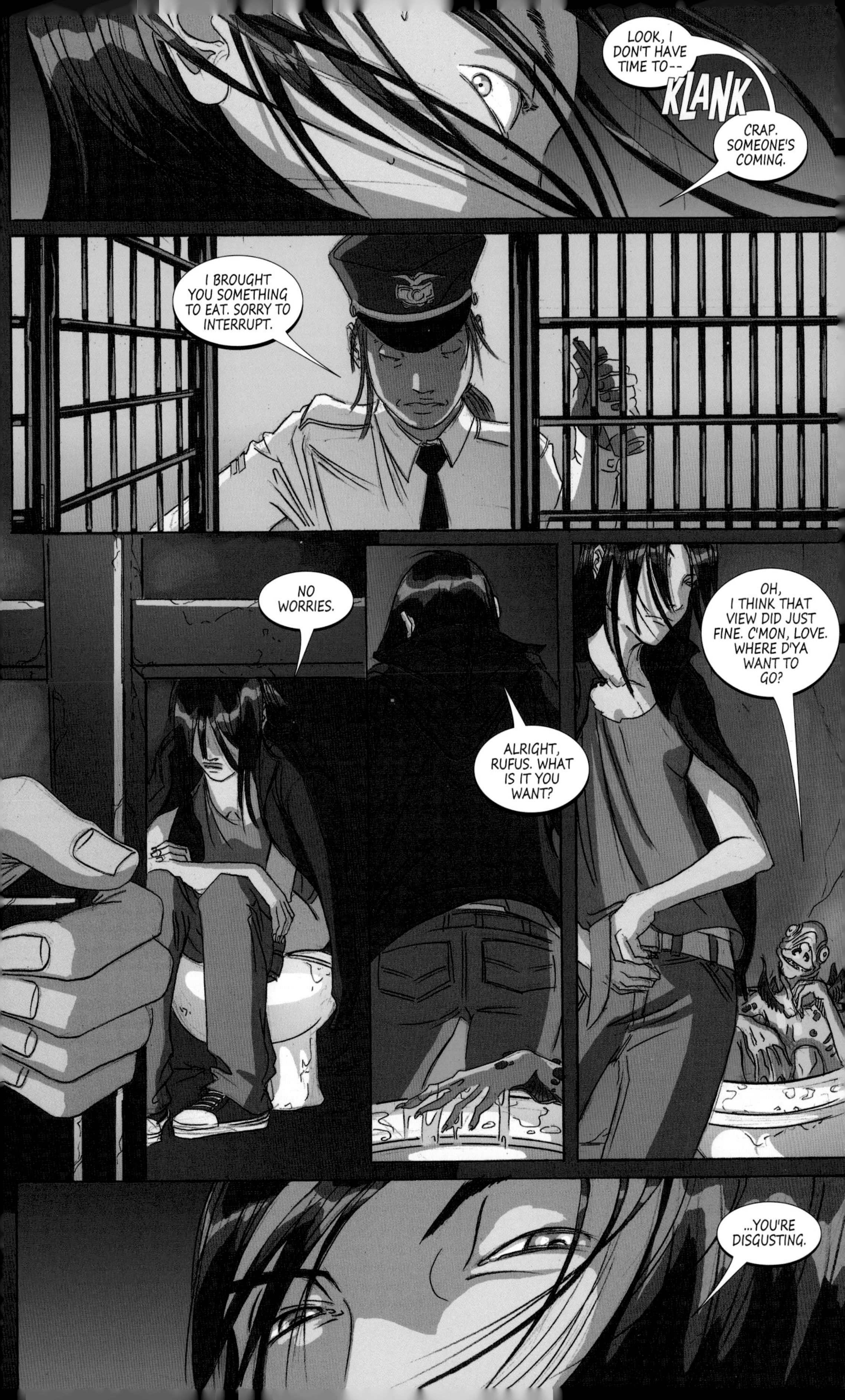
LOOK, I DON'T HAVE TIME TO--
KLANK
CRAP. SOMEONE'S COMING.
I BROUGHT YOU SOMETHING TO EAT. SORRY TO INTERRUPT.
NO WORRIES.
ALRIGHT, RUFUS. WHAT IS IT YOU WANT?
OH, I THINK THAT VIEW DID JUST FINE. C'MON, LOVE. WHERE D'YA WANT TO GO?
...YOU'RE DISGUSTING.

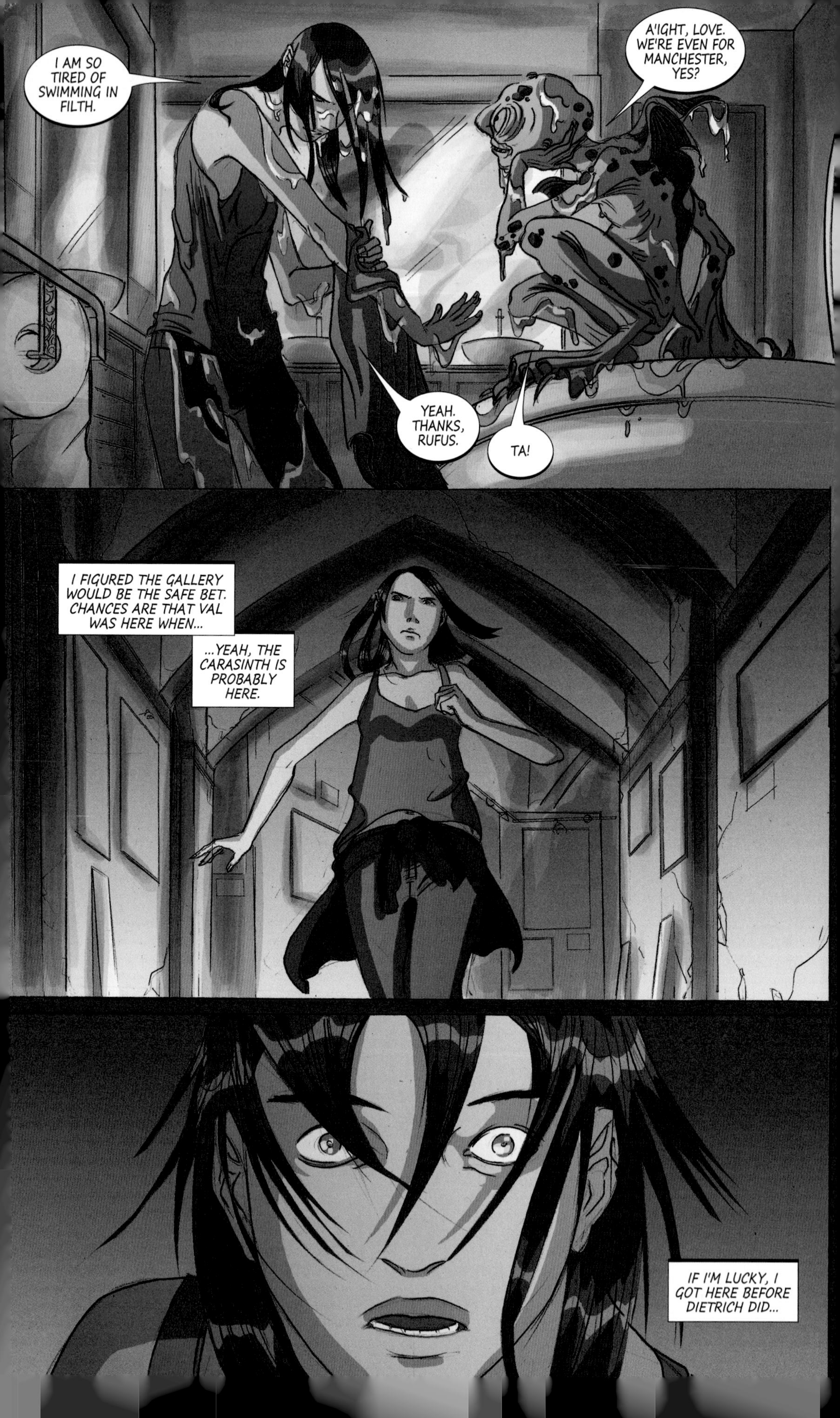
I AM SO TIRED OF SWIMMING IN FILTH.
A'IGHT, LOVE. WE'RE EVEN FOR MANCHESTER, YES?
YEAH. THANKS, RUFUS.
TA!
I FIGURED THE GALLERY WOULD BE THE SAFE BET. CHANCES ARE THAT VAL WAS HERE WHEN...
...YEAH, THE CARASINTH IS PROBABLY HERE.
IF I'M LUCKY, I GOT HERE BEFORE DIETRICH DID...

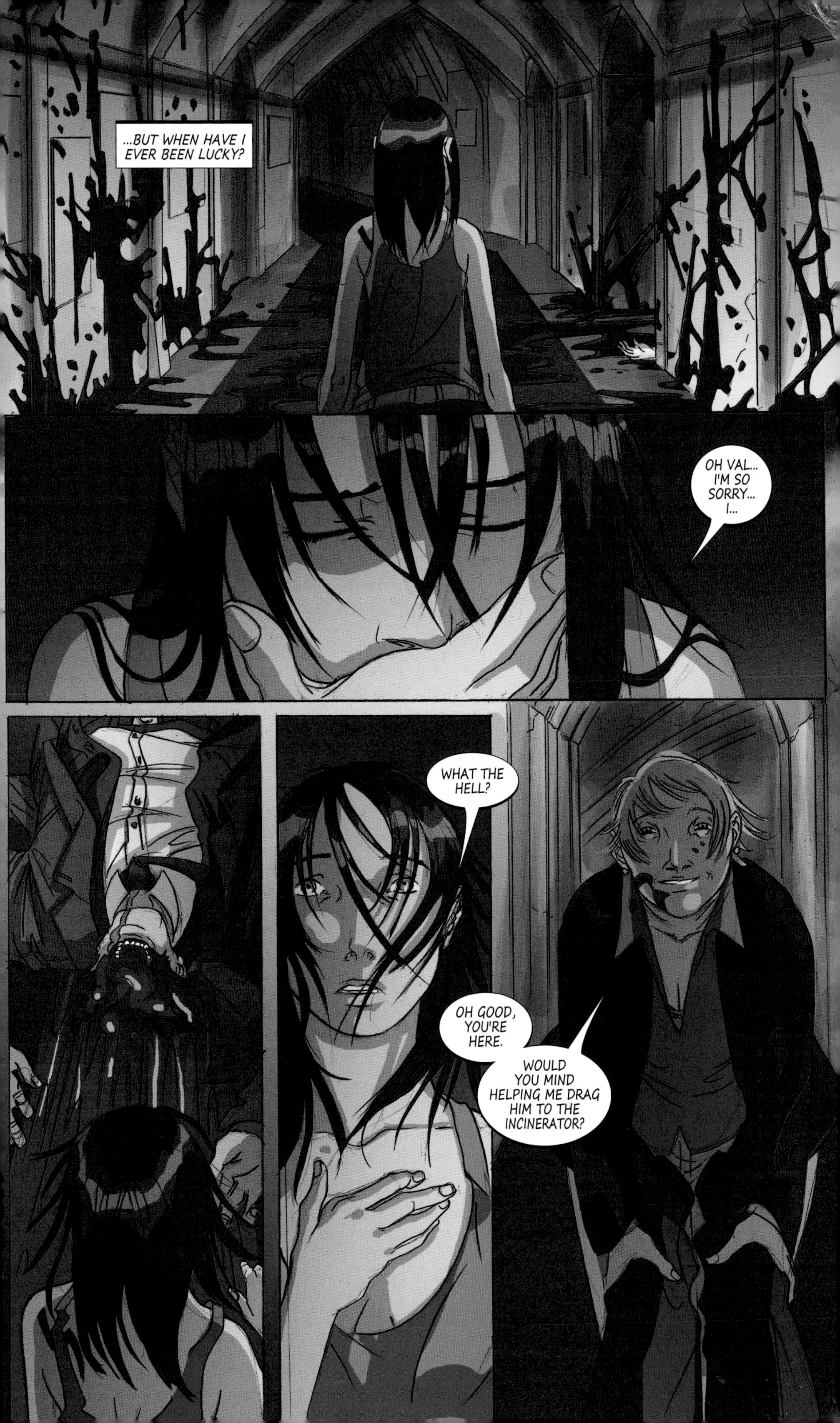
...BUT WHEN HAVE I EVER BEEN LUCKY?
OH VAL... I'M SO SORRY... I...
WHAT THE HELL?
OH GOOD, YOU'RE HERE.
WOULD YOU MIND HELPING ME DRAG HIM TO THE INCINERATOR?

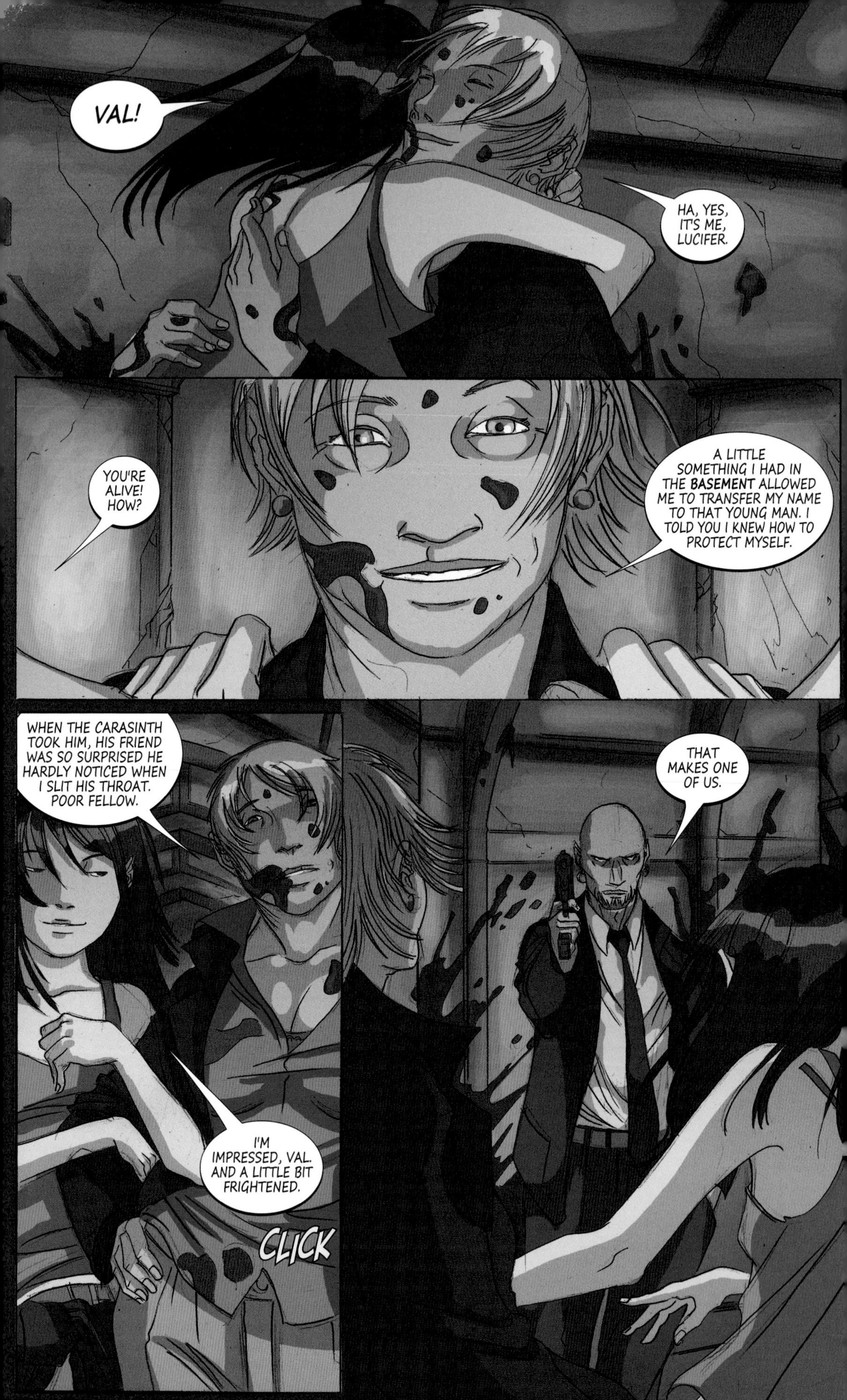
VAL!
HA, YES, IT'S ME, LUCIFER.
YOU'RE ALIVE! HOW?
A LITTLE SOMETHING I HAD IN THE **BASEMENT** ALLOWED ME TO TRANSFER MY NAME TO THAT YOUNG MAN. I TOLD YOU I KNEW HOW TO PROTECT MYSELF.
WHEN THE CARASINTH TOOK HIM, HIS FRIEND WAS SO SURPRISED HE HARDLY NOTICED WHEN I SLIT HIS THROAT. POOR FELLOW.
I'M IMPRESSED, VAL. AND A LITTLE BIT FRIGHTENED.
CLICK
THAT MAKES ONE OF US.

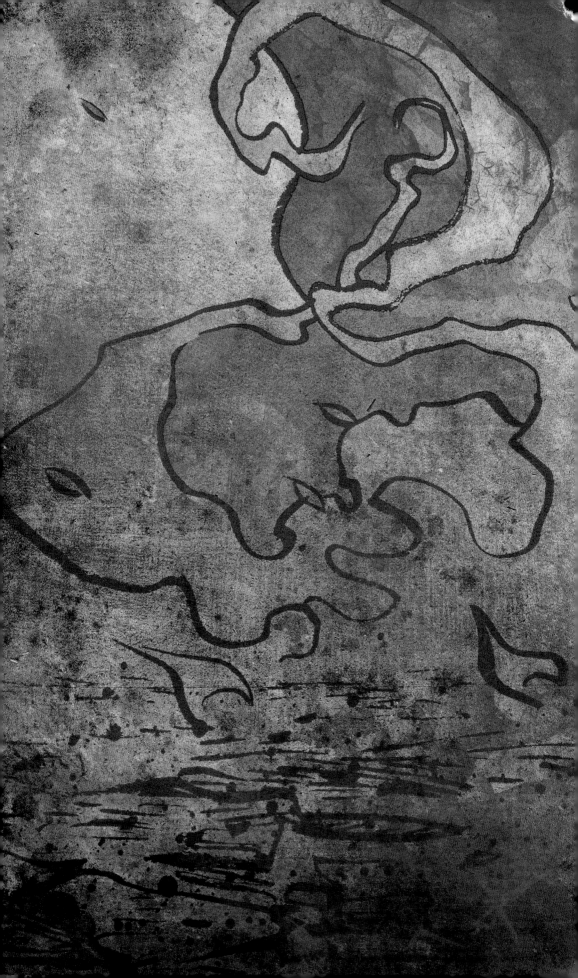

CHAPTER IV

WHEREIN LUCIFER BECOMES A DAY PLAYER
AND FEARS THE NUMBER 30.

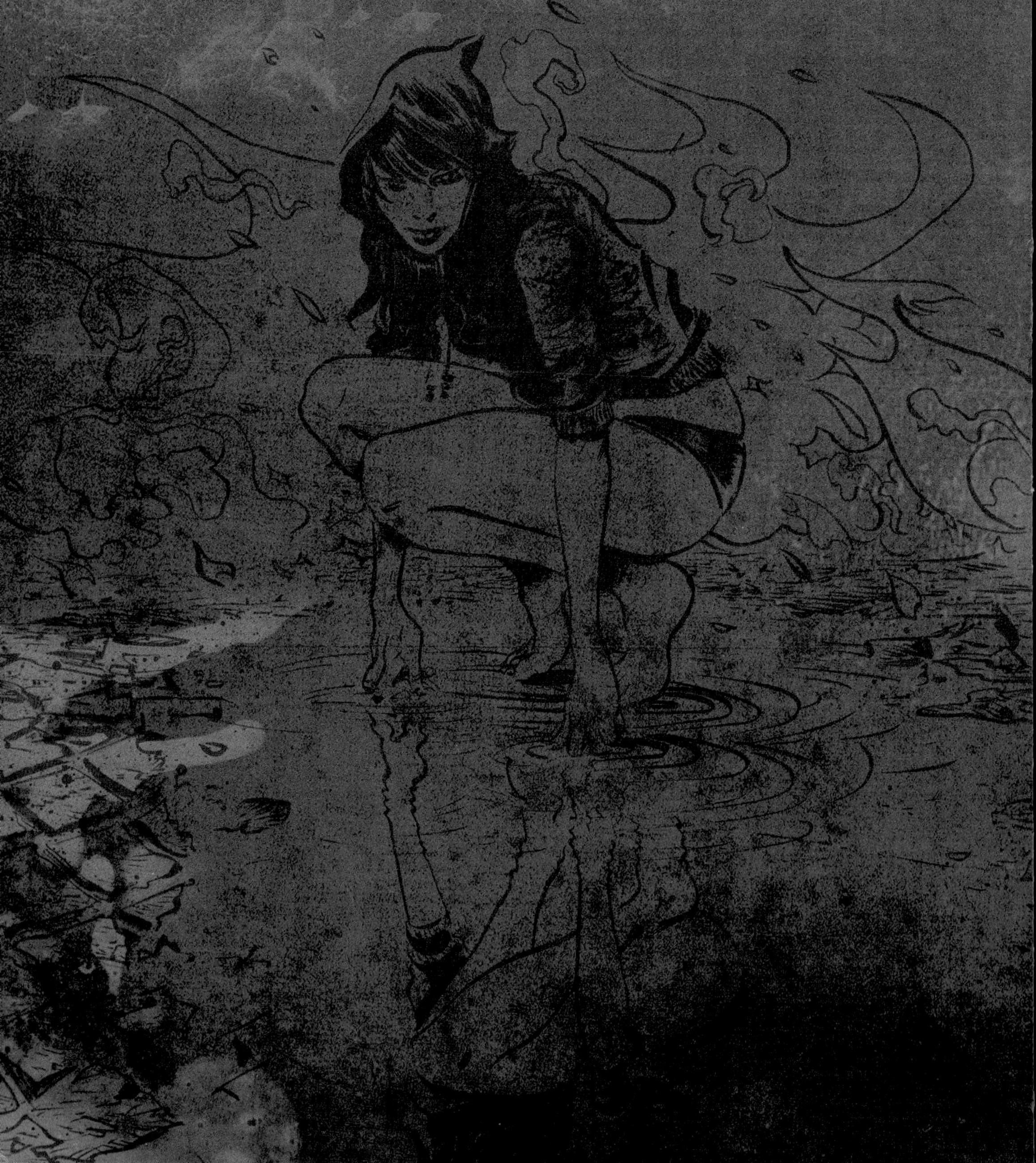

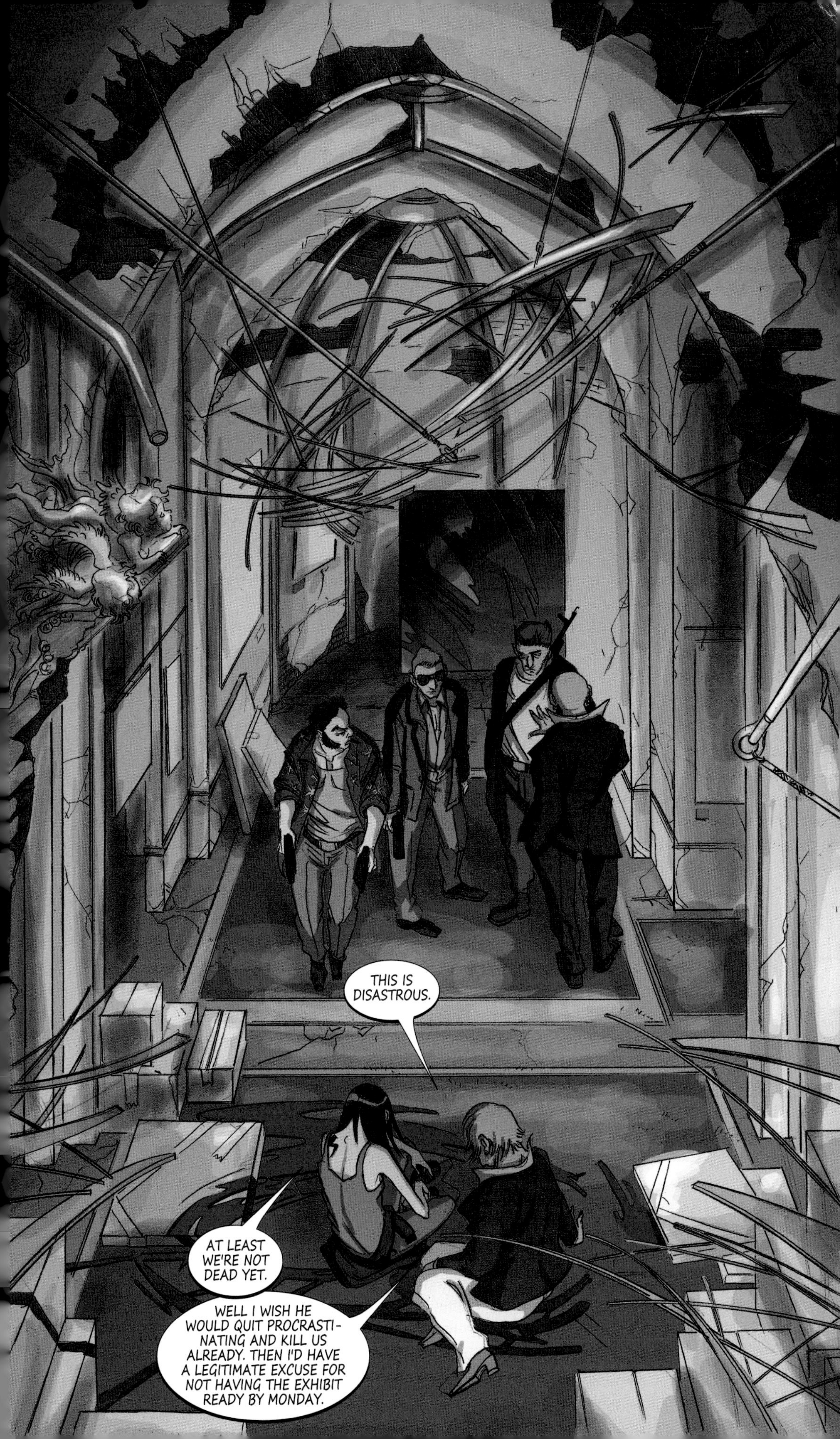
THIS IS DISASTROUS.
AT LEAST WE'RE NOT DEAD YET.
WELL I WISH HE WOULD QUIT PROCRASTI-NATING AND KILL US ALREADY. THEN I'D HAVE A LEGITIMATE EXCUSE FOR NOT HAVING THE EXHIBIT READY BY MONDAY.

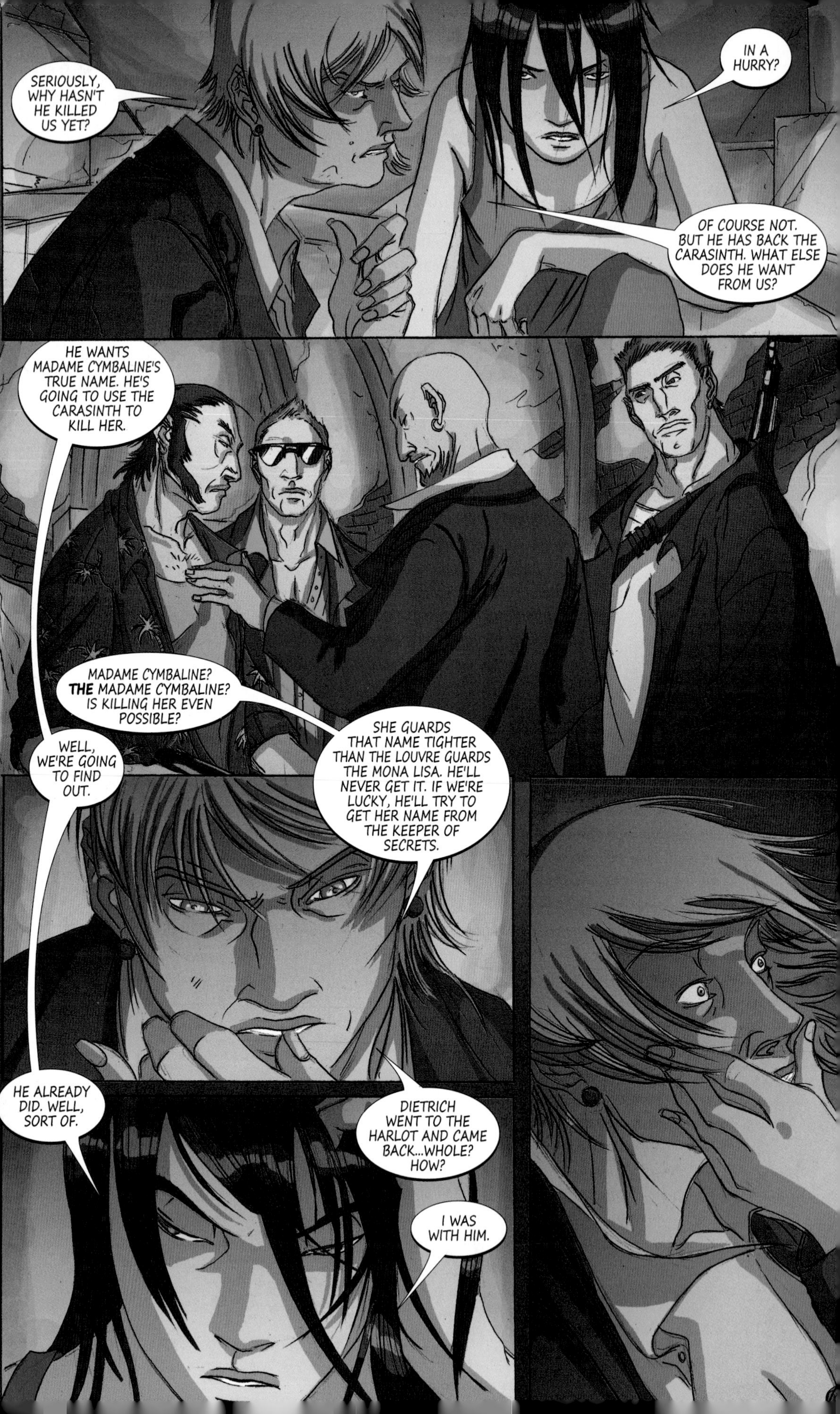
SERIOUSLY, WHY HASN'T HE KILLED US YET?
IN A HURRY?
OF COURSE NOT. BUT HE HAS BACK THE CARASINTH. WHAT ELSE DOES HE WANT FROM US?
HE WANTS MADAME CYMBALINE'S TRUE NAME. HE'S GOING TO USE THE CARASINTH TO KILL HER.
MADAME CYMBALINE? **THE** MADAME CYMBALINE? IS KILLING HER EVEN POSSIBLE?
WELL, WE'RE GOING TO FIND OUT.
SHE GUARDS THAT NAME TIGHTER THAN THE LOUVRE GUARDS THE MONA LISA. HE'LL NEVER GET IT. IF WE'RE LUCKY, HE'LL TRY TO GET HER NAME FROM THE KEEPER OF SECRETS.
HE ALREADY DID. WELL, SORT OF.
DIETRICH WENT TO THE HARLOT AND CAME BACK...WHOLE? HOW?
I WAS WITH HIM.

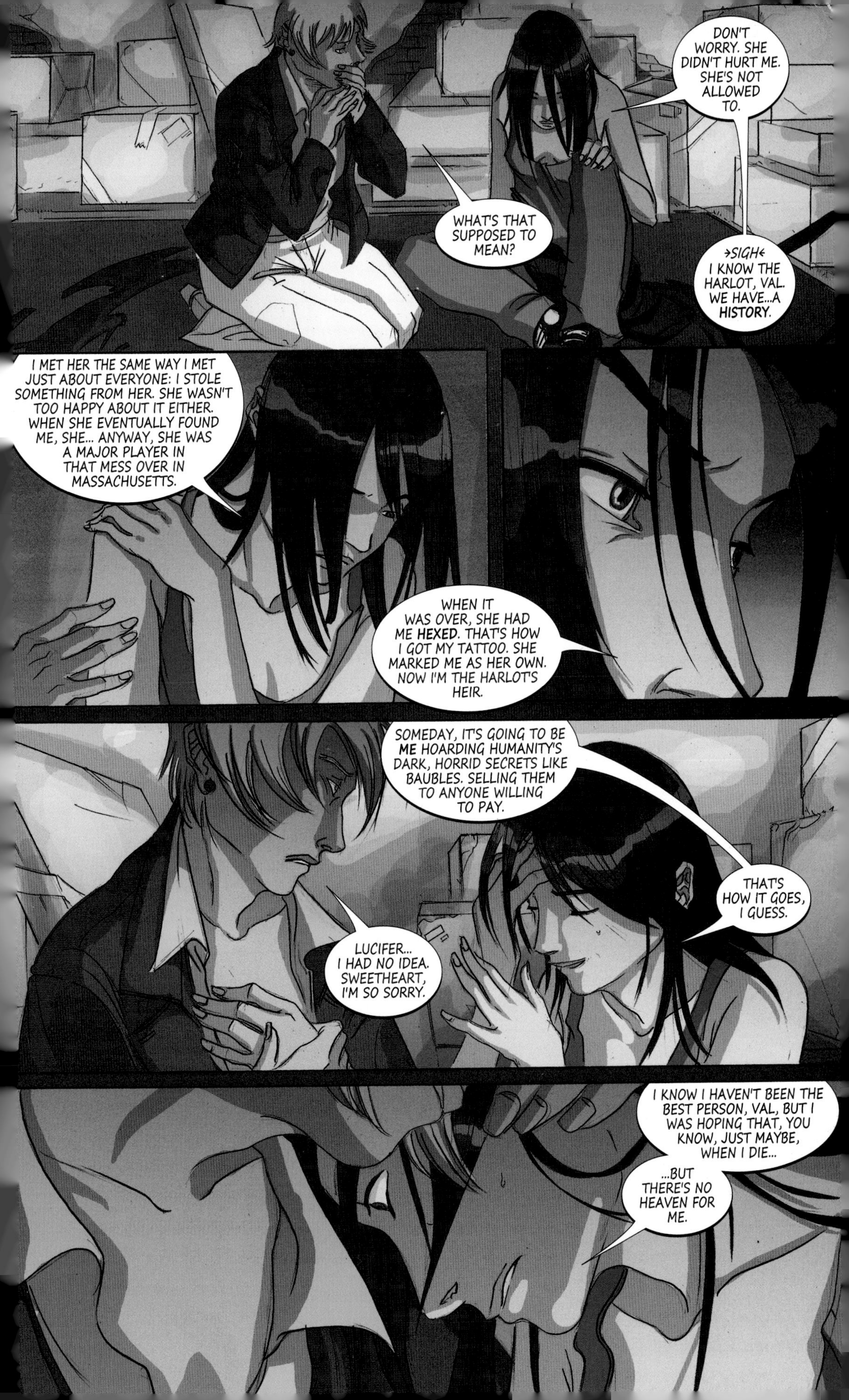
DON'T WORRY. SHE DIDN'T HURT ME. SHE'S NOT ALLOWED TO.
WHAT'S THAT SUPPOSED TO MEAN?
>SIGH< I KNOW THE HARLOT, VAL. WE HAVE...A **HISTORY**.
I MET HER THE SAME WAY I MET JUST ABOUT EVERYONE: I STOLE SOMETHING FROM HER. SHE WASN'T TOO HAPPY ABOUT IT EITHER. WHEN SHE EVENTUALLY FOUND ME, SHE... ANYWAY, SHE WAS A MAJOR PLAYER IN THAT MESS OVER IN MASSACHUSETTS.
WHEN IT WAS OVER, SHE HAD ME **HEXED**. THAT'S HOW I GOT MY TATTOO. SHE MARKED ME AS HER OWN. NOW I'M THE HARLOT'S HEIR.
SOMEDAY, IT'S GOING TO BE **ME** HOARDING HUMANITY'S DARK, HORRID SECRETS LIKE BAUBLES. SELLING THEM TO ANYONE WILLING TO PAY.
THAT'S HOW IT GOES, I GUESS.
LUCIFER... I HAD NO IDEA. SWEETHEART, I'M SO SORRY.
I KNOW I HAVEN'T BEEN THE BEST PERSON, VAL, BUT I WAS HOPING THAT, YOU KNOW, JUST MAYBE, WHEN I DIE...
...BUT THERE'S NO HEAVEN FOR ME.

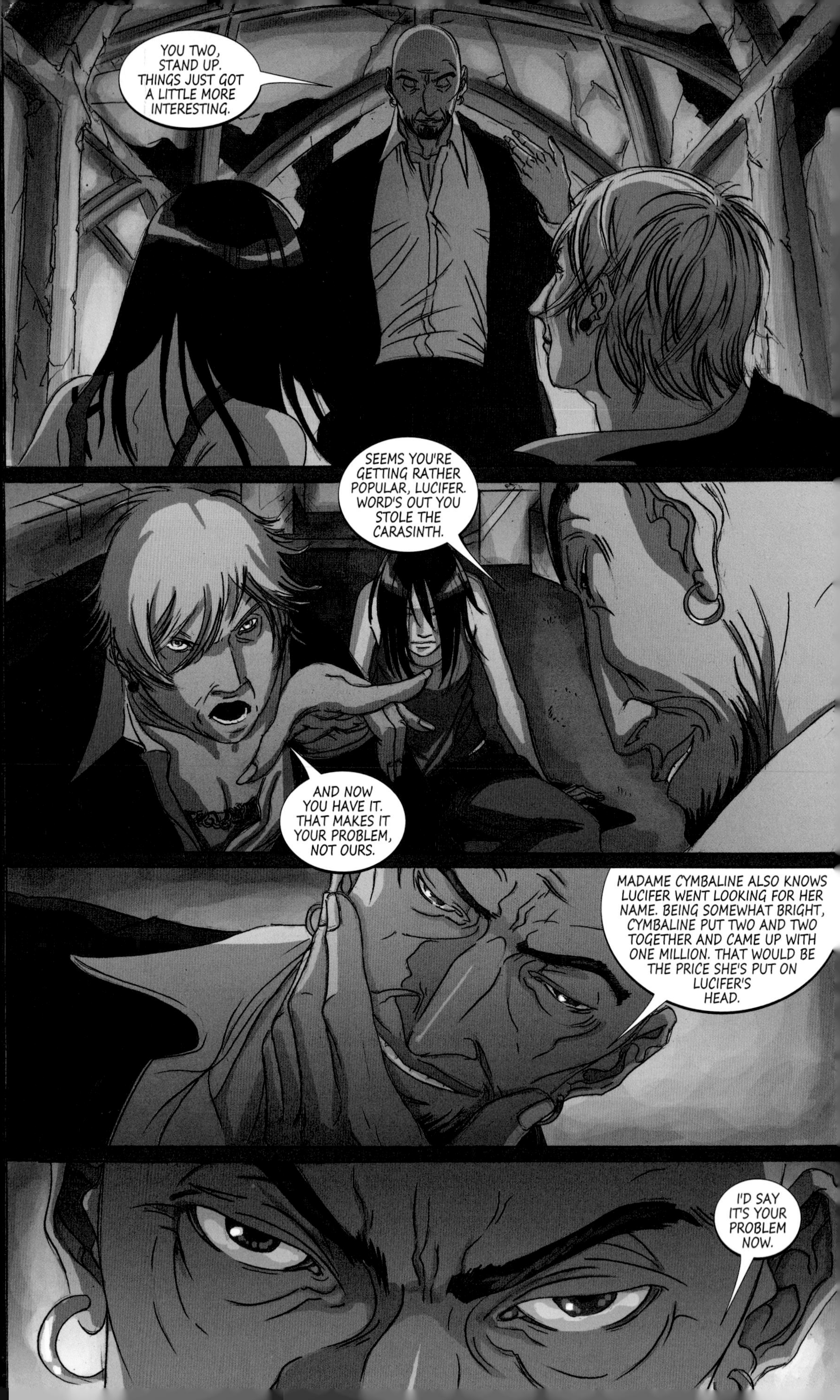
YOU TWO, STAND UP. THINGS JUST GOT A LITTLE MORE INTERESTING.
SEEMS YOU'RE GETTING RATHER POPULAR, LUCIFER. WORD'S OUT YOU STOLE THE CARASINTH.
AND NOW YOU HAVE IT. THAT MAKES IT YOUR PROBLEM, NOT OURS.
MADAME CYMBALINE ALSO KNOWS LUCIFER WENT LOOKING FOR HER NAME. BEING SOMEWHAT BRIGHT, CYMBALINE PUT TWO AND TWO TOGETHER AND CAME UP WITH ONE MILLION. THAT WOULD BE THE PRICE SHE'S PUT ON LUCIFER'S HEAD.
I'D SAY IT'S YOUR PROBLEM NOW.

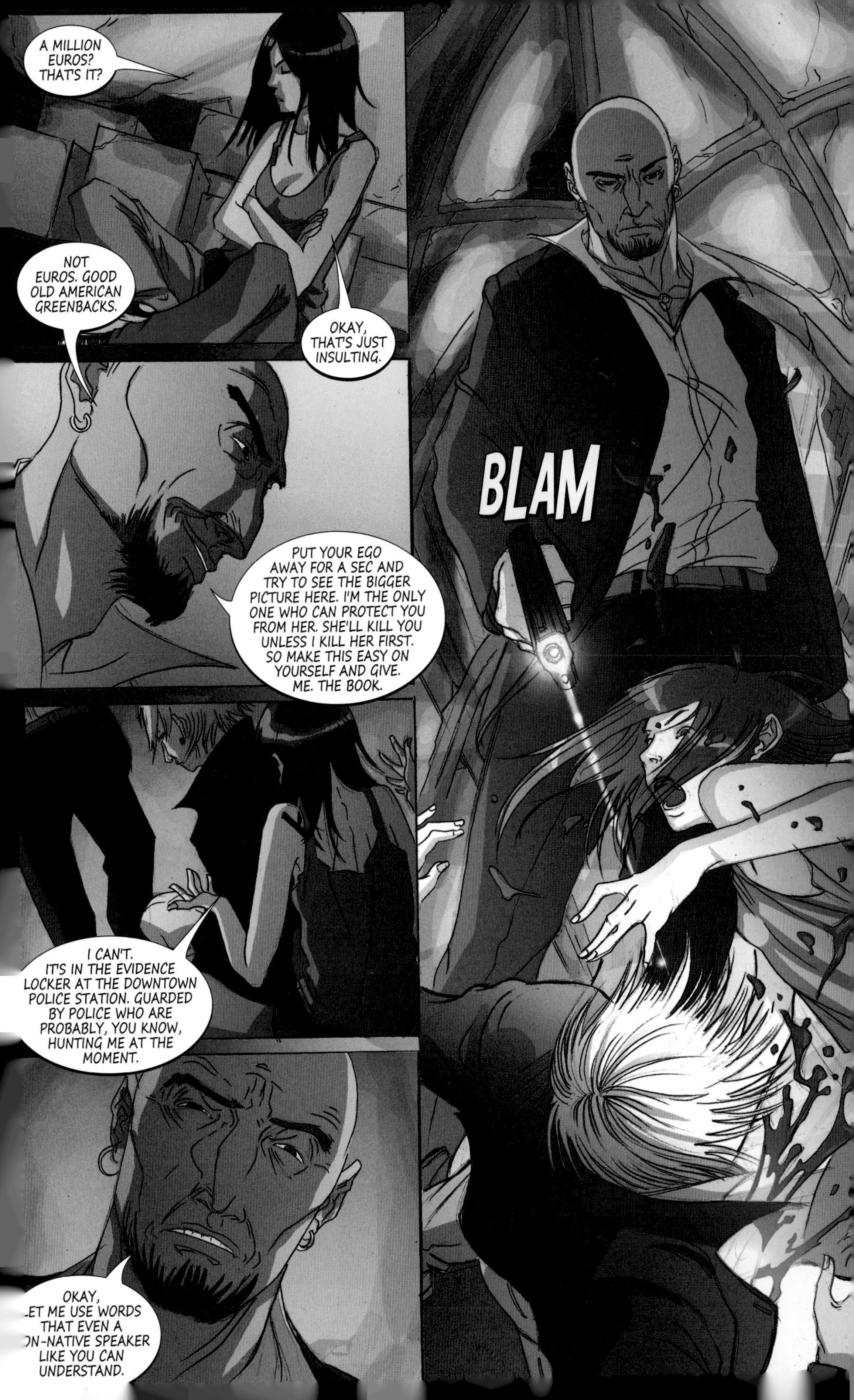
A MILLION EUROS? THAT'S IT?
NOT EUROS. GOOD OLD AMERICAN GREENBACKS.
OKAY, THAT'S JUST INSULTING.
PUT YOUR EGO AWAY FOR A SEC AND TRY TO SEE THE BIGGER PICTURE HERE. I'M THE ONLY ONE WHO CAN PROTECT YOU FROM HER. SHE'LL KILL YOU UNLESS I KILL HER FIRST. SO MAKE THIS EASY ON YOURSELF AND GIVE. ME. THE BOOK.
I CAN'T. IT'S IN THE EVIDENCE LOCKER AT THE DOWNTOWN POLICE STATION. GUARDED BY POLICE WHO ARE PROBABLY, YOU KNOW, HUNTING ME AT THE MOMENT.
OKAY, LET ME USE WORDS THAT EVEN A NON-NATIVE SPEAKER LIKE YOU CAN UNDERSTAND.
BLAM

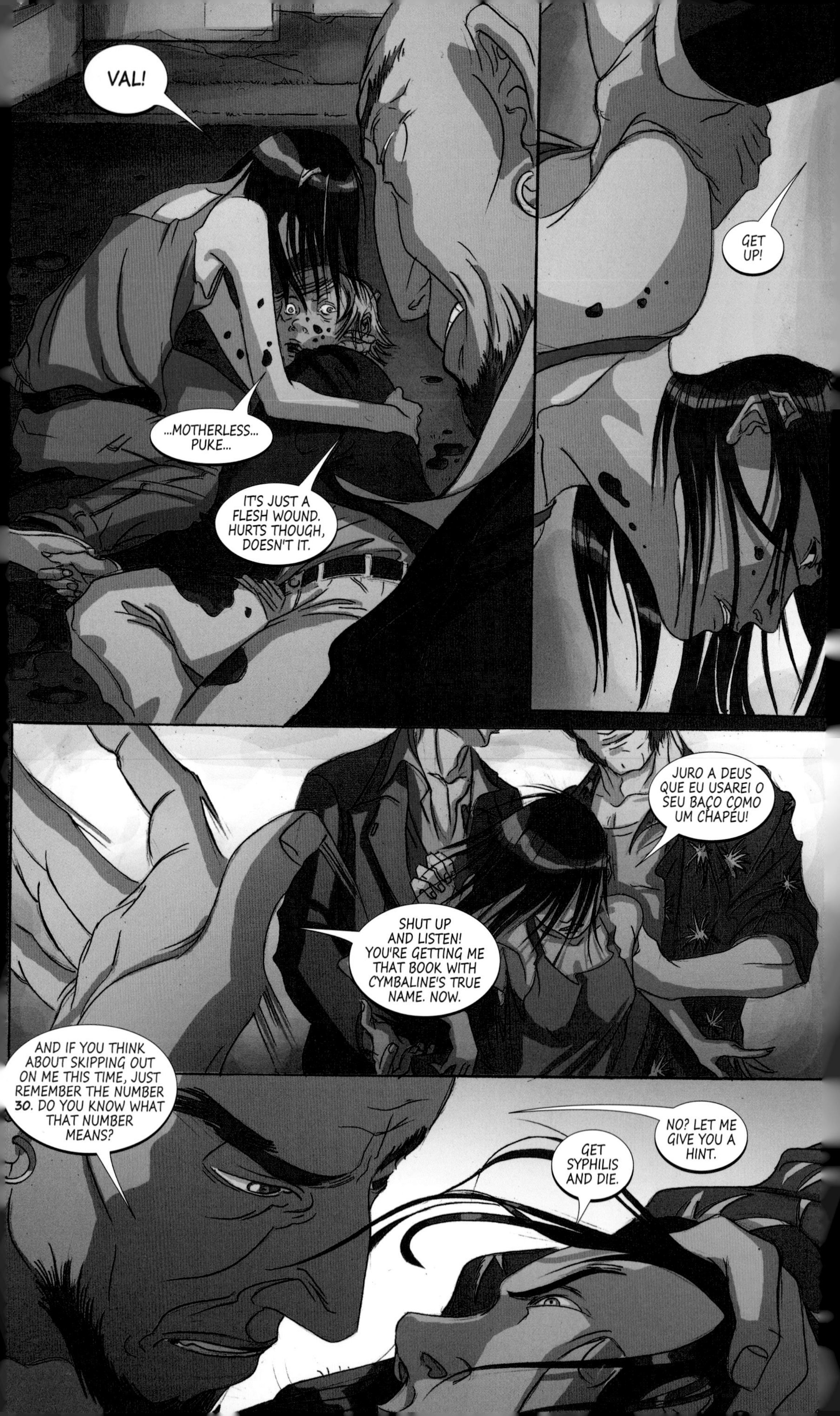
VAL!
...MOTHERLESS... PUKE...
IT'S JUST A FLESH WOUND. HURTS THOUGH, DOESN'T IT.
GET UP!
JURO A DEUS QUE EU USAREI O SEU BAÇO COMO UM CHAPÉU!
SHUT UP AND LISTEN! YOU'RE GETTING ME THAT BOOK WITH CYMBALINE'S TRUE NAME. NOW.
AND IF YOU THINK ABOUT SKIPPING OUT ON ME THIS TIME, JUST REMEMBER THE NUMBER **30**. DO YOU KNOW WHAT THAT NUMBER MEANS?
NO? LET ME GIVE YOU A HINT.
GET SYPHILIS AND DIE.

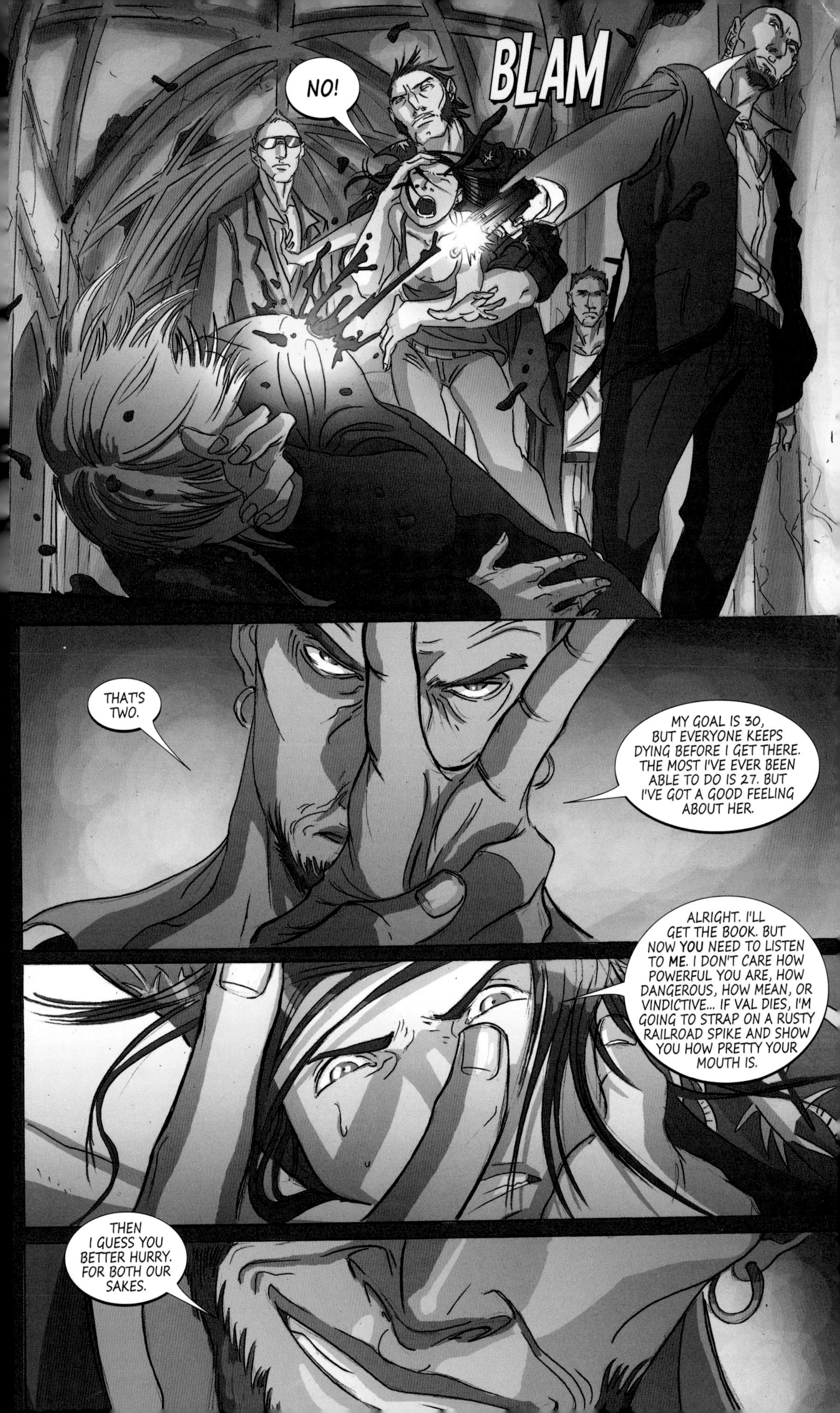
NO!
BLAM
THAT'S TWO.
MY GOAL IS 30, BUT EVERYONE KEEPS DYING BEFORE I GET THERE. THE MOST I'VE EVER BEEN ABLE TO DO IS 27. BUT I'VE GOT A GOOD FEELING ABOUT HER.
ALRIGHT. I'LL GET THE BOOK. BUT NOW **YOU** NEED TO LISTEN TO **ME**. I DON'T CARE HOW POWERFUL YOU ARE, HOW DANGEROUS, HOW MEAN, OR VINDICTIVE... IF VAL DIES, I'M GOING TO STRAP ON A RUSTY RAILROAD SPIKE AND SHOW YOU HOW PRETTY YOUR MOUTH IS.
THEN I GUESS YOU BETTER HURRY. FOR BOTH OUR SAKES.

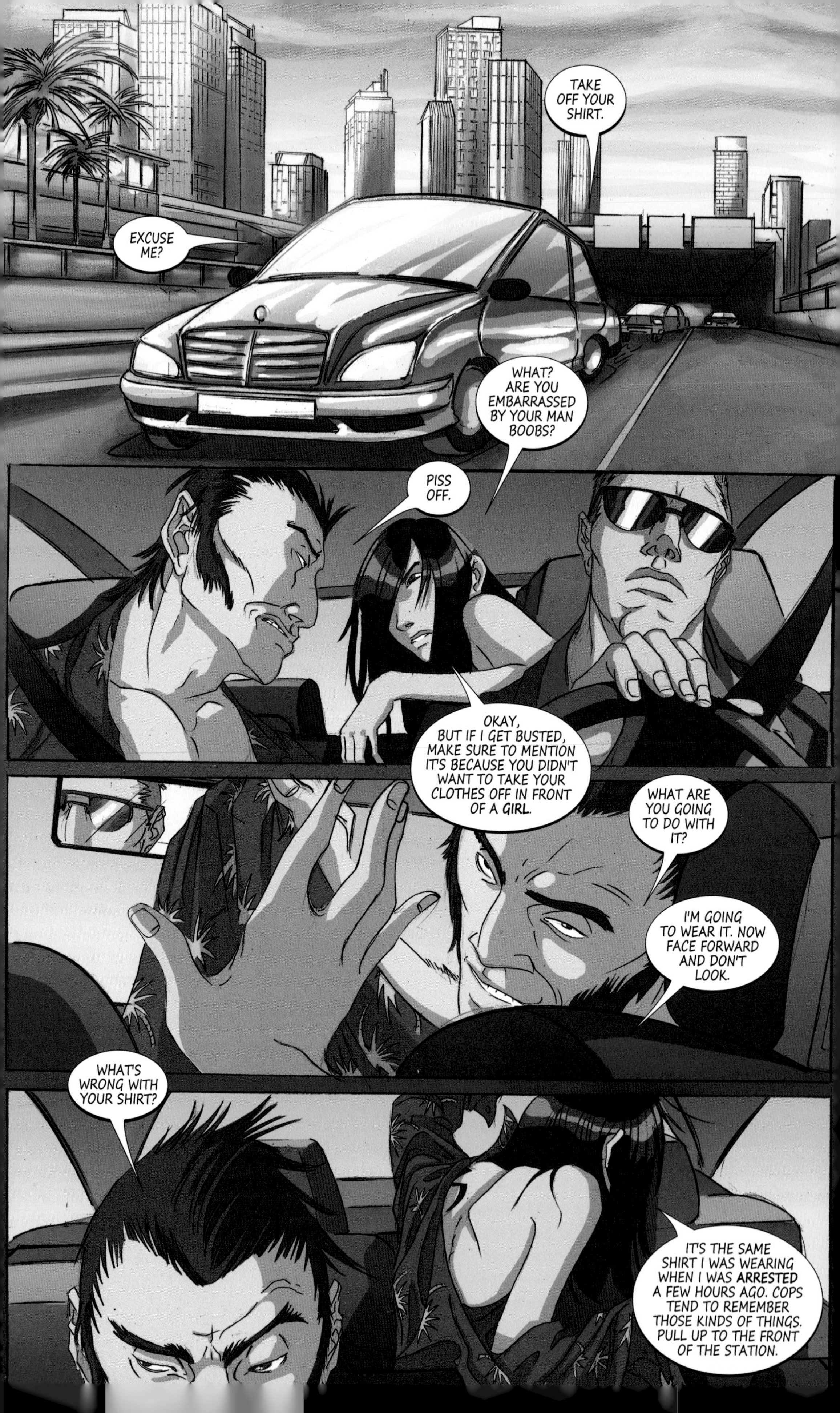
TAKE OFF YOUR SHIRT.
EXCUSE ME?
WHAT? ARE YOU EMBARRASSED BY YOUR MAN BOOBS?
PISS OFF.
OKAY, BUT IF I GET BUSTED, MAKE SURE TO MENTION IT'S BECAUSE YOU DIDN'T WANT TO TAKE YOUR CLOTHES OFF IN FRONT OF A **GIRL**.
WHAT ARE YOU GOING TO DO WITH IT?
I'M GOING TO WEAR IT. NOW FACE FORWARD AND DON'T LOOK.
WHAT'S WRONG WITH YOUR SHIRT?
IT'S THE SAME SHIRT I WAS WEARING WHEN I WAS **ARRESTED** A FEW HOURS AGO. COPS TEND TO REMEMBER THOSE KINDS OF THINGS. PULL UP TO THE FRONT OF THE STATION.

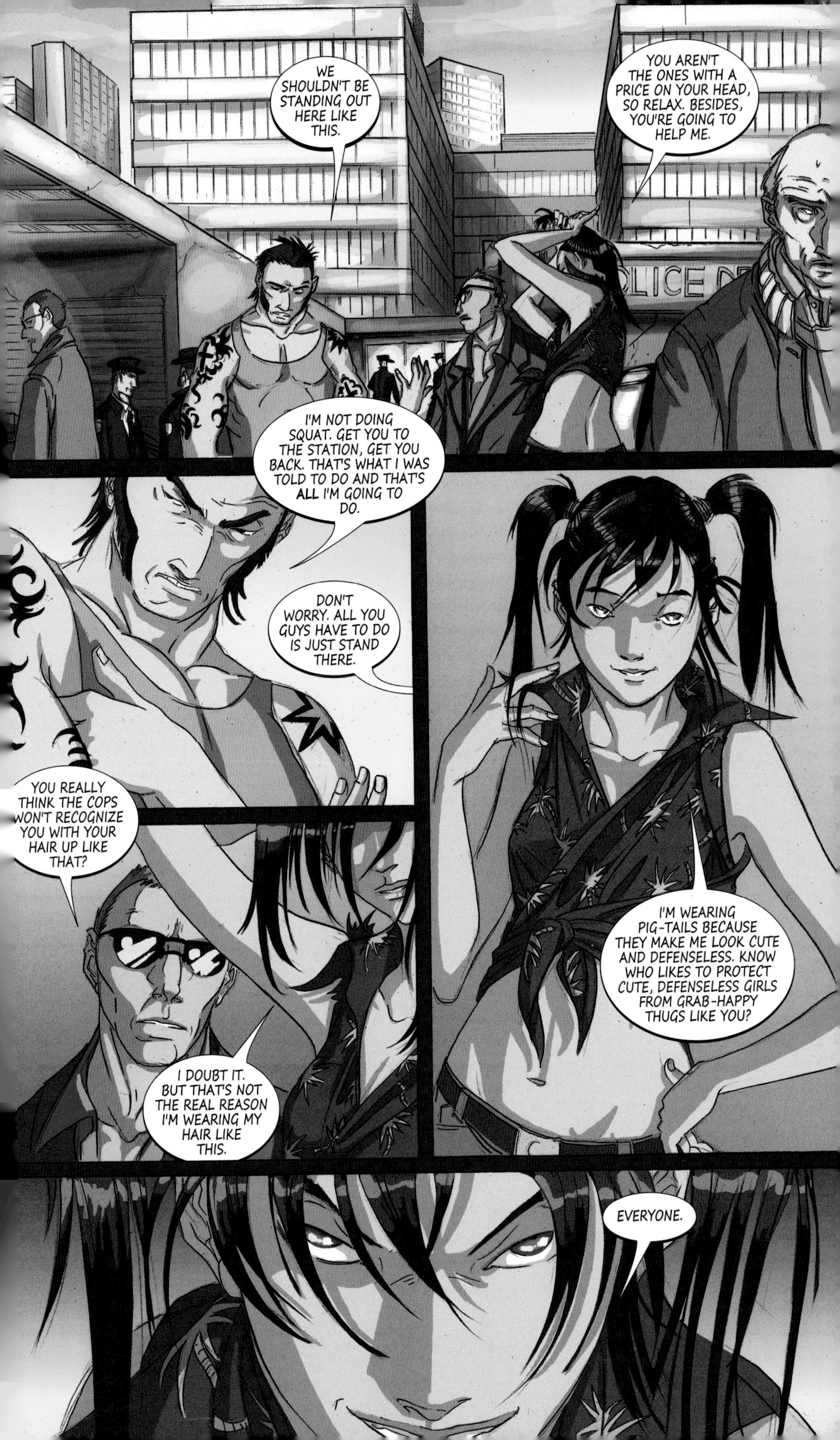
WE SHOULDN'T BE STANDING OUT HERE LIKE THIS.
YOU AREN'T THE ONES WITH A PRICE ON YOUR HEAD, SO RELAX. BESIDES, YOU'RE GOING TO HELP ME.
I'M NOT DOING SQUAT. GET YOU TO THE STATION, GET YOU BACK. THAT'S WHAT I WAS TOLD TO DO AND THAT'S **ALL** I'M GOING TO DO.
DON'T WORRY. ALL YOU GUYS HAVE TO DO IS JUST STAND THERE.
YOU REALLY THINK THE COPS WON'T RECOGNIZE YOU WITH YOUR HAIR UP LIKE THAT?
I DOUBT IT. BUT THAT'S NOT THE REAL REASON I'M WEARING MY HAIR LIKE THIS.
I'M WEARING PIG-TAILS BECAUSE THEY MAKE ME LOOK CUTE AND DEFENSELESS. KNOW WHO LIKES TO PROTECT CUTE, DEFENSELESS GIRLS FROM GRAB-HAPPY THUGS LIKE YOU?
EVERYONE.

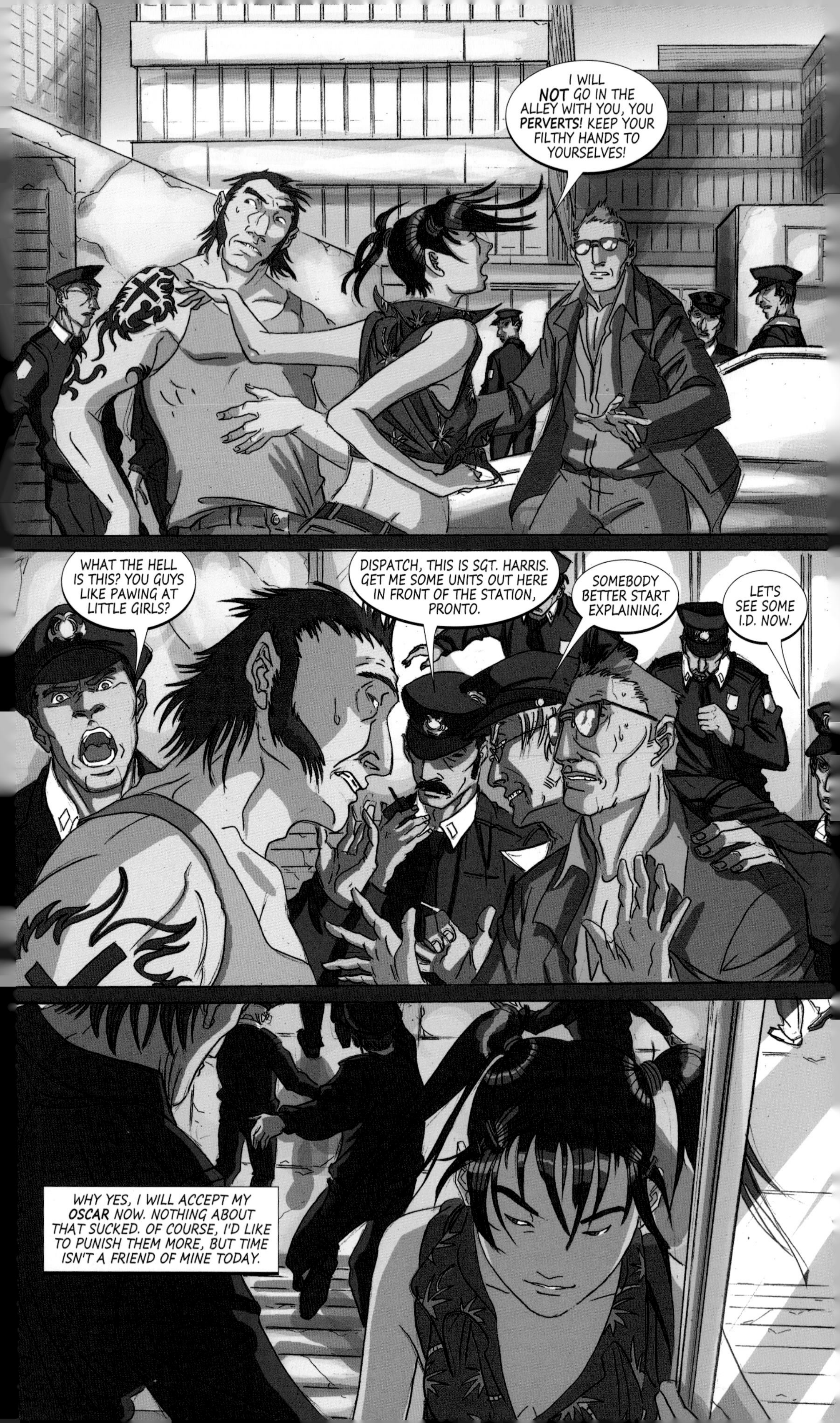
I WILL **NOT** GO IN THE ALLEY WITH YOU, YOU **PERVERTS!** KEEP YOUR FILTHY HANDS TO YOURSELVES!
WHAT THE HELL IS THIS? YOU GUYS LIKE PAWING AT LITTLE GIRLS?
DISPATCH, THIS IS SGT. HARRIS. GET ME SOME UNITS OUT HERE IN FRONT OF THE STATION, PRONTO.
SOMEBODY BETTER START EXPLAINING.
LET'S SEE SOME I.D. NOW.
WHY YES, I WILL ACCEPT MY ***OSCAR*** *NOW. NOTHING ABOUT THAT SUCKED. OF COURSE, I'D LIKE TO PUNISH THEM MORE, BUT TIME ISN'T A FRIEND OF MINE TODAY.*

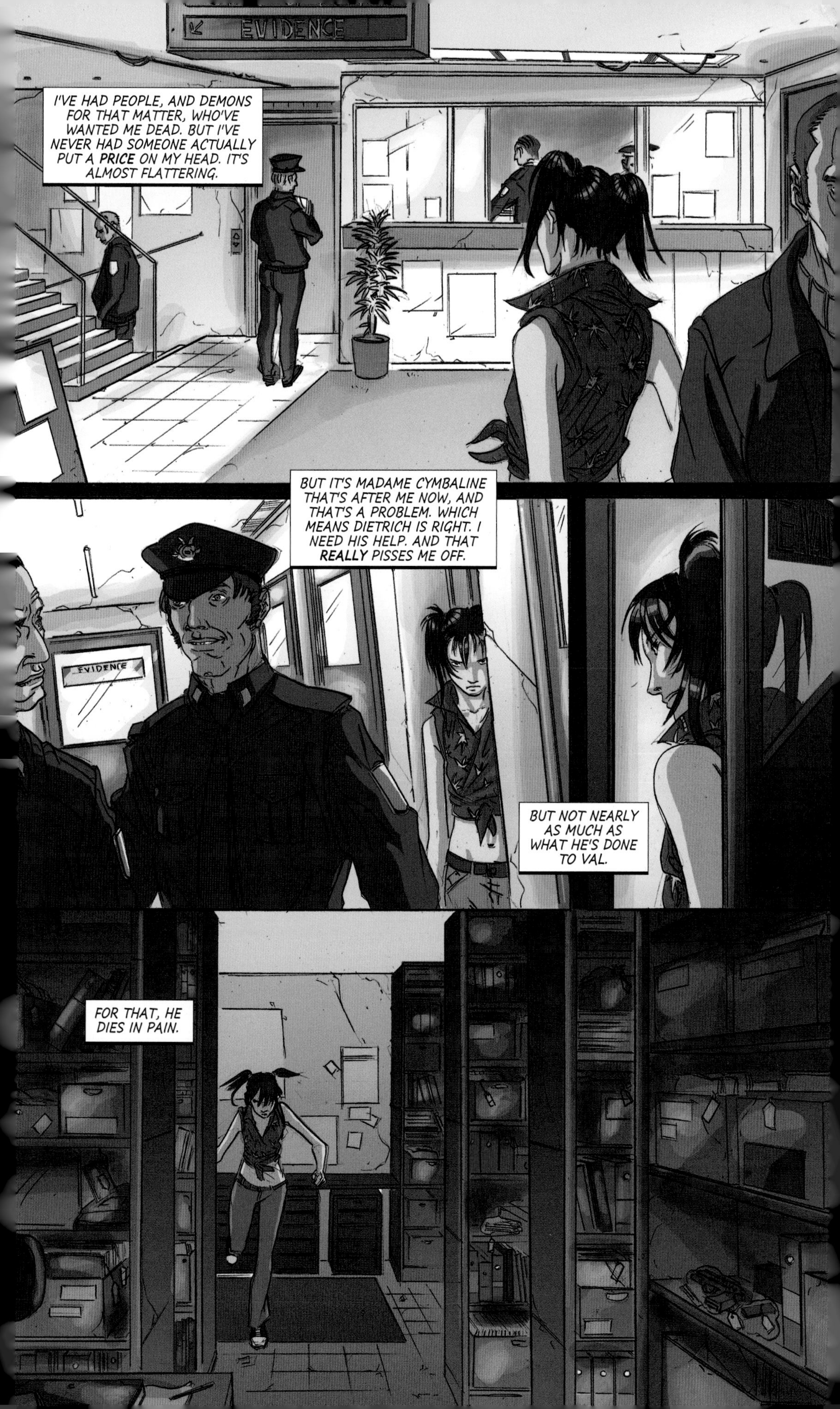
EVIDENCE
I'VE HAD PEOPLE, AND DEMONS FOR THAT MATTER, WHO'VE WANTED ME DEAD. BUT I'VE NEVER HAD SOMEONE ACTUALLY PUT A PRICE ON MY HEAD. IT'S ALMOST FLATTERING.
BUT IT'S MADAME CYMBALINE THAT'S AFTER ME NOW, AND THAT'S A PROBLEM. WHICH MEANS DIETRICH IS RIGHT. I NEED HIS HELP. AND THAT REALLY PISSES ME OFF.
EVIDENCE
BUT NOT NEARLY AS MUCH AS WHAT HE'S DONE TO VAL.
FOR THAT, HE DIES IN PAIN.

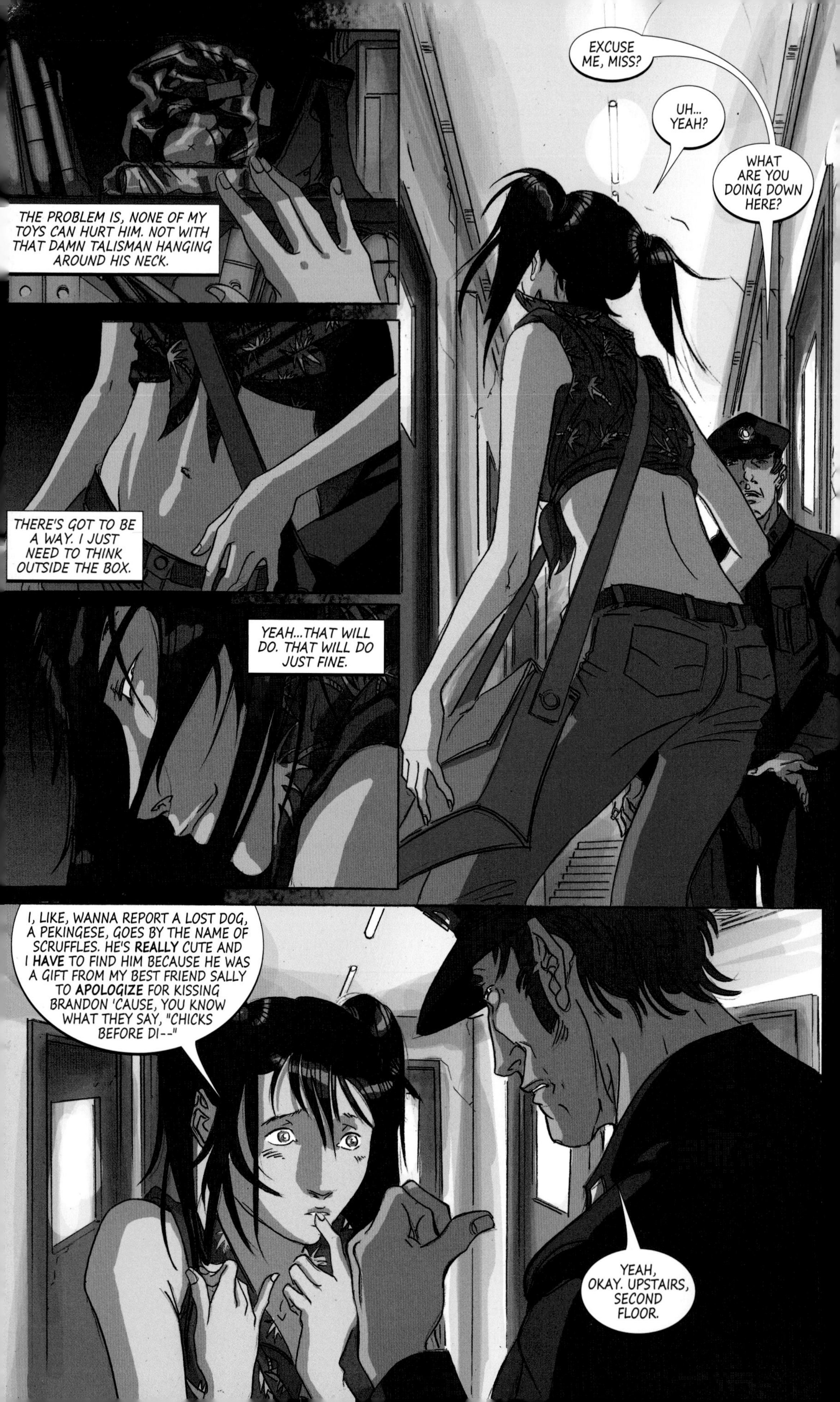
THE PROBLEM IS, NONE OF MY TOYS CAN HURT HIM. NOT WITH THAT DAMN TALISMAN HANGING AROUND HIS NECK.
THERE'S GOT TO BE A WAY. I JUST NEED TO THINK OUTSIDE THE BOX.
YEAH...THAT WILL DO. THAT WILL DO JUST FINE.
EXCUSE ME, MISS?
UH... YEAH?
WHAT ARE YOU DOING DOWN HERE?
I, LIKE, WANNA REPORT A LOST DOG, A PEKINGESE, GOES BY THE NAME OF SCRUFFLES. HE'S REALLY CUTE AND I HAVE TO FIND HIM BECAUSE HE WAS A GIFT FROM MY BEST FRIEND SALLY TO APOLOGIZE FOR KISSING BRANDON 'CAUSE, YOU KNOW WHAT THEY SAY, "CHICKS BEFORE DI--"
YEAH, OKAY. UPSTAIRS, SECOND FLOOR.

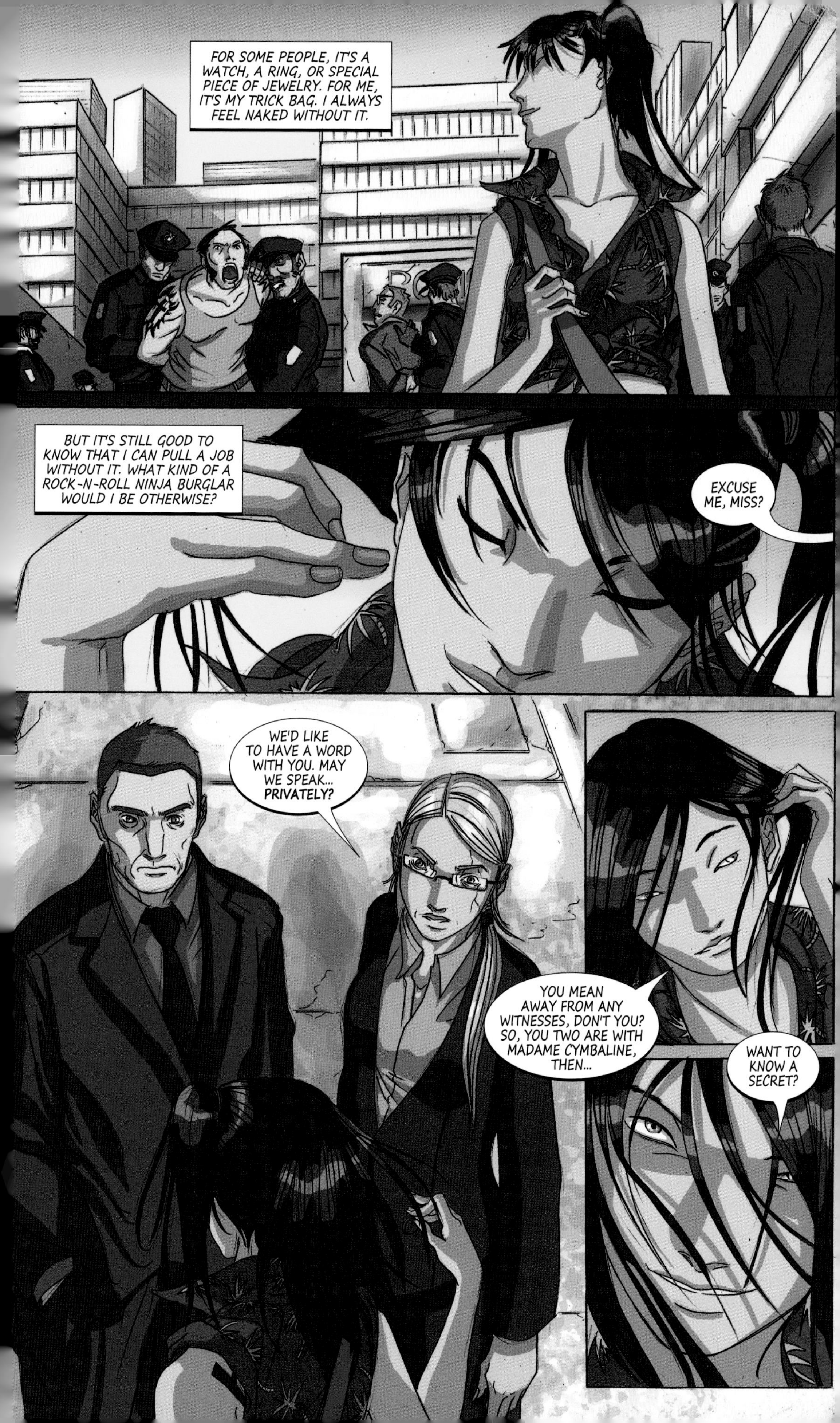

FOR SOME PEOPLE, IT'S A WATCH, A RING, OR SPECIAL PIECE OF JEWELRY. FOR ME, IT'S MY TRICK BAG. I ALWAYS FEEL NAKED WITHOUT IT.
BUT IT'S STILL GOOD TO KNOW THAT I CAN PULL A JOB WITHOUT IT. WHAT KIND OF A ROCK-N-ROLL NINJA BURGLAR WOULD I BE OTHERWISE?
EXCUSE ME, MISS?
WE'D LIKE TO HAVE A WORD WITH YOU. MAY WE SPEAK... PRIVATELY?
YOU MEAN AWAY FROM ANY WITNESSES, DON'T YOU? SO, YOU TWO ARE WITH MADAME CYMBALINE, THEN...
WANT TO KNOW A SECRET?

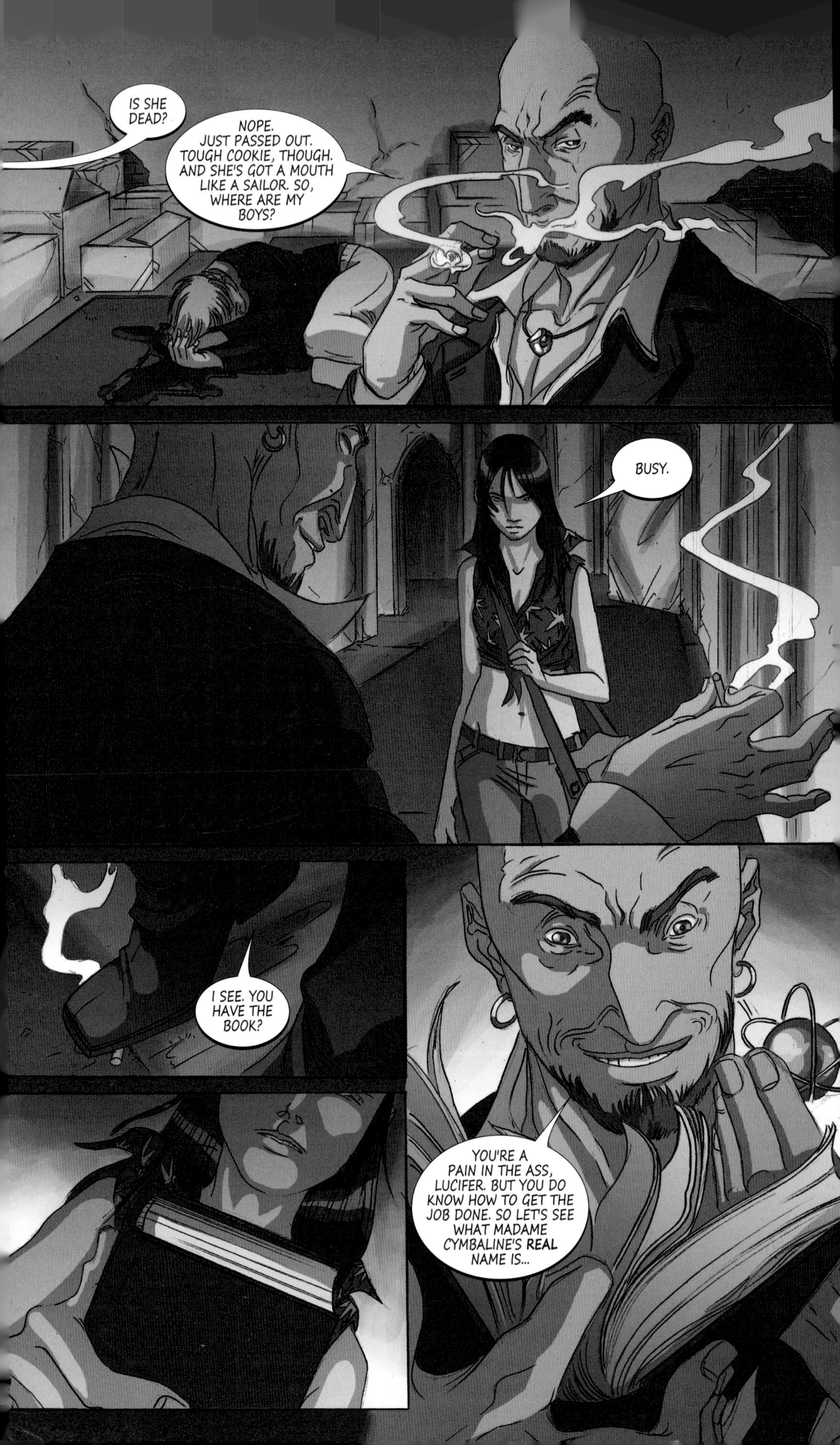

IS SHE DEAD?
NOPE. JUST PASSED OUT. TOUGH COOKIE, THOUGH. AND SHE'S GOT A MOUTH LIKE A SAILOR. SO, WHERE ARE MY BOYS?
BUSY.
I SEE. YOU HAVE THE BOOK?
YOU'RE A PAIN IN THE ASS, LUCIFER. BUT YOU DO KNOW HOW TO GET THE JOB DONE. SO LET'S SEE WHAT MADAME CYMBALINE'S **REAL** NAME IS...

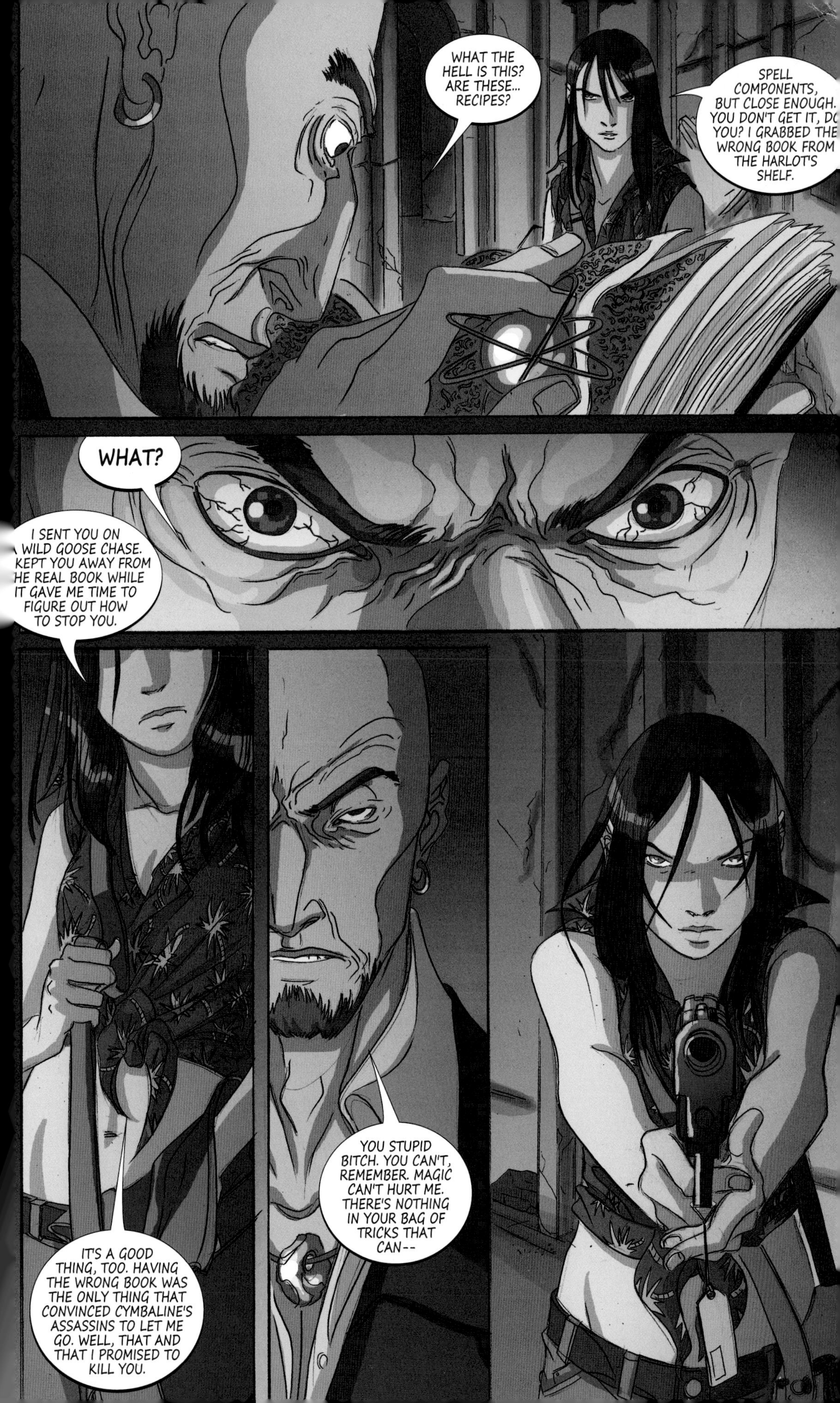

WHAT THE HELL IS THIS? ARE THESE... RECIPES?
SPELL COMPONENTS, BUT CLOSE ENOUGH. YOU DON'T GET IT, DO YOU? I GRABBED THE WRONG BOOK FROM THE HARLOT'S SHELF.
WHAT?
I SENT YOU ON A WILD GOOSE CHASE. KEPT YOU AWAY FROM THE REAL BOOK WHILE IT GAVE ME TIME TO FIGURE OUT HOW TO STOP YOU.
YOU STUPID BITCH. YOU CAN'T, REMEMBER. MAGIC CAN'T HURT ME. THERE'S NOTHING IN YOUR BAG OF TRICKS THAT CAN--
IT'S A GOOD THING, TOO. HAVING THE WRONG BOOK WAS THE ONLY THING THAT CONVINCED CYMBALINE'S ASSASSINS TO LET ME GO. WELL, THAT AND THAT I PROMISED TO KILL YOU.

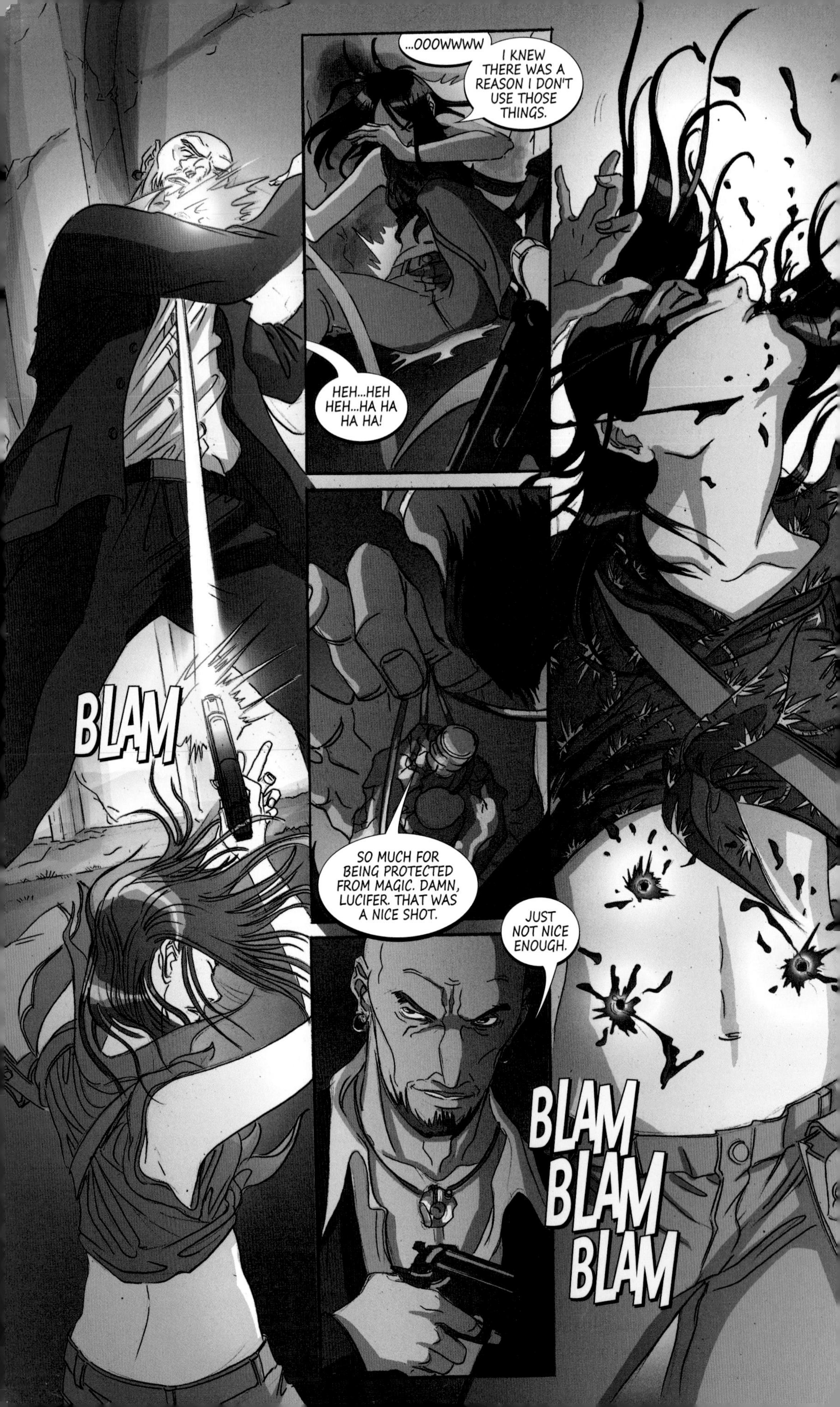
...OOOWWWW
I KNEW THERE WAS A REASON I DON'T USE THOSE THINGS.
HEH...HEH HEH...HA HA HA HA!
BLAM
SO MUCH FOR BEING PROTECTED FROM MAGIC. DAMN, LUCIFER. THAT WAS A NICE SHOT.
JUST NOT NICE ENOUGH.
BLAM
BLAM
BLAM

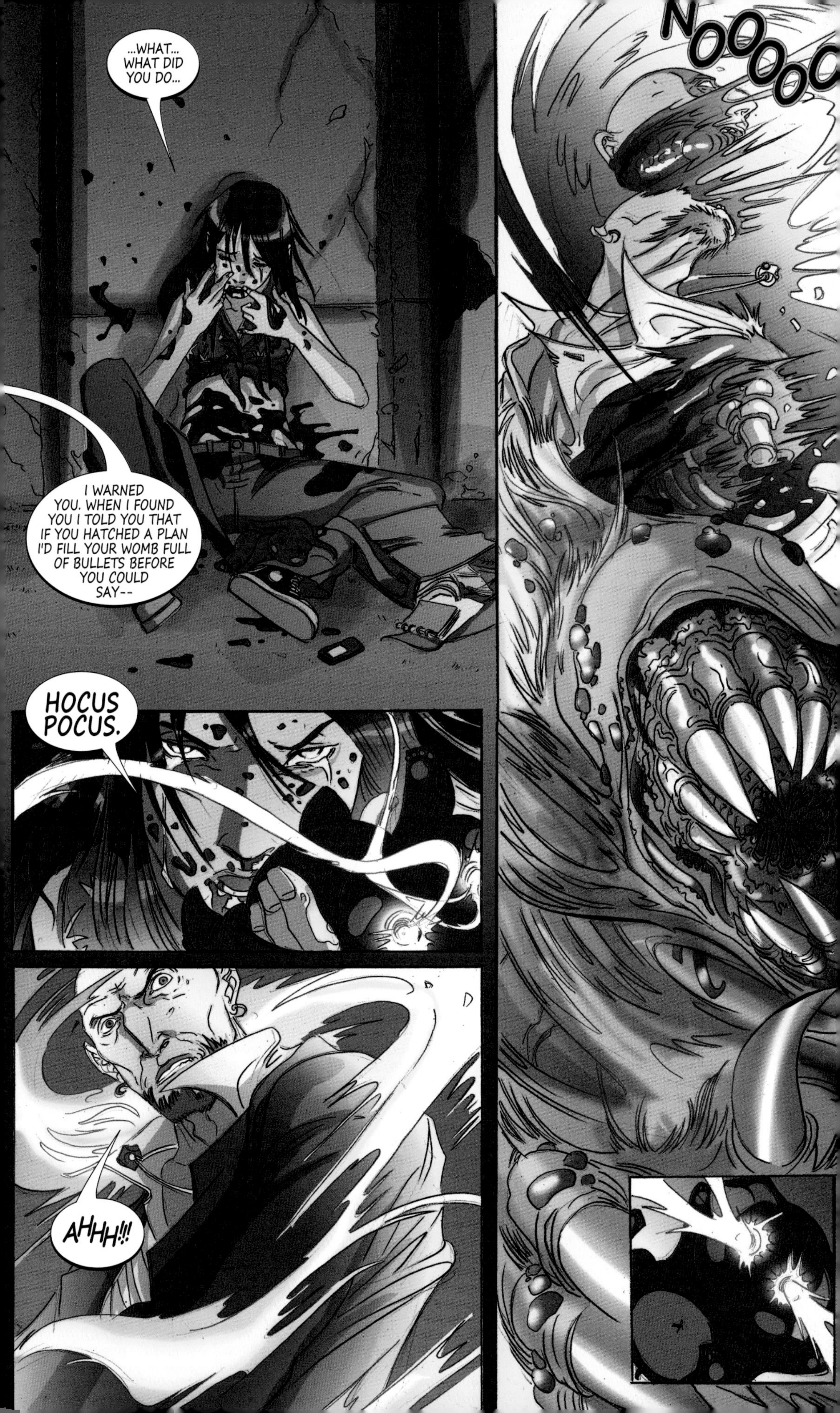

...WHAT... WHAT DID YOU DO...
I WARNED YOU. WHEN I FOUND YOU I TOLD YOU THAT IF YOU HATCHED A PLAN I'D FILL YOUR WOMB FULL OF BULLETS BEFORE YOU COULD SAY--
HOCUS POCUS.
AHHH!!!
NOOOOO

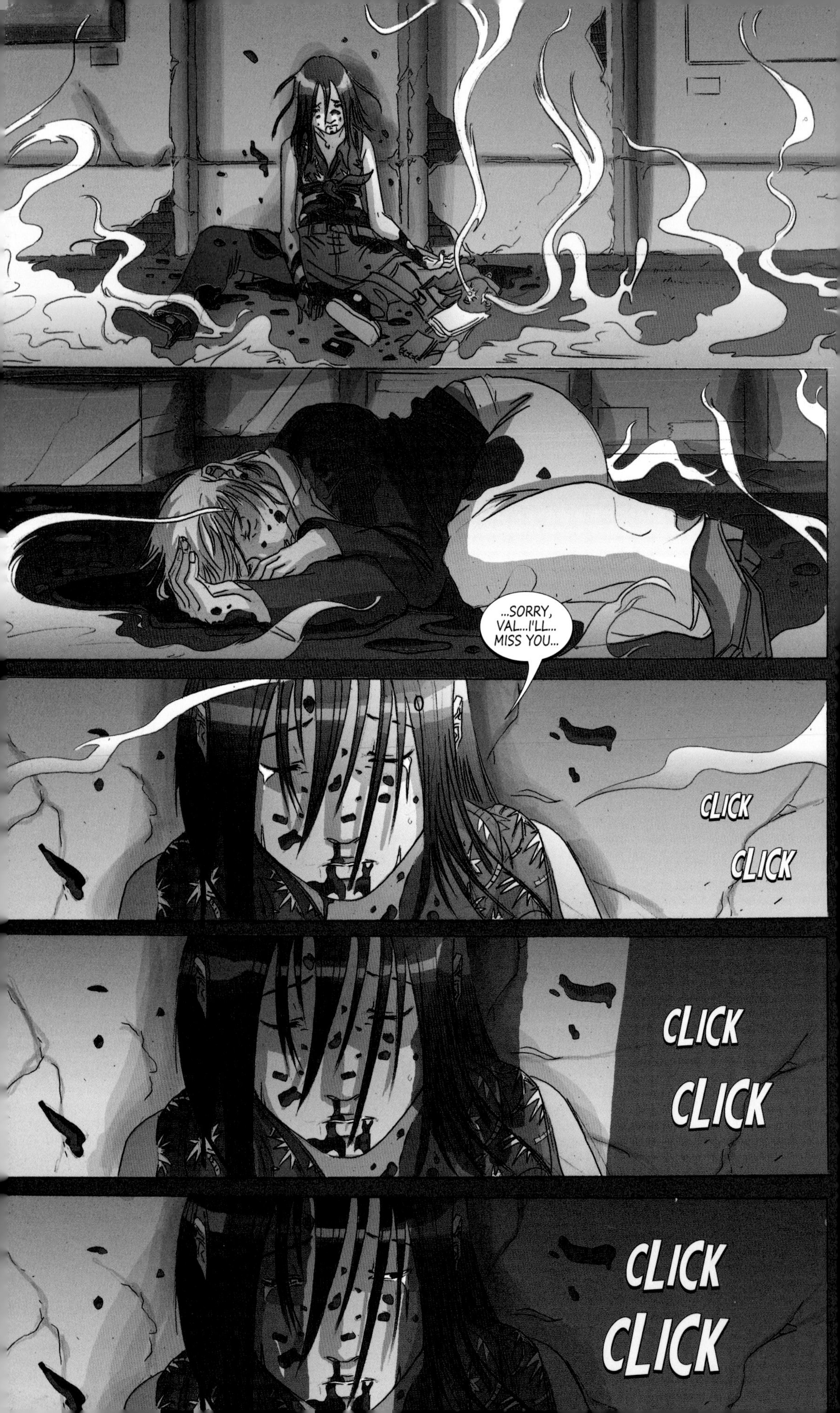
...SORRY, VAL...I'LL... MISS YOU...
CLICK
CLICK
CLICK
CLICK
CLICK
CLICK

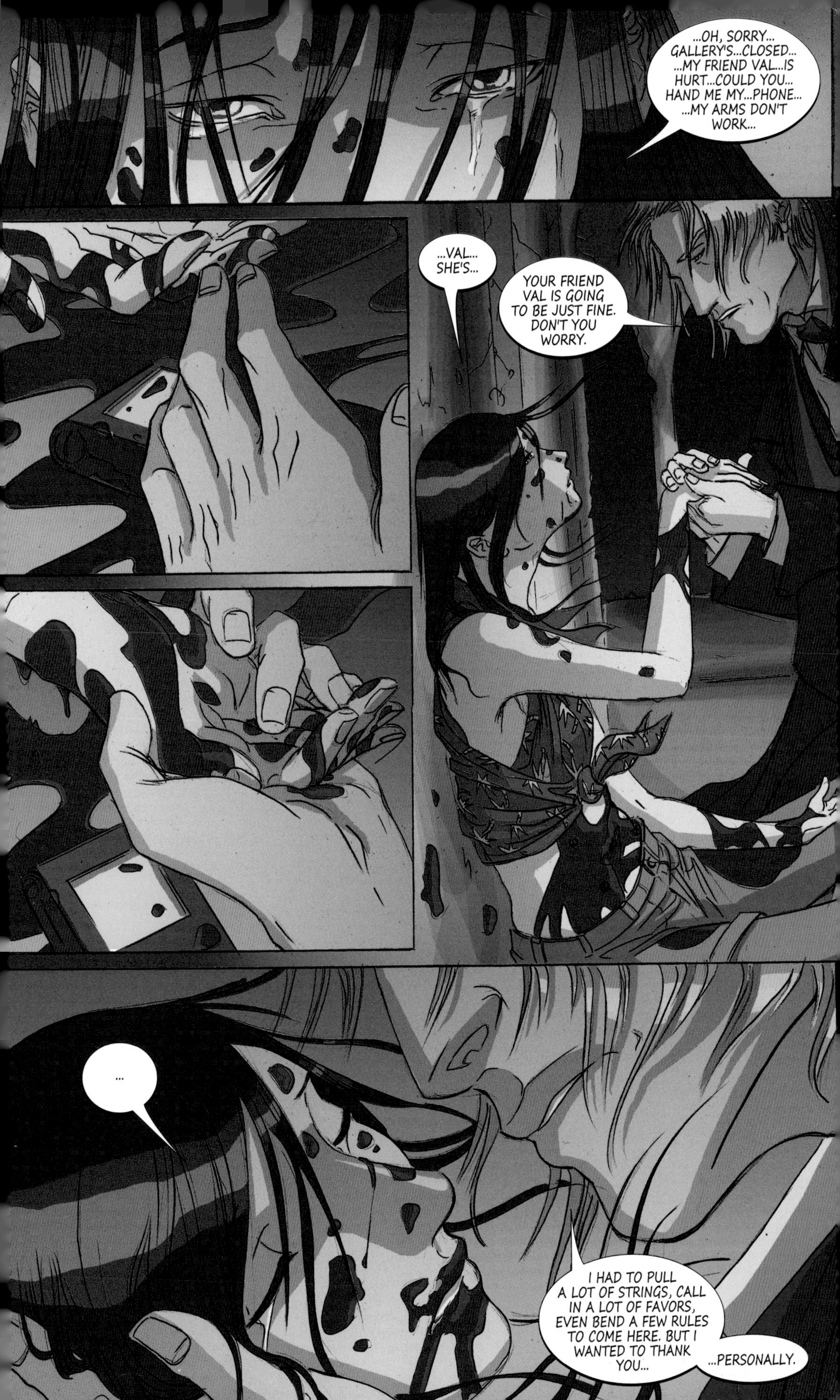
...OH, SORRY... GALLERY'S...CLOSED... ...MY FRIEND VAL...IS HURT...COULD YOU... HAND ME MY...PHONE... ...MY ARMS DON'T WORK...
...VAL... SHE'S...
YOUR FRIEND VAL IS GOING TO BE JUST FINE. DON'T YOU WORRY.
...
I HAD TO PULL A LOT OF STRINGS, CALL IN A LOT OF FAVORS, EVEN BEND A FEW RULES TO COME HERE. BUT I WANTED TO THANK YOU...
...PERSONALLY.

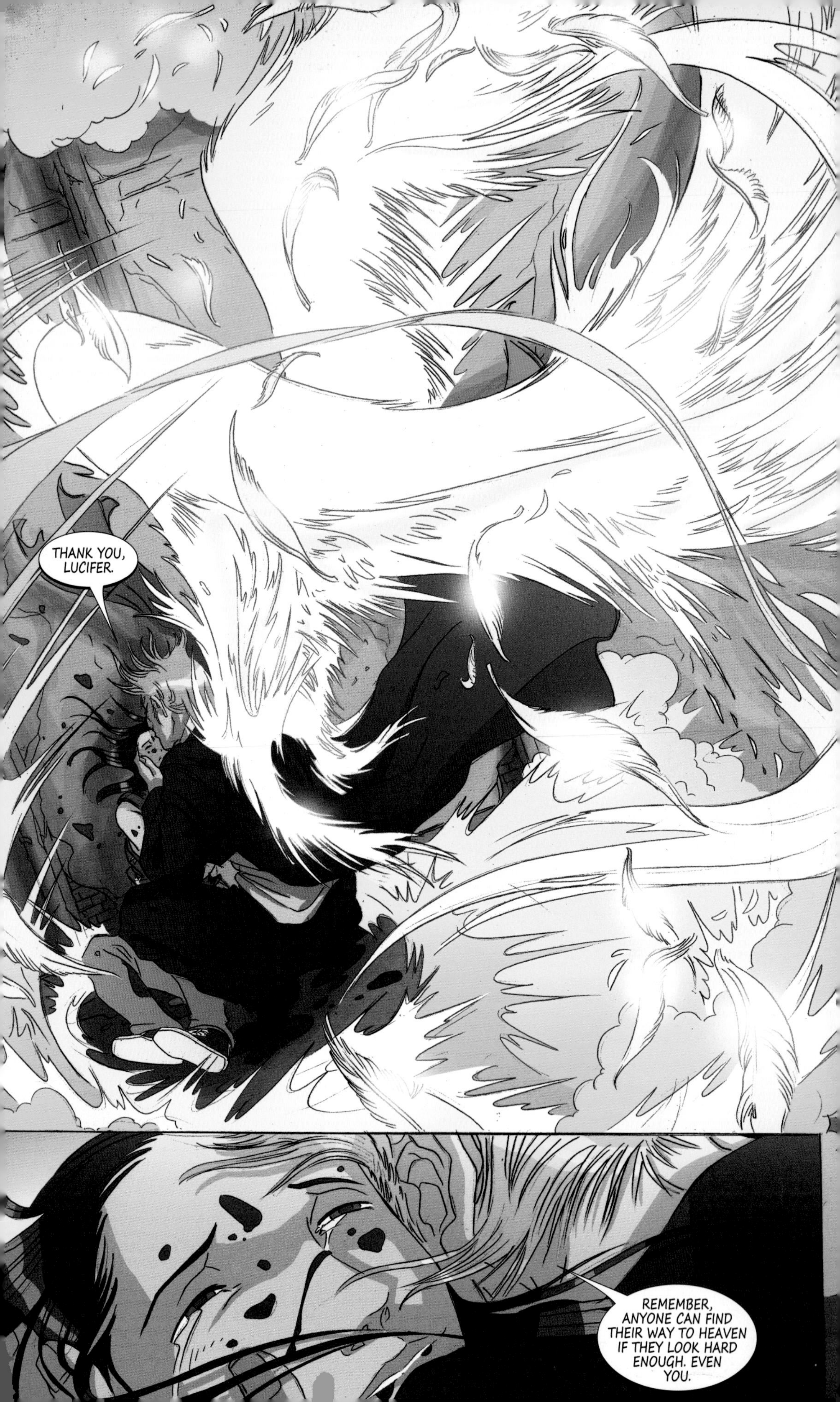
THANK YOU, LUCIFER.
REMEMBER, ANYONE CAN FIND THEIR WAY TO HEAVEN IF THEY LOOK HARD ENOUGH. EVEN YOU.

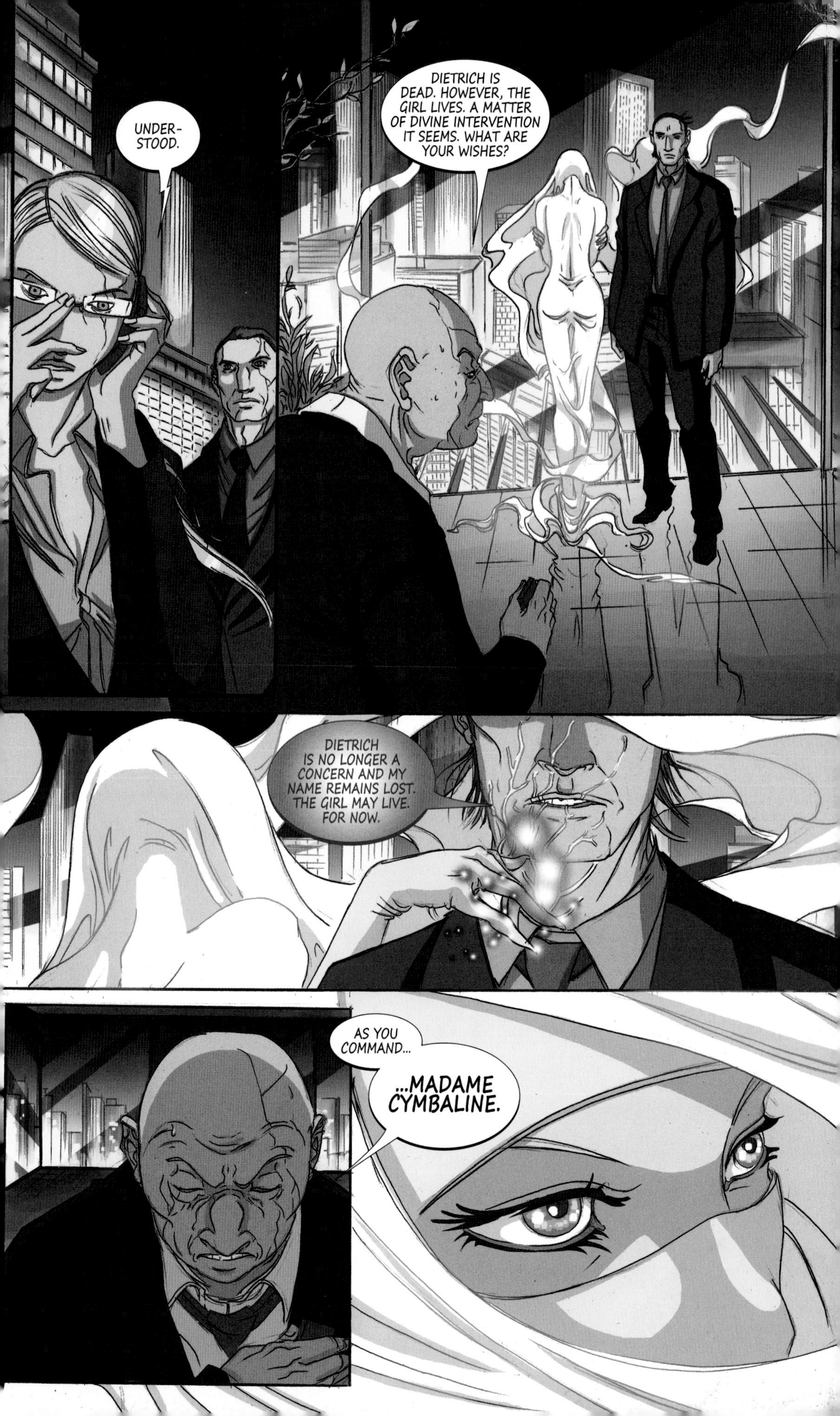
UNDER-
STOOD.
DIETRICH IS DEAD. HOWEVER, THE GIRL LIVES. A MATTER OF DIVINE INTERVENTION IT SEEMS. WHAT ARE YOUR WISHES?
DIETRICH IS NO LONGER A CONCERN AND MY NAME REMAINS LOST. THE GIRL MAY LIVE. FOR NOW.
AS YOU COMMAND...
...MADAME CYMBALINE.

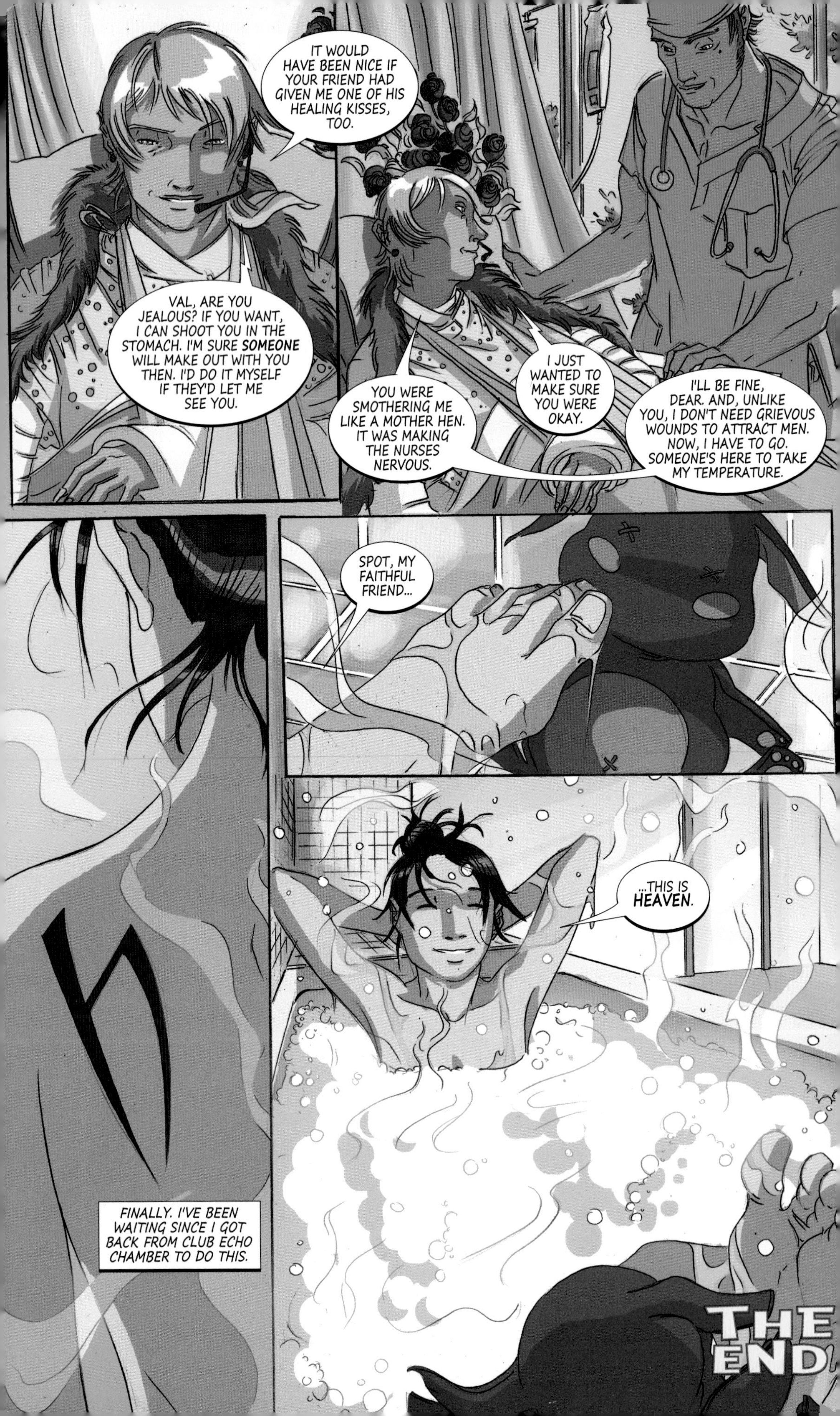
IT WOULD HAVE BEEN NICE IF YOUR FRIEND HAD GIVEN ME ONE OF HIS HEALING KISSES, TOO.
VAL, ARE YOU JEALOUS? IF YOU WANT, I CAN SHOOT YOU IN THE STOMACH. I'M SURE **SOMEONE** WILL MAKE OUT WITH YOU THEN. I'D DO IT MYSELF IF THEY'D LET ME SEE YOU.
I JUST WANTED TO MAKE SURE YOU WERE OKAY.
YOU WERE SMOTHERING ME LIKE A MOTHER HEN. IT WAS MAKING THE NURSES NERVOUS.
I'LL BE FINE, DEAR. AND, UNLIKE YOU, I DON'T NEED GRIEVOUS WOUNDS TO ATTRACT MEN. NOW, I HAVE TO GO. SOMEONE'S HERE TO TAKE MY TEMPERATURE.
FINALLY. I'VE BEEN WAITING SINCE I GOT BACK FROM CLUB ECHO CHAMBER TO DO THIS.
SPOT, MY FAITHFUL FRIEND...
...THIS IS **HEAVEN**.
THE END

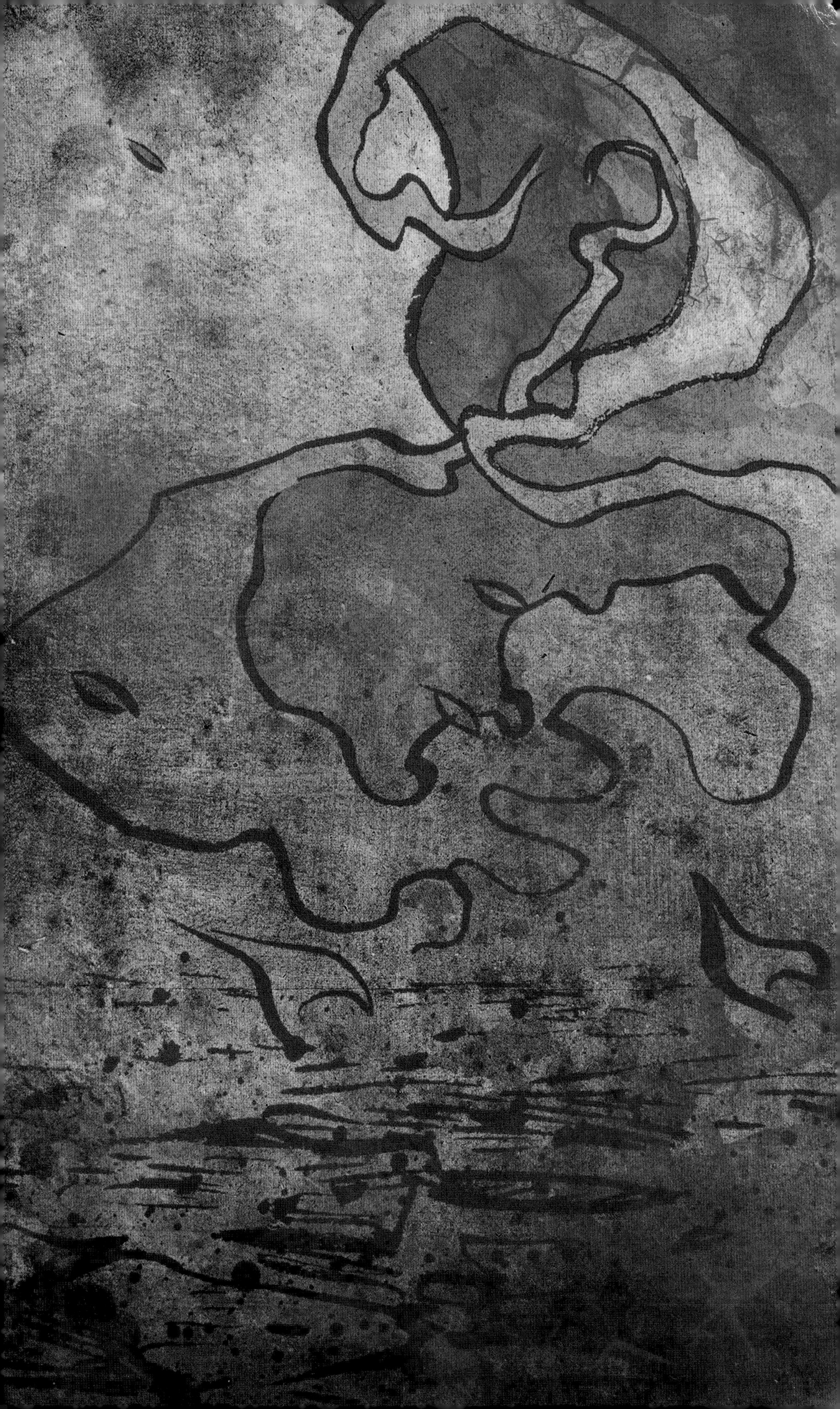

COVER GALLERY

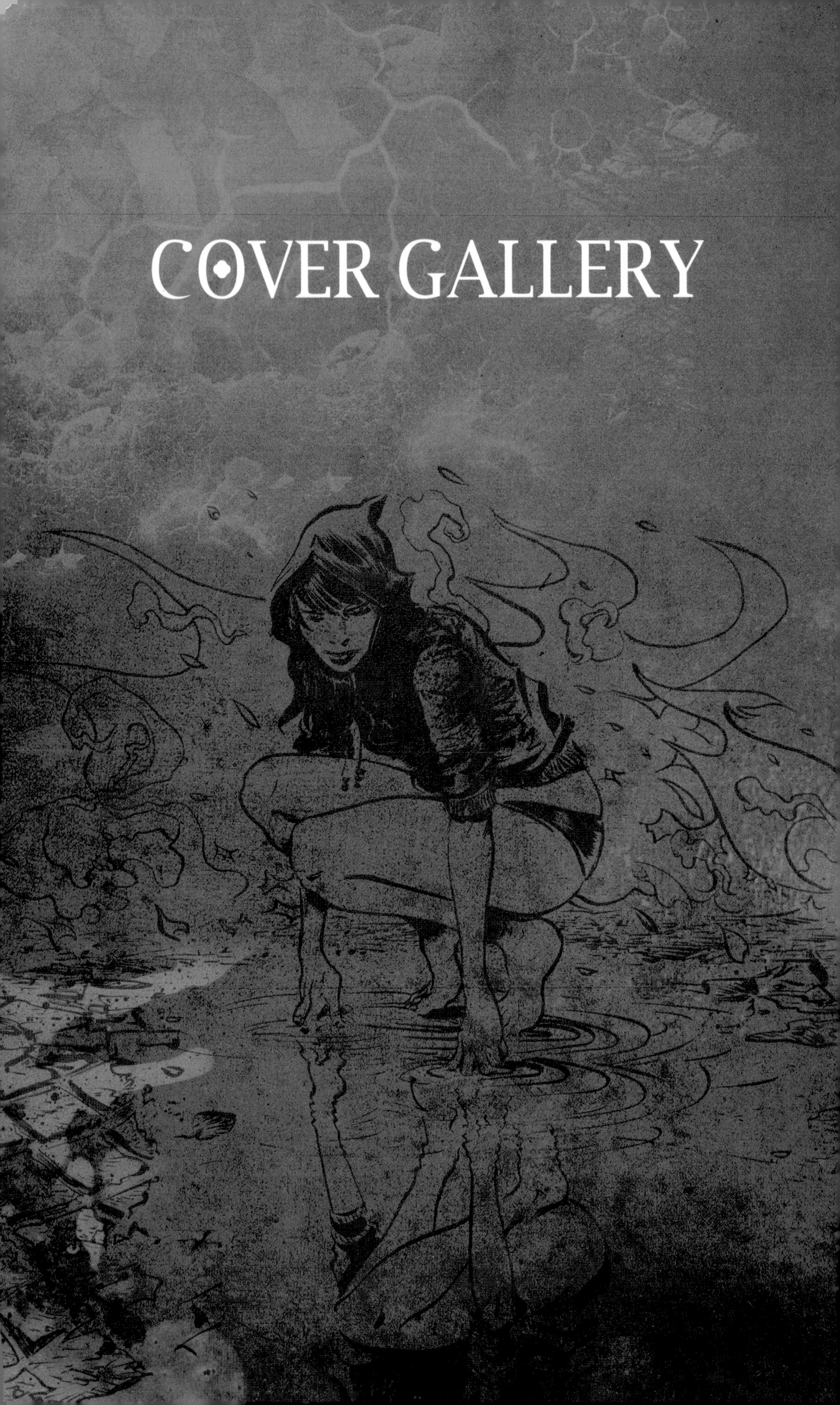

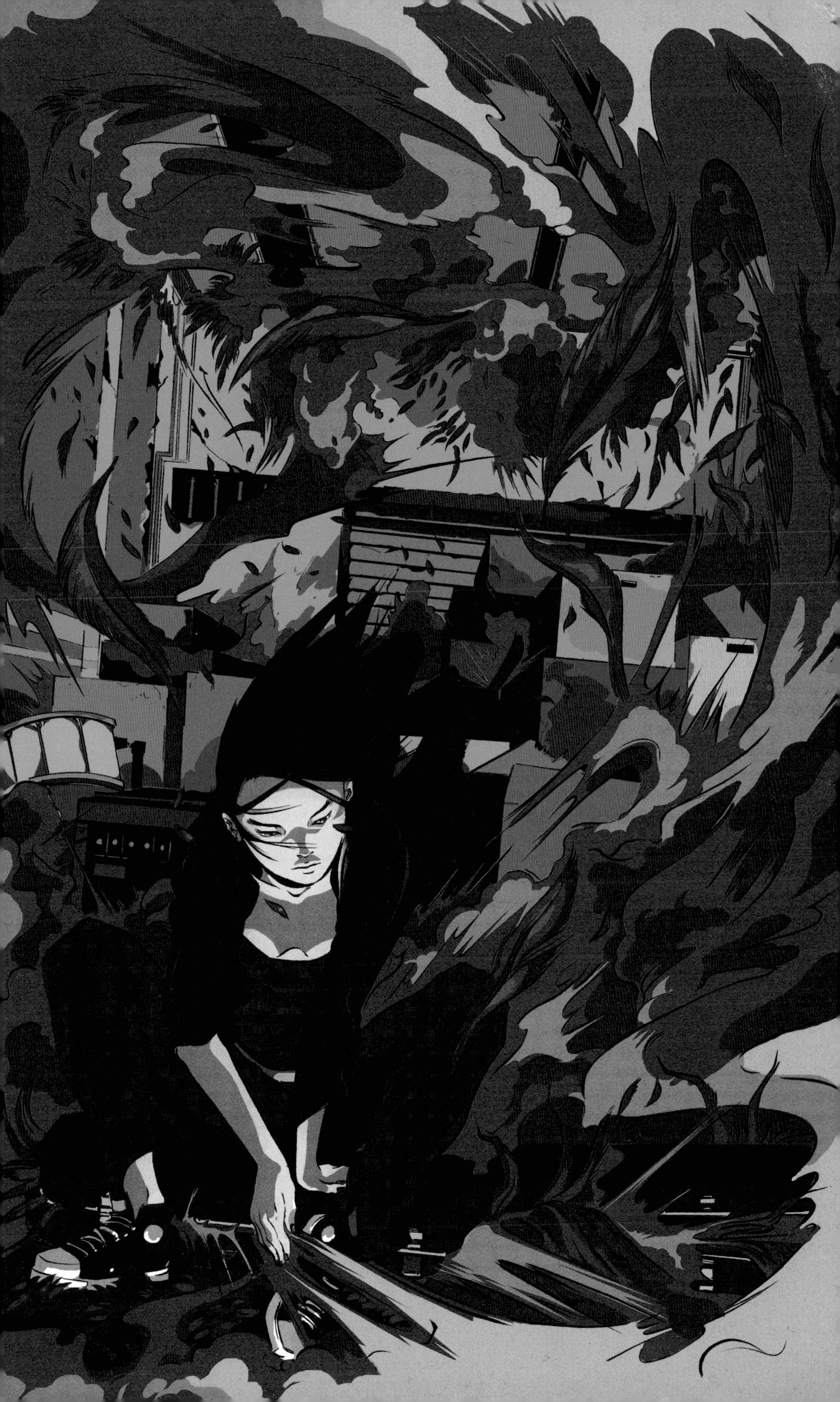

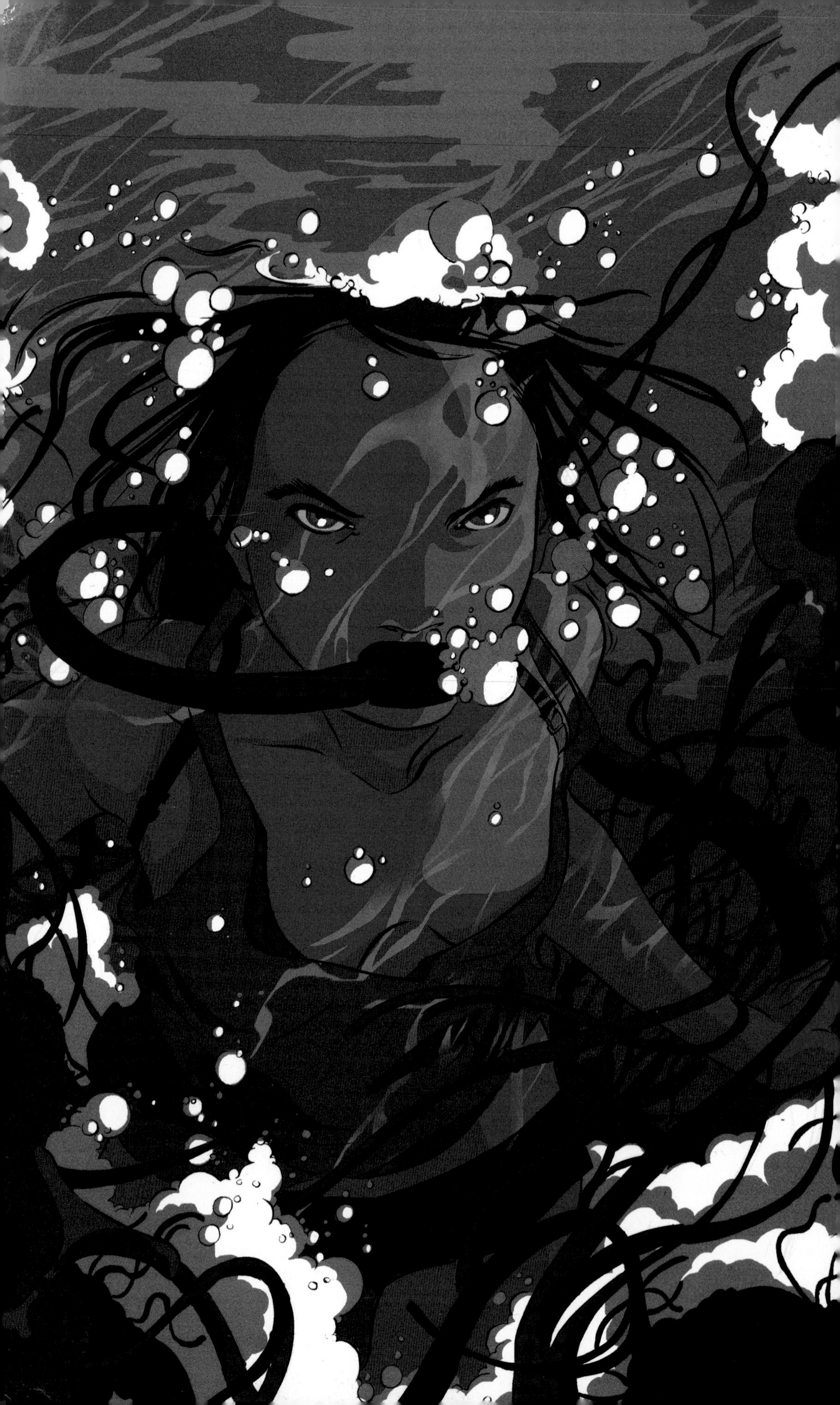

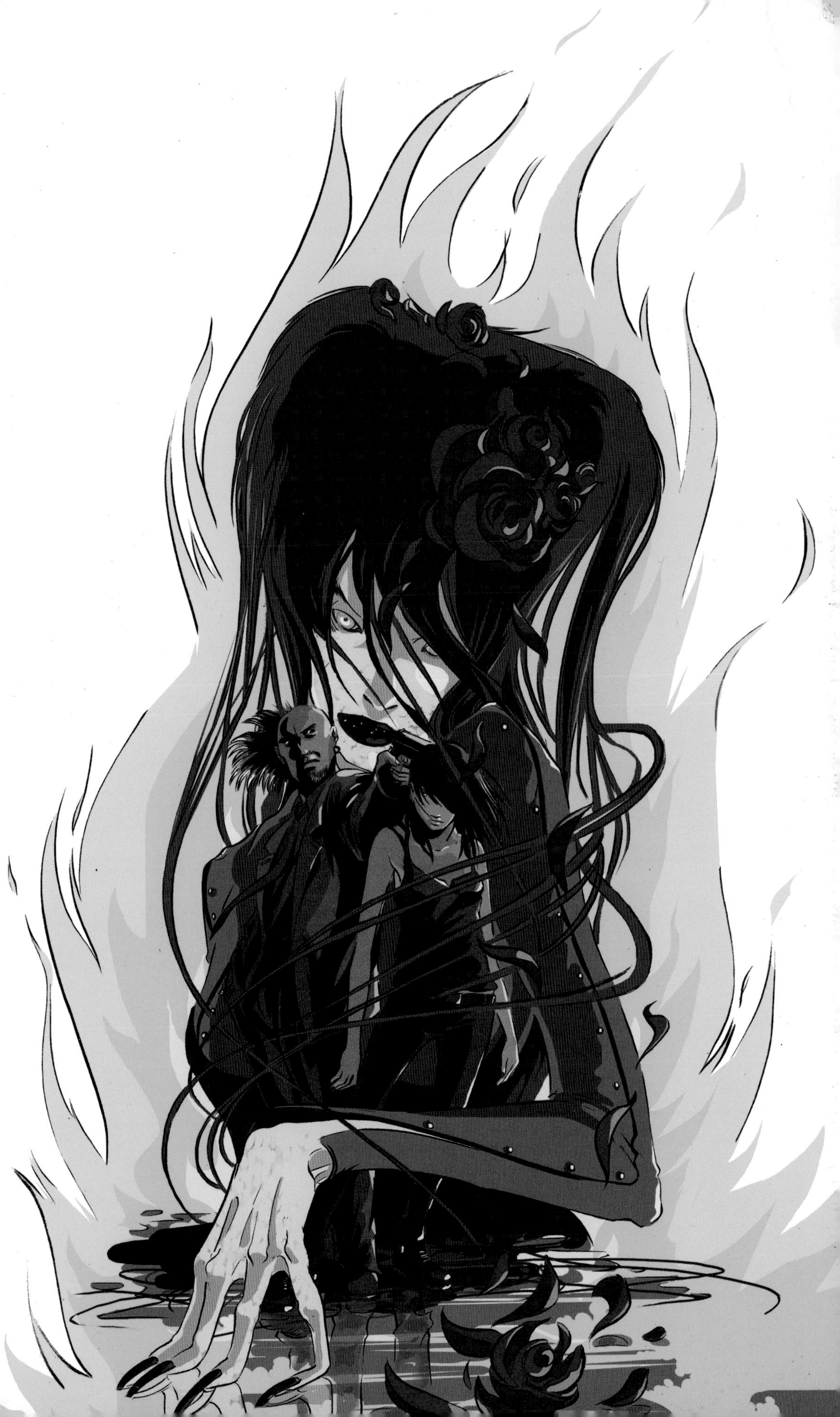

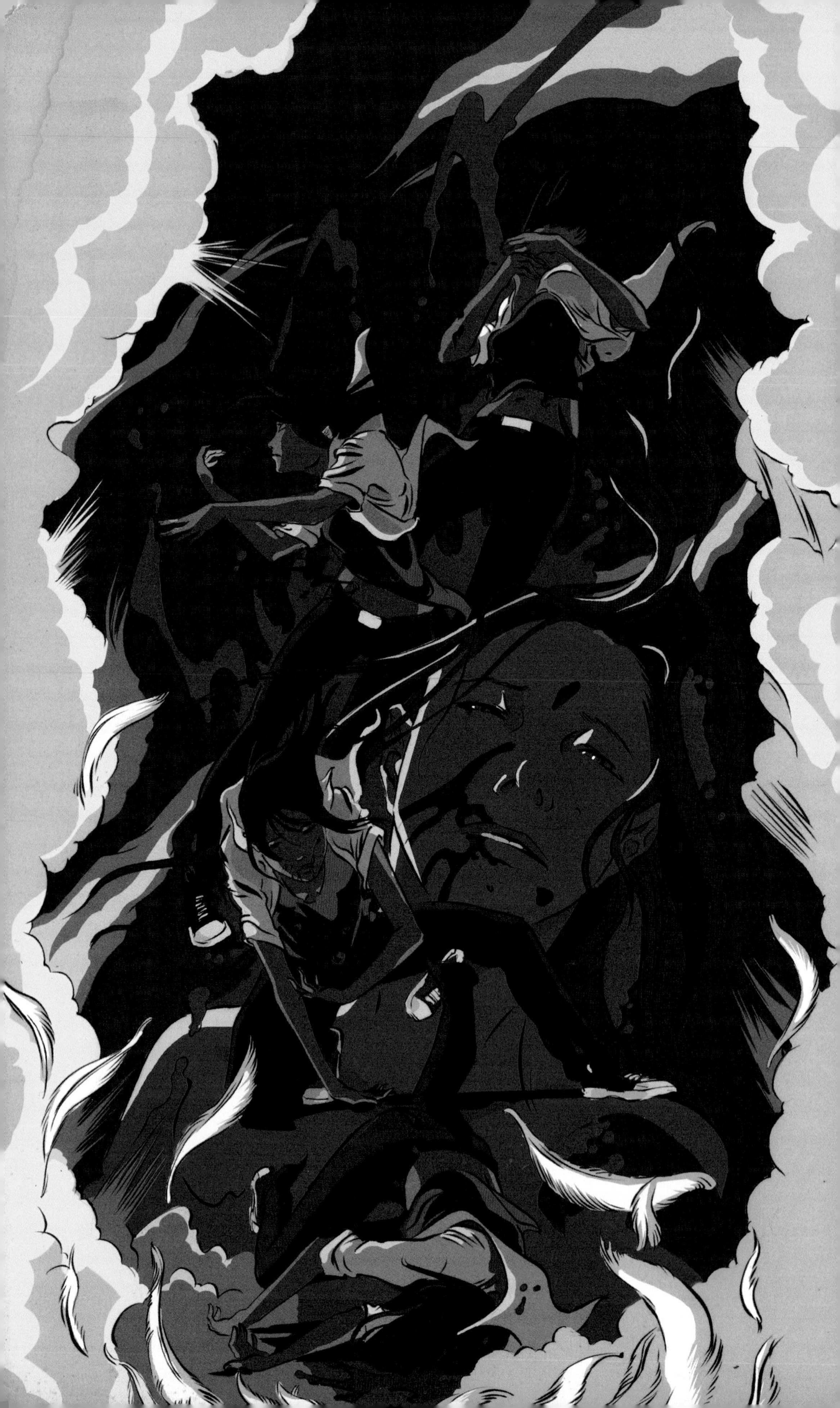

AFTERWORD

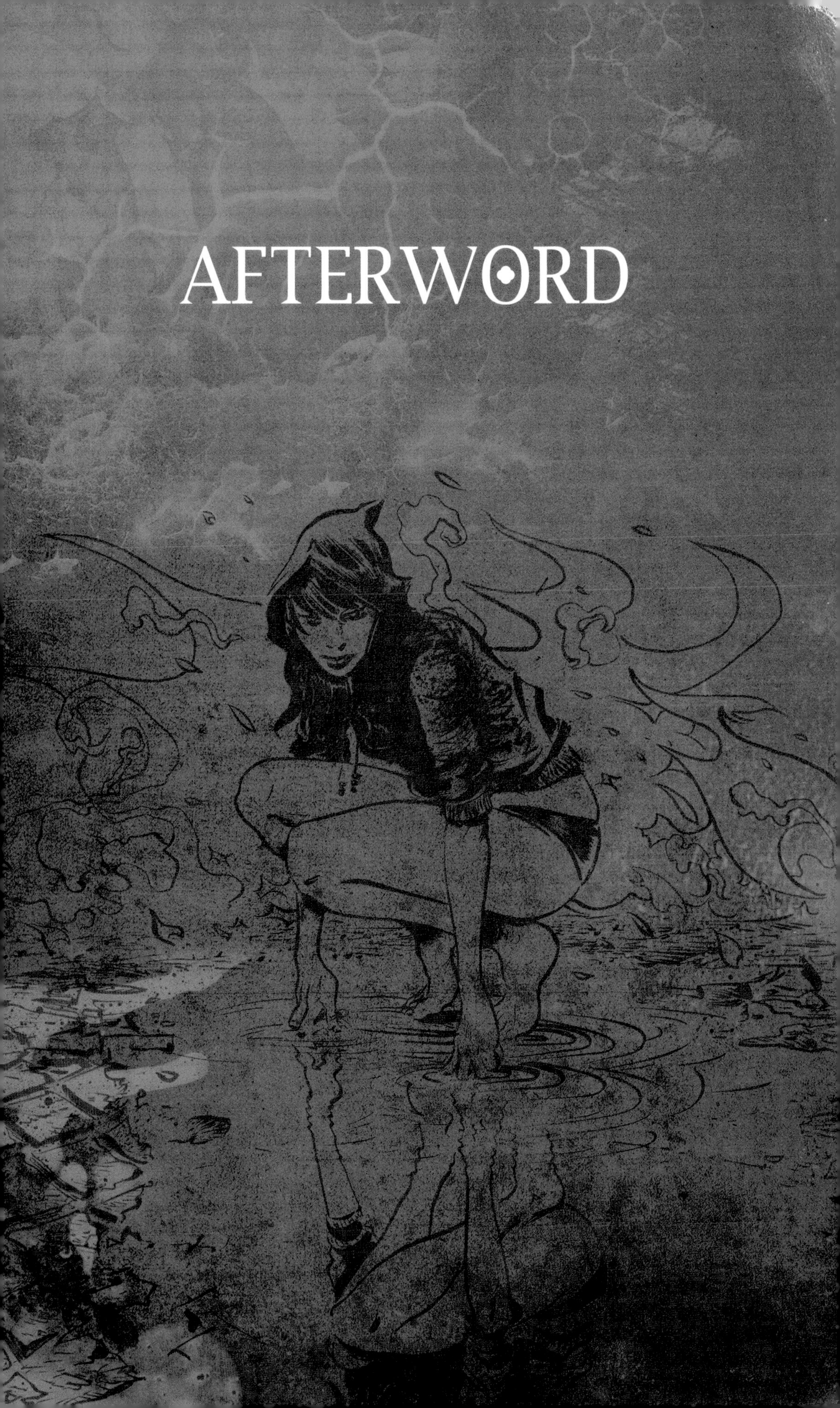

There's magic in the world.

That's quite a bold statement, I must admit, but it is, nevertheless, true. How do I know? You're holding the proof of it in your hands right now.

Alright, be honest. For a moment, you thought I meant the kind of magic that makes shapely assistants disappear, sends fireballs hurtling from one's fingertips, or binds ferocious witch-hounds inside pink and cuddly prisons. No, I'm talking about something else, something even more wondrous. I'm talking about the kind of magic that happens when an idea blossoms into something beyond even one's highest expectations. It doesn't happen very often, but when it does, it is, in the truest sense of the word, awesome.

The idea for the character Lucifer came to me in a fit of panic. I needed to think of some cover concepts for the third arc of my series FALL OF CTHULHU; but unfortunately, I wasn't sure what the story was going to be. Nothing was coming to me. Yet, as I tried to work a story through in my head, an image kept floating in my mind: there was a teen-aged girl sitting on the floor of a jail cell, drawing dark and ominous symbols in the dust around her. There she was, in my mind's eye, looking up at me as she scrawled runes on the floor,

daring me to ask her questions. What did those symbols mean? Why was she in jail? And above all, who was she? For the life of me, I had no idea what my story was going to be, but I knew that it simply had to be about her.

As I developed her character and her story in FALL OF CTHULHU, Lucifer had become an amazingly rich and compelling character. She was strong, capable, and knew how to survive in a dangerous and terrifying world. And she did it all by herself. No super powers, no innate magical prowess, just her wits and the skills honed by the unforgiving mistress of necessity. And she had become more than just an interesting part of an ensemble that included deities with a fan base decades in the making. True to her name, Lucifer had become the star.

But she was a star in someone else's sky.

No matter how much I made FALL OF CTHULHU my own, how deeply I populated it with my own original characters, how much of my own voice shined through the story, I was still playing in Lovecraft's sandbox. Call it selfish, but I wanted Lucifer to walk in a world wholly of my own creation, a place that wasn't so immured in shadow and despair. Rather, I saw her in a world with humor, compassion, and a beauty hidden beneath the horrors (it's no coincidence that Lucifer works for the curator of an art gallery). In short, I wanted the chance for Lucifer to have a happy ending. But it's one thing to talk about a world of beautiful horror. It's another to actually make one.

That is, unless there's magic in the world.

Open this book up to any page and you can see the magic, weaving itself among the images, permeating through the paper like soft, cherubic whispers. Cris Peter's colors rise from the page like the grand finale of a master illusionist and every pencil stroke sings the delicate song of a complex spell, proving that, without a doubt, Emma Rios is nothing short of a sorceress.

Emma and Cris gave HEXED a depth and vision beyond anything I could have hoped for. And they did it by doing what I thought was impossible: they created a world of beautiful horror.

My ego would love nothing more than to lie and tell you that it was I who had the inimitable vision to bring together these two sisters of the arcane. However, that honor belongs to my editor Matt Gagnon, a man who helped me shape this book into something more than just another story about a pretty girl fighting evil. He saw what HEXED could be and knew exactly how to make it happen.

It's a rare and wonderful thing when so many variables come together to make such a powerful piece of art. And I can think of no words exalted enough to praise the team that made HEXED into the stunningly beautiful story you hold in your hands. Because of them, HEXED is not just special.

It's **magical.**

Michael Alan Nelson
Los Angeles - July 2009

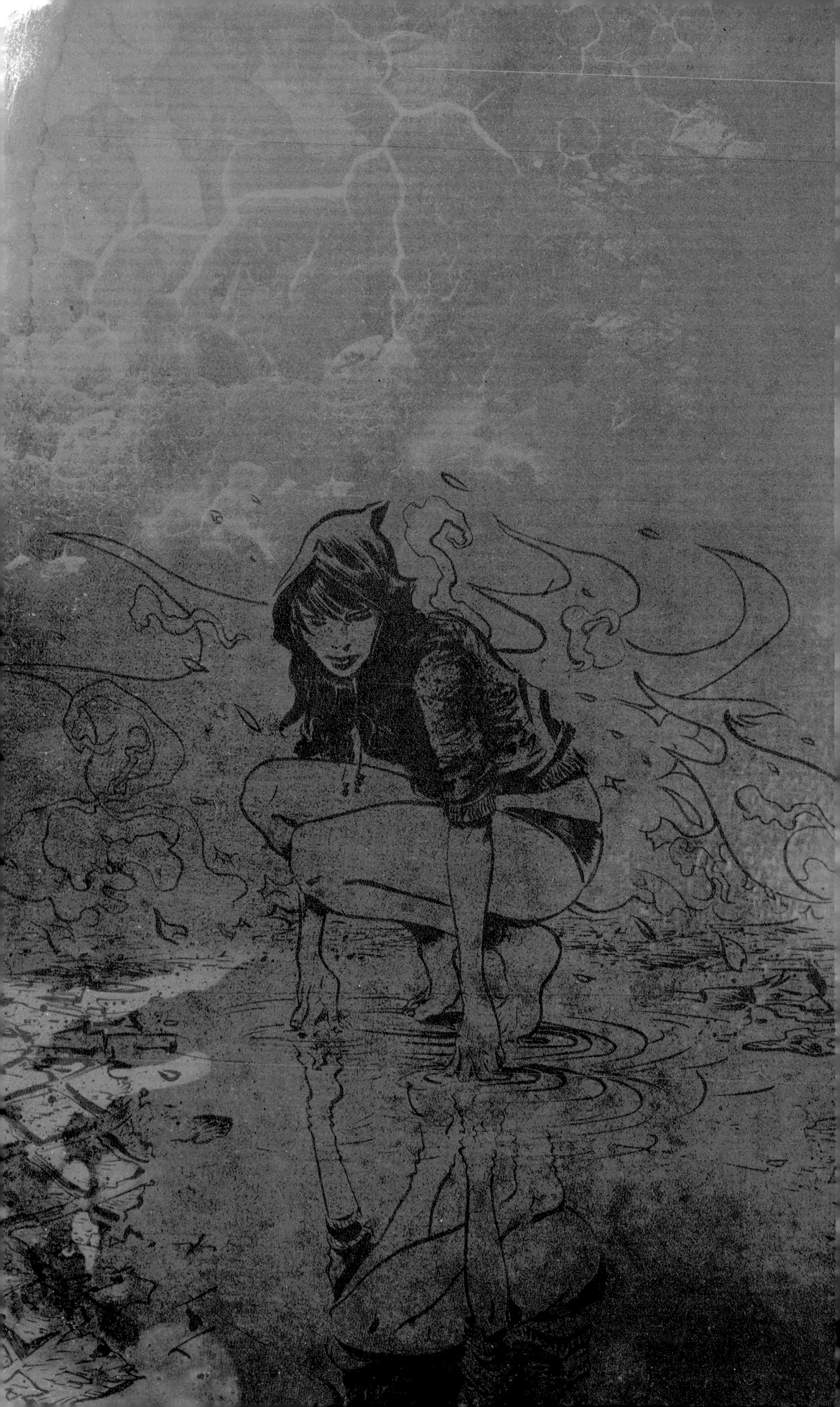